Redeeming the Past

Redeeming the Past

My Journey from Freedom Fighter to Healer

MICHAEL LAPSLEY

With Stephen Karakashian

ORBIS BOOKS

Maryknoll, New York   10545

Founded in 1970, Orbis Books endeavors to publish works that enlighten the mind, nourish the spirit, and challenge the conscience. The publishing arm of the Maryknoll Fathers and Brothers, Orbis seeks to explore the global dimensions of the Christian faith and mission, to invite dialogue with diverse cultures and religious traditions, and to serve the cause of reconciliation and peace. The books published reflect the views of their authors and do not represent the official position of the Maryknoll Society. To learn more about Maryknoll and Orbis Books, please visit our website at www.maryknollsociety.org.

Published by Orbis Books, Box 302, Maryknoll, NY 10545–0302.

Manuscript editing and typesetting by Joan Weber Laflamme.

Manufactured in the United States of America

Library of Congress Cataloging-in-Publication Data

On file with publisher.

ISBN: 978–1–57075–992–5
EISBN: 978–1–60833–227–4

For all those who still wait
For someone to listen to their story.

Contents

Part IV
A Worldwide Mission

Foreword

ARCHBISHOP EMERITUS DESMOND TUTU

I have known Fr. Michael Lapsley since he first came to Lesotho after being expelled from South Africa in late 1976. Those were very hard times, when we all lived under the brutal heel of apartheid. Even though he was a young priest, he had been speaking out with great courage against repression and was rewarded for his efforts by being banished from the country. Instead of going home to the safety of New Zealand, he moved to Lesotho, where I was bishop at the time. There he stayed with the liberation struggle with great determination and became an ambassador across the world on behalf of freedom and justice in South Africa. In 1990, while living in Zimbabwe, he paid a heavy price for his commitment when he was sent a letter bomb that did him very considerable damage. After he recuperated from his injuries and returned to South Africa, I invited him to become a priest in my diocese, the Anglican Diocese of Cape Town, a position that I am happy to say he holds to this day.

A little more than a year ago I had the great pleasure of officiating at a mass of thanksgiving at St. George's Cathedral in Cape Town on the twentieth anniversary of Fr. Michael's bombing. We gave thanks for his survival and celebrated the work he has been doing through the Institute for Healing of Memories that he founded and of which I am a proud patron. For some time I have hoped that he would write a memoir of his life's journey doing God's work, and I am delighted to have been asked to write the Foreword.

Since his bombing Fr. Michael has become a marvelous advocate for healing and reconciliation in South Africa and other strife-torn regions of the globe. He has truly become a citizen of the world, and I have watched his work with a growing sense of awe and admiration. Although he was broken physically, he has become the most whole person I know, truly a wounded healer. His memoir will bring his message to many more people throughout the world and will help create new opportunities for the Institute's work. That will be a great blessing.

Preface

The story of South Africa is a parable for a world in need of hope. After a long and bitter struggle, a system of constitutionally sanctioned racism gave way, apartheid ended, and a many-hued democracy took its place. It was a victory not without cost for the country and for myself. My own journey mirrors that of my adopted country. As a young Anglican priest originally from New Zealand, I was sent by my religious order to live in South Africa at the height of white supremacist repression. I joined the liberation struggle, went into exile, and became a thorn in the side of the apartheid regime. I was sent a letter bomb that took away my hands and one eye but failed to kill me, just as the brutality of apartheid failed to crush the aspirations of the South African people. I returned to South Africa, where I soon saw that everyone had been damaged by the apartheid years and had a story to tell, and I resolved to become a healer of the nation. This memoir, then, recounts my journey from freedom fighter for the liberation of South Africa to a wounded healer with a global mission.

The apartheid regime often attempted to justify its repression by a perverse reading of the Bible. It was a choice for death carried out in the name of the gospel of life. My role as a priest in the liberation movement directly challenged the religious and moral legitimacy that the government claimed. After a profound crisis of faith, I reluctantly abandoned pacifism and embraced the armed struggle as necessary for the liberation of South Africa's people. I was expelled from the country by the apartheid government and went into exile, first in Lesotho and subsequently in Zimbabwe, where I was sent the letter bomb that left me with a serious, permanent disability. My convalescence coincided with the negotiations that ended apartheid and ushered in democracy, so when I recovered I was able to return once again to South Africa. There I became chaplain of Cape Town's Trauma Centre for Victims of Violence and Torture and later founded the Institute for Healing of Memories.

Across the globe, wherever there is violence, poverty, and repression, South Africa's journey continues to inspire human beings injured in body, mind, and spirit. In our darkest hour the forces of good proved stronger than the forces of evil—apartheid fell and justice triumphed. So too, people draw courage from my own story. The bomb that failed to kill me left me with my tongue, which was my only weapon against apartheid. My visible brokenness creates a bond with others whose brokenness is often less visible than mine but just as real. The truth is that pain unites human beings. In my work as a healer, many people say they can trust me because I know pain. In the end, though, what matters most is whether we are able to transform pain into a life-giving force. That can be a journey of many steps. In our Healing of Memories work we offer people an opportunity to begin.

This memoir is in four parts. Part I recounts the pivotal event of my life, the bombing that took away my hands and an eye. It then continues through my long convalescence and adjustment to my disability. Part II tells the story of my life as a freedom fighter. But first it circles back to my childhood growing up in New Zealand and the development of the religious faith that has shaped every aspect of my existence. I then recount the shock of my encounter with apartheid South Africa and how my faith was shaken by that experience, my banishment from South Africa, and the years as a freedom fighter in Lesotho and then in Zimbabwe. Part III briefly revisits the bombing and then describes how my life changed as I moved from being a freedom fighter to becoming a healer and eventually founding the Institute for Healing of Memories. The remainder of the memoir, Part IV, focuses on the Institute's work worldwide, first in South Africa and later reaching across the globe for those who are in need of help and healing. There are stories of our work with Australian Aborigines, with survivors of the genocide in Rwanda and the ongoing repression in Zimbabwe, and with war veterans in the United States. Appropriately, my role in this part of the narrative becomes more a part of the background, as remarkable people we have worked with move forward with stories of their own, some of which are included alongside mine.

I like to say that the time for Healing of Memories has come in the world. In our work we raise important questions that people the world over grapple with in the context of their own struggles. What is healing? Will the wrong that has been done to us ever be acknowledged? What do we do with terrible memories? What is the role of faith? Should we forgive? And can forgiveness be reconciled with the struggle for justice? Our workshops speak to people in many different cultures. They provide a wide container that allows participants to bring whatever content, both personal and cultural, has meaning to them. We work with a great variety of people, including victims of violence and human rights abuses, people experiencing discrimination and injustice, war veterans, prison inmates, and people living with HIV/AIDS. In a world of limited resources and burgeoning need, our success points a way forward. For both practical and theoretical reasons, human rights and trauma workers and caregivers more generally are increasingly recognizing that culturally sensitive, community-based methods of healing pain like Healing of Memories are the wave of the future.

In conclusion I would like to return to faith, which is the central unifying strand of my life. In a sense, this memoir is the story of my call to live out my faith as part of the liberation of all God's people. While not everyone is religious, all of us are spiritual beings in that we seek to understand and find meaning in our lives. For most people, as for me, this is a lifelong quest and not necessarily an easy one. Not wishing to trumpet my religious faith, I have tried instead to let my actions bear it witness. My own faith journey has encompassed the simple faith of a child, the precocious piety of an adolescent, a crisis engendered by the conflict between pacifism and the armed struggle, long patient years in the liberation movement, recuperation from a bomb that nearly killed me, and finally a more mature healing faith that, while firmly rooted in the Christian tradition, embraces the full range of human spiritual experience. In our Healing of Memories work we have created a powerful method that honors people for their sacrifices and yet encourages them in the fullness of time to lay down their burdens and integrate their pain into a new life. In this way none of us need remain imprisoned by the past; rather, we can become agents of the future, helping to shape and create a better world. For me, this is the meaning of liberation, and I believe it is God's dream for the human family.

Acknowledgments

I would like to acknowledge the pivotal and major role played by Steve Karakashian, who with great generosity of spirit dedicated more than two years of his life to writing this memoir.

I wish to thank Sr. Janice McLaughlin, MM, president of the Maryknoll Sisters, and the Maryknoll Fathers and Brothers for welcoming us for two months at Maryknoll as we began work on the memoir, and my friend Madoda Gcwadi for his assistance.

I will always be grateful to the African National Congress of South Africa for accepting my membership application and thereby giving me a unique opportunity to participate in the liberation struggle.

Thank you to the Society of the Sacred Mission, the Sally and Dick Roberts Coyote Foundation, and the World Council of Churches for financial contributions and encouragement.

We are grateful to the Rockefeller Foundation for a residency in idyllic surroundings at the Rockefeller Bellagio Center in Italy, where the first draft of the manuscript was completed, and to Brother Nkoenyane Maroka, SSM, for assisting me.

Many thanks to Paul and Sally Bermanzohn, Pedro Hinestroza, Immanuel Hlabangana, the late Johnny Issel, Marlene Jackamarra, Alistair Little, the late Ndukenhle Mtshali, Karin Penno-Burmeister, Deon Snyman, Christo Thesnaar, and Michael Worsnip. All of you generously agreed to add your stories to mine. They have greatly enriched this memoir.

Thank you to Thulani Xaba, Madoda Gwadi, Ntsikelelo Mateta, and Themba Lonzi, who have crisscrossed the world spreading the gospel of Healing of Memories, and similarly Brenda Rhode, Victor Cervati, Nceba Mkwalo, and Jonah Sithole.

I appreciate the huge supportive role played by my personal assistant, Eleanor Kuhn, and before her by Shanti Mather.

My life has been shaped by my forty-one years as a member of the Society of the Sacred Mission, and I am thankful to generations of members of the Society for their love and support. In particular I wish to thank the Brothers of the Southern African Province for embracing my work.

I owe a special debt of gratitude to Tiro Motaung, my companion and friend, for more than ten years of life-giving love and support.

My mother, until her death last year, was my greatest supporter, even complaining that local TV stations did not give me enough air time. I thank all my siblings for their support, in particular since the bombing, but especially my older sisters, Helen and Irene.

I appreciate greatly the unequivocal support for this memoir from the board of the Institute for Healing of Memories under the leadership of Canon Delene Mark and previously Glenda Wildschut. Equally enthusiastic has been the board of IHOM-North America chaired by the Rev. Margaret Fell and previously the Rev. Paul Feuerstein.

My colleagues at the Institute for Healing of Memories have always encouraged the writing of this memoir even though it has increased their own work loads, especially that of my deputy Alphonse Niyodusenga and our KwaZulu-Natal manager Mpendulo Nyembe.

My dear friend Fatima Swartz was particularly helpful and encouraging with the Cuba chapter.

Through the years the Institute has relied on the contribution of volunteer facilitators and no more so than the long-term commitment of Sr. Jacinta Bannon, IBVM, and Dick Herbert.

Thank you to Orbis Books and especially to Robert Ellsberg for agreeing to publish and for his helpful advice and encouragement.

Very many friends over the years have encouraged me to write my version of my life, including the story of the Institute for Healing of Memories. Well, here it is.

With my friends Ntsikelelo Mateta and Stephen Karakashian.

PART I

THE BOMBING
AND ITS AFTERMATH

◇ 1 ◇

The Bombing

◇◇◇◇◇◇◇

IT WAS APRIL 28, 1990, and I had just sat down in my living room in Harare, happy and a bit tired after a lovely farewell party that my friends had given for me. I was sorry to leave them and to leave Harare, a city that had been my home for several years, but I looked forward to my new job as a parish priest in Zimbabwe's second city, Bulawayo. As I chatted with Andrew Mutizwa, the young man who shared my house, I reached over to a neglected pile of unopened mail and picked up a large manila envelope that had arrived from South Africa. Inside I found two religious magazines wrapped in plastic, one in Afrikaans, the other in English. Peeling away the plastic, I opened the English-language magazine and thereby completed the circuit.

The force of the blast struck me full on. I felt myself hurtling backward as if I were falling into unending darkness. If my eardrums hadn't been shattered, I would have heard the crash of the ceiling falling all around me; if my eyes hadn't been blinded, I might have made out what remained of my living room amid the rubble; but as it was, I entered a world of silence, darkness, and excruciating pain. Instinctively I knew that I had been bombed by the apartheid regime. I was in extraordinary pain, and I remember screaming to the strangers who arrived to help me from the hotel across the street, "I'm a member of the ANC. You must get help for me." I now think it was a blessing that I couldn't see, because it spared me from the sight of the blood and the stumps where my hands had been. The room was almost completely destroyed. There were huge holes in the floor and the ceiling above where I had been sitting. When one regards the destruction, it is hard to comprehend that I survived.

Alone in that emptiness, I felt the presence of God surrounding me and I knew that Mary, who had watched her son being crucified,

3

understood what I was going through. I remained conscious, though I was losing much blood, and gradually I became fully aware of the horror that had befallen me. Chaos swirled around me as my friends Rebecca Garrett and Hugh McCullum arrived and struggled to transport me to the nearest hospital. The ambulance they called never came, and so they took me to the hospital in their own car. Rebecca remembers me screaming in pain when she reached out her hand and touched me. Nevertheless, God accompanied me through the harrowing hours that lay ahead as the medical staff worked to save my life and minimize the damage to my body. Thank goodness for shock, which dulls the senses. Even so, I had pain on a scale that I don't think any human being should have to endure. Yet God's promise had been kept, the great promise of the Christian scriptures. It is not a promise that we will not suffer, but a promise that, "lo, I am with you always, even to the end of the age." I am not among those triumphalist Christians who would claim a monopoly on human wisdom or an understanding of who God is. But that is my tradition, and in that moment I went to its depths.

My close friend Jenny Hanekom is a physical therapist. She knew that the surgeon on duty that day at the Harare hospital had the reputation of being "a butcher," as she later put it somewhat indelicately. She told the medical staff firmly, "You can't operate until I find someone else." She had no real standing as a family member, but her tone of authority carried the day. Her intervention could not have been more important, but it had the effect of delaying the surgery. I was badly burned and had broken bones and wounds all over me. Since pain medication would have interfered with the anesthetic, I remained in great pain for several hours. While the staff tried to stop the bleeding, Jenny located Dr. Glenn Gordon, a visiting surgeon from the United States who was nearing the end of his appointment at the medical school. Dr. Gordon rushed to the hospital and undertook the surgery to, as he put it, "save everything I could." In a recent letter Dr. Gordon described my injuries:

When I reached his gurney in the emergency room, his condition was critical. His face was deeply cut by multiple shrapnel. One eye was virtually destroyed. Both ear drums were torn. His hands were both partially blown away with fleshless bones open to the air. Much of his upper torso and arms received shrapnel also. Amazingly, he was alert and able to communicate in a calm, clear manner. Surgery to repair the multiple lacerations over his face and body took most of the night.

A day or two later Dr. Rita Quaas, a physician from the German Democratic Republic, had to remove my right eye, which had been hopelessly damaged. She spoke movingly to me about what a terrible thing it was for her as an eye specialist to have to remove an eye that cannot be saved. At that point a little vision had returned to my left eye, so I was no longer in complete darkness, and I could hear if people shouted. Having lost one eye and seeing only a little out of the other, I feared at first that I might become permanently blind, but with the sight in my remaining eye gradually returning, I felt greatly relieved. Losing my hands was major, but if I had been blind as well, that would have been another ballgame altogether. Even so, my vision remained very poor for many weeks.

The night of the bombing, my friend Phyllis Naidoo rushed to the hospital. Phyllis is what I would call a "retired Catholic." I asked her to say the Lord's Prayer, which she had probably learned at her mother's knee, but which she nevertheless struggled to complete. When she got to "deliver us from evil," which is how the prayer ends in the Roman Catholic tradition, I remember saying, "No, no, Phyllis, you can't stop with 'evil.' We have to go on to, 'For thine is the kingdom, the power, and the glory forever.'" So even then, lying there broken as I was, I felt a sense of victory. I had won by thwarting the attempt that the "Boers" made to kill me. I was alive, and I suppose my work over the months and years since that day has been about appropriating that victory.

I had never made a distinction between human liberation and my Christian witness. For me, they are one and the same. The agents who sent the letter bomb would no doubt have viewed what they did as a political act by which they attempted to eliminate someone who was a danger to the state. Others, however, saw what had happened to me through quite a different lens. My friend and fellow priest Michael Worsnip visited me in the hospital three days after the bombing, and in the biography of me that he later wrote, he described what he saw in explicitly religious language. I quote his comments with a sense of humility and the awareness that they equally well describe the sacrifice of countless others.

I saw Christ there. Not in Michael . . . well yes, perhaps in Michael. Christ in pain. Christ with his hands blown off. Christ speaking to us through bleeding lips. Christ with one eye. Christ with a tooth missing from his mouth. Yes, I saw Christ lying there in that bed and I felt Christ minister to me. It was perhaps one of the most extraordinary spiritual experiences of my entire life. I saw not one single sign of bitterness or hatred. And that is God, is it not? I stood and could but watch and listen as this extraordinary distinctly Christian drama took the form of human flesh—scarred, burnt dismembered human flesh in the form of a friend, pastor, fellow priest and comrade.[1]

All of us in the liberation struggle had lived with the reality that a fate like this could befall us, as it had so many of our comrades. South African hit squads were relentless in hunting down their targets, and many succeeded. The military had made attacks as far afield as London. Murder, car bombing, and harassment were common. Toward the end of the time I lived in Lesotho, where South African exiles were especially vulnerable, we sometimes slept in different houses every night when there was a rumor of attack, and I always checked for bombs under my car before starting the engine. So, with the apartheid regime on the rampage across the world, this wasn't mindless paranoia. Though some comrades were dismissive of the danger with a certain bravado, it was the prudent thing to do. Years later I learned that I had indeed been singled out by South African agents. During the Truth and Reconciliation Commission hearings I obtained access to my security file, and there I found an account of an agent who had been tailing me on a speaking tour of Canada. Unfortunately for my ego, his report was that I was a very boring speaker. I was tempted to put an indignant note in my file saying, "It's not true actually. I was not a boring speaker!" On a more chilling note, in an investigative file of the Truth and Reconciliation Commission on death squads, I found reference to a communication by a certain "Colonel Hammer," so called because it was said that he would use a hammer to kill a fly. In a remarkably prescient statement, he advocated considering other methods of eliminating me, because he was concerned that a letter bomb might not actually kill me and that I would survive and come back to haunt them, which indeed I did.

My life continued to be in danger after I moved from Lesotho to Zimbabwe. I will always remember when Zimbabwean intelligence agents told me that I was on a South African government hit list. Time froze and I remember vividly the loneliness of that moment. This wasn't someone else I had read about in the newspaper; they were after me! Sometimes I would wake in the night startled by a sound and think, "Why am I awake? Is there an attack?" I learned how to

---

[1] Michael Worsnip, *Priest and Partisan: A South African Journey* (North Melbourne: Ocean Press, 1996), 15.

roll out of bed and onto the floor. I never sat or stood up, because that is when they would shoot a person dead. The Zimbabwean government's response to the hit list information was to put me under a twenty-four-hour armed guard. That, along with speaking at the funerals of comrades who had been killed, was a constant reminder that the struggle could cost me my life at any moment. I had lived with this possibility for a long time, and it forced me to ask myself, "What is it that I am living for such that the South African government wants to kill me? What are my deepest values? What do I believe in?" I knew I was prepared to die for the cause of liberation, yet fear is a very human emotion. I think people who do not feel fear are not fully human, and so I always prayed that I would have the courage to act as I believed and not shrink because of my fear. Despite all this, I had never really considered that surviving with a permanent, major physical disability might be part of the bargain. Yet here I was; the worst had happened, and I knew almost immediately that I was going to live, and despite great pain, I felt victorious for having survived.

I thought of what happened after the horrible 1982 massacre in Lesotho when South African troops invaded the country in the dead of night and killed forty-two people, citizens of Lesotho and South African members of the ANC. Many children and adults died in their beds. I was out of the country, and when I returned I found that some people had begun to suspect others of treachery. If a person had survived, what did that mean? Why didn't they get that person? The questions were left unanswered, but it was as if the only decent thing was to be dead. Phyllis Naidoo herself had been injured by a letter bomb in 1979 in Lesotho, and her son Sahdhan had been murdered in cold blood by an agent of the South African government in Lusaka only the year before my bombing, so Phyllis too knew suffering. That night when she prayed with me in the hospital, I realized that seeing me a mass of bloody bandages must bring back painful memories for her. The sadness of her loss overcame me, and I felt a need to say to her, "I'm sorry I survived"—to apologize to her that I had lived while her precious son had not, and we cried together.

Given how common assassinations were, the most startling element in my bombing was not that it occurred, but its timing. Negotiations were about to begin between the ANC and the apartheid government, and there were assurances from South African Defense Minister Magnus Malan that there would be no further attacks in neighboring countries. We kept telling ourselves we shouldn't be naive, but despite that we relaxed our vigilance a bit, including the Zimbabweans who removed my armed guards. Nelson Mandela had been released from prison not quite three months earlier, the ANC and other political organizations had been unbanned, and only four days after I was bombed on April 28, 1990, representatives of the apartheid government and the ANC sat down in Cape Town for the first time to talk about normalizing their relationship. There had been secret negotiations before, but this was the first time they had spoken publicly. It said to the world that both sides were serious about finding a negotiated settlement. These discussions culminated on May 4 in a communiqué that is known as the Groote Schuur Minute, and it laid the groundwork for the negotiations that followed.

Needless to say, there was opposition from many quarters in the white community to these developments, and some people have suggested that my bombing may have been intended to delay or scuttle the talks. Then too, there was a particular resentment, even hatred, against white people like myself who were seen as "race traitors" by supporters of apartheid. My own view is that these explanations, however flattering, give me entirely too much importance. It is equally likely that there was a completely banal reason; I may have been on a hit list, and perhaps my bombing was simply unfinished business by low-level operatives who may have been under the illusion that they could prevent the talks. Regardless of the reason, the attack on me was a straw in the wind, because in South Africa during the next few years all hell broke loose. The government killed defenseless people on an unprecedented scale, while at the same time negotiations between the ANC and the government continued and eventually led to full democracy.

In view of all this, the Zimbabweans were taking no chances. After Dr. Gordon had done his work and the surgery was completed, I was put in a military section of the hospital with a policeman stationed outside my door. The Zimbabwean authorities worried that the apartheid regime might try to finish me off, so they kept most visitors away for what they saw as my own good. Understandable as that was, it was very difficult for me, and those visitors who made it through the security gauntlet were as good as medicine. My friend Geraldine Fraser-Moleketi later said she knew I was going to be fine when I turned to her and asked how I looked. When I made the mistake of asking my friend Phyllis Naidoo the same question, she told me that I was as ugly as ever. I knew then she thought I was going to be all right. A couple of my visitors were from the Zimbabwean Central Intelligence Organization. Ironically, years later I found that a transcript of my hospital interview with them had been inserted into my South African security file, indicating that at least one of them was a double agent. So much for my security!

My bombing was news on radio broadcasts throughout Zimbabwe and indeed across the world. In the four weeks that I remained in that Harare hospital, messages from friends and supporters streamed in. My two sisters, Helen and Irene, and a close family friend, Charles Hamilton, arrived, two from Australia and one from London, along with the head of my order and other members of my religious community. For a time I had been a parish priest in a township outside of Harare, and many former parishioners came, especially the youth, but also some elderly folks who walked long distances in the hot African sun. Unfortunately, they were not allowed to see me.

A few days after the bombing there was a prayer service at the Anglican Cathedral in Harare, and people from all over the country made their way there to pray for my recovery. I managed to dictate a message to the congregation that was read out by my sister Helen. At the service one of the speakers said of me:

He ministered to exiles from South Africa in all parts of the world. He ministered to nationals of the country he worked in. He buried our dead, visited our sick, married our comrades, christened our babies, and found scholarships for so many South Africans. He provided a home for all. He comforted us in good times and bad. But mostly this stranger came to us and gave us his love and won ours. We are beggars in the face of his courage. The Boers will not win in the face of such indomitable courage.

The ambassador of Cuba visited and invited me to Cuba for free medical treatment, as did the governments of Sweden and Norway. The Palestinian ambassador said, "Any support you need, we will give you." In all, seven countries offered free medical treatment. To my great delight, my former boss from the Lutheran World Federation, Wolfgang Lauer, contrived to bring in whiskey, which was quite sensitive of him, I thought. Unfortunately, after a while the whiskey before supper had to stop because doctors feared it would interfere with my other medications. Highly regrettable!

My friend Sr. Janice McLaughlin, a Maryknoll Sister from the United States, came to the hospital with Fr. Cas Paulsen and Fr. Dick O'Riordan, and along with Dr. Gordon, my surgeon, and his wife, Sue, we all—Anglicans, Methodists, and Catholics—celebrated the Eucharist together in my hospital room as soon as I was able. Though

I had only bloody stumps I could still manage the sign of the cross. After the mass Dr. Gordon sang and played the guitar for us all. On another occasion we ended the communion service by singing "Nkosi Sikelel' iAfrika," now South Africa's national anthem, and I gave the power salute at the end.

For my family in New Zealand the bombing was perhaps what they had long feared. Though they didn't speak of it, they knew about the police guards and the threats I lived under. My father especially was a very emotional person like myself. My mother often said she was glad he wasn't alive because she didn't think he could have coped. She was already in her seventies when I was bombed, and it certainly shook her very deeply as well. The family was besieged by the press because I was well known in New Zealand for my antiapartheid work. Family members protected my mother. She was a private person and would not have had any desire to speak publicly about the terrible thing that had befallen her son. She was also a woman of deep religious conviction, and I believe she was engaged in her own inner faith journey with respect to what happened to me. I felt a need to speak with her, and she mothered me by telephone in my hospital bed as soon as I was able to talk. As we spoke, I had the sense that a sword had pierced her heart. Later on, she flew to Australia to visit me in the hospital there.

As I grew stronger, a part of me began to feel some of the time that I had gotten off lightly. The apartheid regime had failed twice over. Not only had they failed to kill me, I had no major internal injuries and my mind was as clear as ever, and though they had taken my hands and my eye and shattered my skull, they had left my tongue intact. That, after all, had been my only weapon. Ever since, my body has been a testimony to the brutality of apartheid. Nevertheless, I was still very weak and swathed in bandages. In truth, I was as helpless as a newborn baby; I could do nothing for myself. There were more than a few bleak moments when I thought surely it would have been better to be dead. Will life ever be life again? How will I live a life with no hands? Will I ever be independent and able to drive a car? How can I possibly celebrate the Eucharist? Touching people was my way of expressing love and affection. Now what will I do? I still could not see well, and with each day that passed, my fear grew that I would never read again. That would have been a terrible blow! It was quite a triumphant moment when later in Australia the doctors realized that with glasses I would indeed be able to read. Just as wonderful was the news that my sight would be within the legal requirements to drive a car.

When visitors were expected, the hospital staff usually got me all tucked up and ready for company. Of course, under the circumstances there was a limit to what they could do to make me presentable. I must have been a frightful sight. I remember one couple that came, and I must not have been as nicely tucked up as usual, and they really freaked out. So I found myself becoming the pastor to them and saying, "There, there, it's not so bad. It could have been much worse; after all, I'm alive." So I was the victim ministering to the witnesses. But they found it very difficult to cope with the visual reality of what had happened to me. And if truth be known, later on when I could see better, I had the same difficulty myself.

Some of the time I found myself playing the sort of self-blaming mind games that victims do. Perhaps I deserved to be bombed. I was tempted to go through the catalog of the sins I'd committed since childhood. This wasn't a dominant feeling and it certainly isn't my theology, but for me, like other trauma survivors, these feelings surfaced nonetheless. In those darker moments I relied on my simple childhood faith in a loving God and in Jesus who suffered like me and was crucified. In my years of training as a priest, I had been steeped in the psalms. I turned to them for consolation and support, and I drew comfort from the knowledge that people had done so for four thousand years before me. But above all, an avalanche of prayers and love from supporters around the world lifted me up. I have scrapbooks full of the messages that kept flooding in. In some ways I feel that when I die I won't need a funeral because people said all the nice things then. It was quite extraordinary.

As the recipient of a letter bomb, I had become the object of evil. It is evil to create and send letter bombs to other human beings and to type an address on an envelope knowing it is designed to kill someone. Yet at the same time I also became the beneficiary of all that is beautiful in the human family, the ability to be tender, loving, and compassionate.

With my mother, Laura, in New Zealand.

◇ 2 ◇

Recovery

◇◇◇◇◇◇◇

THE NURSES AT PARIRENYATWA HOSPITAL had fussed over me with great love and kindness, and the doctors had patched me up. My life was no longer in danger, but a month on, my wounds were still jagged and raw. I needed much more surgery to facilitate proper healing and to prepare my body to accept the prostheses that I would have to wear for the rest of my life. I decided to go to Australia for further treatment. My sister Helen taught health economics at the University of New South Wales in Sydney and made arrangements for me to be admitted to Prince of Wales Hospital, a large teaching facility there. I would be close to her and her husband, Clive, and not far from the Brothers of my religious community and friends from my theological student days, so Australia was the obvious choice. Besides excellent medical care, I was going to need support and companionship through what was certain to be a long convalescence. There was some nervousness on the part of the airline about whether taking me on board would constitute a security risk. After all, I had just been bombed by the South African government, and perhaps it would take the opportunity to finish the job aloft that it had botched on the ground. Nevertheless, the airline eventually relented.

Flying from Harare to Sydney by way of Perth required nearly twenty-four hours, because there were no direct flights, and it is exhausting under the best of circumstances. In my case, sitting up in a normal airline seat was out of the question. Arrangements were made that I would travel in a portable bed with a member of my order and a nurse accompanying me. Selecting the nurse was easy; I chose the one who gave the least painful injections. During the month since the bombing I had scarcely been out of my hospital room except to be wheeled for surgery and medical tests. Everything was done to and for me. What a drastic change from the active, independent life I had led! Even as a schoolboy in New Zealand I had quite an independent streak and tried in my small way to fight racism and advocate for justice. As an adult I thought for myself, I acted according to what I saw as right, and I had something of a reputation for challenging authority and its abuse. I had had my battles, not only with the South African government, but with church officials whom I sometimes perceived as narrow minded or self-interested, if not racist. I saw the struggle for the soul of South Africa as a moral issue for the whole world, and although my role was modest, I had sometimes flown on long trips representing the ANC to faith organizations abroad. Planes were nothing new to me, but now, outside the hospital for the first time since the bombing, I found myself strapped immobile on a stretcher and placed on a wooden pallet ready to be loaded like so much cargo into a jumbo jet. As I lay there on the tarmac looking up at the sky, I thought, "What kind of world is possible for me? Will I ever have a meaningful life again?"

The flight was as grueling as I feared. Sedation took the edge off my discomfort, but I rested only a little. On many previous trips I had dreamed about how nice it would be to have a bed on these long flights. But lying in a stretcher, weak, swathed in bandages, and perched precariously atop six airplane seats was another story altogether. I was physically uncomfortable and dependent on the nurse for my smallest needs. I had fought so hard during these past weeks to live, and friends had showered me with so much love and encouragement. Now, in these rather bizarre circumstances I felt exposed and vulnerable.

When we finally arrived in Sydney, an ambulance was waiting on the tarmac, and I was duly delivered to the hospital. The fact that I arrived on a stretcher with bandages where my hands should have been did not daunt the admitting officer who detained me with a long series of questions, I suppose to see if my brain was still working. I believe psychologists call this a mental-status inventory. "What is your name?" they wanted to know. In my current state I was lucky to remember. "What day is it?" Ironically, I had just crossed the international date line though I'm not sure whether the admitting officer would have appreciated that. "Why are you in the hospital?" At that, I thought to myself, "Oh, dear God, isn't it reasonably obvious?"

By midnight I was finally assigned a room and settled into bed. The nurses did their best to make me comfortable, but I had been in transit for more than twenty-four hours and was completely exhausted. In the Harare hospital I had been surrounded by friends much of the time and protected by police and soldiers outside my door. Here on my first night in the Sydney hospital I was alone without any security whatever. It was all too much to cope with in my weakened state. The little energy that remained drained out of me and I had no reserves left. I was seized with the premonition that I might die that night. I never even told my sister this, but in my despair I asked the nurses to please telephone a few Australian friends and ask them to pray for me. Unfortunately, they were not able to reach anyone. I tried to stay awake all night so I wouldn't die, but I knew it was impossible. Spiritual strength alone would have to sustain me; there was nothing else. As the darkness of night settled over the hospital, I lay in my bed silently repeating, "I can't survive without help. I can't survive without help." It was a prayer.

The next morning I learned that the nursing sisters had realized the urgency of my distress and had later found a way to contact my friends Helen and Jim Tregea in Wagga Wagga. Jim had been the parish priest under whom I'd done a curacy as a newly ordained priest many years earlier, and he and Helen had become lifelong friends. When they paid me a visit not long after, they told me that they had organized a Eucharist in their home in response to the hospital's call and had sat up all night praying for me.

The next evening, still shaky from my ordeal, I suddenly noticed a shadowy figure appear outside the window of my room. In my vulnerable state I completely freaked out. I was sure the enemy had finally caught up with me. The shadow turned out to be a window cleaner, but my fear was not unfounded. After all, my being alive represented a failure on the part of the regime that wished to kill me. South Africans had recently exploded a bomb in Australia, and ANC members had been attacked in France and Brussels. Bombings and assassinations were all too real. Some time later the Australian government sent around a security adviser. He said words to the effect that if I put myself in a cupboard and closed the door, I would be completely safe, and then he left me to draw my own conclusion. It was clear that that would not be a life worth living. I had to be sensible but not imprisoned by fear. Why survive if my life is bound up with worry that they might kill me? There were indeed threats from time to time. Three years later, in 1993, on the night when Chris Hani, a much-beloved leader of the armed struggle, was assassinated, an anonymous caller phoned and said, "We will get you!" That unnerved me more than a little, but I never retreated from my decision to move forward undaunted.

About two weeks after I arrived at the hospital in Sydney, I dictated a letter that my friend George Makoko sent out to friends and supporters around the world:

Dear Friends,

On Saturday evening, April 28, I opened a letter bomb which had been sent from South Africa to kill me. I am alive! My physical body is scarred, but then I had never been in danger of winning a beauty contest.

My spirit at one level is as fragile as anyone in the human community. And yet at another level, my spirit is stronger, deeper, and more resolute than ever before in the commitment I share with the people of South Africa for a new and full liberated South Africa, whose birth pangs are still proving to be so painful and so costly to so many. Hopefully and prayerfully, all that has happened to me will make me a more sensitive and compassionate human being.

My personal road back to a full contribution to the struggle and more complete healing seems likely to be quite lengthy. I have wept and been overwhelmed and strengthened a thousand fold by the messages of love, of prayer, of support, and solidarity that have poured in from all over the globe. To say "thank you" seems such a trite and inadequate response in the face of what you have given me. One day I will try and tell the story as I remember it of what happened on that fateful night and the story of some of the many people who saved my life.

Many of you will know that for some considerable time I have been a member of a number of families. Firstly, and obviously, there is my natural family. Then there is the Society of the Sacred Mission, the religious community of which I am a member. And there is the wider family of the African National Congress of South Africa that is leading South Africa's liberation struggle, of which I have been a member for a number of years. For six and a half years, the Basotho people have shared their lives with me. Since 1983 Zimbabwe and her people have been home to me in ways too numerous to mention. People from many other struggles and all corners of the globe continue to enrich my life. At my own personal moment of need all these different families have become as one, and so together we shall survive and we shall win.

As always, still in struggle, and with much love,
Michael Lapsley, SSM

My brother-in-law Clive, Helen's husband, knowing me to be a news junkie and still unable to read, thoughtfully recorded onto tape excerpts culled from the day's leading newspapers. That helped me to while away the time. In all, I spent seven months in two Australian hospitals, and I faced a long series of surgeries. There were operations to clean up the stumps of my arms so they would accept the prostheses and others to prepare my eye socket to be fitted with an artificial eye. The two operations on my ears were not fully successful; to this day the range of what I can hear is limited. I faced these many surgeries with dread and anxiety. Being bombed is one thing, but going into the operating theater again and again is another sort of trauma altogether; there is too much time to anticipate what is coming. Fortunately, the Australians were superb at pain management. When it is not handled properly, amputees can suffer phantom pain, sometimes for the rest of their lives. I have never experienced this because of the skill with which the doctors administered the pain medication and then incrementally withdrew it when it was no longer needed.

The hospital decided to send a psychologist to help me cope with my surgeries. When she arrived, she turned out to be a white South African. What was startling was that our meeting was a crisis for her. She felt that her own people had bombed me, so even though she was the psychologist and I was the patient, I ended up being a priest and ministering to her. I said, "Well, look, I don't have a problem with your being a white South African. Some of my best friends are white. I happen to be white myself, but I do have a problem if you are personally committed to apartheid." She carried a heavy burden of collective guilt and shame for what had happened to me at the hands of what she experienced as her people.

When the hospital chaplain appeared, he asked me, "Do you think you upset the South African government?" I was so taken aback that for once I was tongue-tied. What I should have said was, "I bloody well hope so!" Another day he said, "Of course, opinion is divided about apartheid." This time I was ready and I replied, "Well, yes, the international community says it's a crime against humanity; the Christian community says it's a heresy. Then there are the supporters." He never came back. I was in that ward for four months, and when I misbehaved one nursing sister said with a twinkle in her eye, "You really are being rather difficult today. If you aren't careful, we'll call the chaplain." The ultimate threat!

Eventually the hospital organized a psychiatrist, Dr. Murray Wright, to see me. He was kind and helpful, and we bonded immediately. I saw him every week for four months. It was so valuable to have an independent person with whom I could share whatever was driving me crazy at the moment—the anxiety I felt about living with disability, and the ordinary things of life in a hospital and relationships with family. These were things I wouldn't have said to people I was intimate with for fear of hurting or offending them, but I needed to say them somewhere that was safe. Dr. Wright played a very beneficial role, for which I was grateful. When I was about to be discharged we had lunch together, and he told me that, for the first time in his professional career, he had not taken notes after the first visit because, as he put it, "I thought you were an exceptionally well-balanced person. The way you've coped with this trauma is quite extraordinary." Then he confessed that he'd enjoyed our sessions so much he kept them going for weeks longer than he thought necessary.

Because I had a broken right arm, I received first the prosthesis for my left arm and thus began the difficult process of coming to terms with my disability. I was confronted with the need to accept the change in my appearance and body image. I had to recognize how, completely unaware, I had internalized the attitudes of people around me. I remember a friend in Lesotho discovering that a young woman he was interested in had a disability. His attitude immediately changed. "Of course I couldn't have a relationship with her," he said. These negative feelings seep into all of us and I was no exception. The prosthetist helped me by arranging a meeting with a young man who had lost his hands in an accident and who was getting on with his life. I was grateful to have such an important role model.

My sister Helen visited soon after I was fitted with the second prosthesis. I was horrified when I looked at myself in the mirror and thought, "Oh, my goodness, this is what I'm going to appear like for the rest of my life." Helen was quite wonderful at that moment. She agreed that they were ugly, and we sat and cried together and shared a strong drink. The unspoken sentiment was, "OK, this is the way it is. Let's not pretend it's beautiful." It continues to be true that I am reminded a thousand times a day that the hands won't ever return. Just as one mourns the loss of a loved one who is also a part of who we are, one mourns the loss of a limb. It affects every single part of your life every single day. It's not all consuming or overwhelming, but it's always there.

The healing journey is a zigzag road, two steps forward, one step backward. The first task is one of accepting the reality of disability; the next is functional—learning how to get on with the tasks of life. Initially I very much wanted to get a set of prostheses that looked like hands and I did. In fact, I still have them. But the reality was that they were quite impractical. I wore them on one or two occasions, but in the end functionality won over aesthetics, and I decided to opt for the hooks that I use now. My friend Bishop John Osmers had one arm blown off by a parcel bomb in Lesotho many years before. I quickly realized that losing both hands was a hundred times worse than losing one hand, because John was able to do almost everything with his good hand. John, like most people who have lost only one hand, had a prosthesis that remained in his drawer. He never used it. In my case the task was much more difficult because I had to use the prostheses for every aspect of daily life.

The second step is the task of everyday living. The physical therapists first focused on the basics of self-care, things such as using the toilet, showering, and getting dressed, but what was especially notable after that was how sensitively they tailored their work to the particulars of my job and what would enhance the quality of my everyday life. Since I am a priest, they asked, "What do you need to do as a priest? What does that require?" I said I needed to celebrate the mass. I needed to drive a car. They also inquired about what makes my life enjoyable. I said I liked to take photographs, and they said, "Bring the camera." I did, and they added an attachment that allowed me to hold it, which would have otherwise been completely impossible. They might easily have reduced me to just a body, taught me the mechanics of using my prostheses, and sent me on my way. Instead, they affirmed me as a person by asking what would help improve the quality of my life and give it meaning.

The third and perhaps most important task is spiritual. Without intending to be overly dramatic, an injury as severe as this is cataclysmic, and no one can know in advance how he or she will respond. In my life till then, I had staked out my own ground. To be sure, I had had my share of trials and I had demonstrated a certain strength of character in the face of adversity, but this was a challenge in a completely different league. Despite my seeming toughness, part of me has always been conscious of my fragility and vulnerability. I was never someone who coped easily with pain. Yet after the bombing I experienced pain that is hard to believe a human being could endure. Somewhere I found strength in me that I didn't know was there. But now I faced a different challenge. How would I come to terms with my physical limitations? Could I learn to accept help for the rest of my life? In the West we often take the desire for independence to absurd lengths. Of course, wherever possible we need a measure of independence. However, I have realized that not only I but all people need to develop a healthy interdependence as well. As the weeks passed I went a long way down the road of struggling with patience. Sometimes we fail and sometimes we succeed, but no matter, the reality is that we've lost a level of independence that we never recover and we never completely stop grieving the loss. There are a million tiny things we do for ourselves in our own way. When people help us, they do them their way not our way, and we have to accept that. At times it is a hard thing to learn. My existence was going to be radically different now, and I had to ask myself what was important in this new life. Ultimately, this is a spiritual question, and it opened a new and deeper chapter of my faith journey.

As a piously religious boy completely devoted to my faith, I had once fantasized about the possibility that devout Christians could develop what are called stigmata, which are marks on the believer's body of Christ's crucifixion. Stigmata have been reported through the ages, especially by members of religious orders, which of course I intended to join. In my case these were the precocious ideas of an adolescent smitten with religiosity, but the great irony is that I did end up with visible traumatic marks of a sort of crucifixion. Even from a mature faith perspective this was one way of making sense of what happened to me.

As so often in these cases, God speaks through human voices. Throughout my convalescence, messages of prayer, love, and support continued to flow in, and I remember particularly the role that children played in my healing. The walls of my hospital room were covered with pictures and drawings that were sent by children from Australia and Canada and my lovely little niece, Lizzie Bick. I had met the Canadian children when I had spoken at their school in North Bay only a few weeks before I was bombed. They were stunned by the news because they knew me and felt a personal connection with me. The Australian children, on the other hand, had never met me but were moved by my story nevertheless. People of faith and people with none sent messages of love and goodwill. That, then, was the vehicle that God used to enable me to make my bombing redemptive, to bring life out of death and good out of evil. Well-meaning Christians sometimes say, "It was God's will." I emphatically reject that! My response is to say, "Oh, you mean that God makes letter bombs?" When I say I have made my bombing redemptive, it is not to say that evil isn't evil.

Obviously my losses are permanent, but so too are the gains for myself and for others. The truth is that in the bombing I lost a lot, I still have a lot, and I have gained as well. I am immeasurably richer for the journey I've traveled, and so my life is not full of regrets. Of course part of me says, "If only I had realized it was a bomb and not opened it," but God has enabled me to make my bombing redemptive. Some people who have had horrible things happen to them are, to be sure, survivors, but they remain prisoners of a moment in their past. I think there is another step that requires moving away from being an object of history—someone to whom something terrible has been done—to becoming a subject of history once more. This means becoming someone who once again participates in shaping and creating the world. Therefore, I began to realize that if I were consumed by hatred, bitterness, and a desire for revenge, I would be a victim forever. The oppressors would have failed to kill my body, but they certainly would have killed my soul. The outpouring of love and support I received enabled me to walk a journey from victim, to being a survivor, to finally becoming a victor. This did not happen quickly or easily; it was a long road, and it continues to this very day. The first step was the struggle to get well, to return to my life, and then to live it as fully and joyfully as possible. That would be my victory.

People often say very generous and kind things about me and sometimes hold me up as a role model. Part of that is appropriate and part of it, though well meant, is dehumanizing. I couldn't be who I am now without the support of the many, many people who have loved and cared about me. So it was not only my victory but also theirs. I think we often do that to people whom we admire. We turn them into plastic. But I am no sort of plastic saint. Ask the person who stays with me and he would say that there is nothing saintly about me. I can be more of an example to others with my many human weaknesses than as a plaster saint who has overcome it all, free of distortions and contradictions. When I walk the streets of South Africa, my appearance confronts people with the truth of who we are as a people and what we've done to one another. So, yes, I am a sign of triumph over adversity, but I am also, with my humanness and my limitedness, a sign that compassion and gentleness are stronger than evil, hatred, and death. This is possible for all God's people in the fullness of their humanity, not just for a sainted few. I am victorious, but the marks of the past remain on me. In that way, as with so many others, my journey from being a freedom fighter to being a healer parallels that of South Africa. We needed to struggle and ultimately slay the monster that was apartheid, but then we had to begin the long journey of healing ourselves and building a new nation where all people have a chance to live their life to the fullest. And that can only happen when one is not imprisoned by the past.

◇ 3 ◇

Disability—Accepting Brokenness

◇◇◇◇◇◇◇

LEAVING THE HOSPITAL IN AUSTRALIA after seven months was a triumph. I had not only survived a bomb intended to kill me and more surgeries than I care to remember, but I was now back on my feet and ready to get on with my life. My resilience surprised many people, but I never had any doubt. It was just a question of doing, medically speaking, what had to be done. Even though the immediate outlook was uncertain, I knew I had a future, though what that might look like, I couldn't yet discern. In one way I was still very much the independent and resourceful person I had always been; at the same time, everything had changed. Negotiating the world without hands was a bit like starting all over again. I felt both fragile and confident.

The next weeks and months were a crash course in managing a life with a major disability. It was a steep learning curve. In the hospital, help was always available. Now it was up to me to arrange the assistance I needed. There were intensely frustrating moments when I was alone and unable to perform simple tasks that I once could have done without a thought. The physical therapists had meticulously trained me on the use of my prostheses, but nothing can prepare us for the challenges presented by the myriad things we do with our hands every day that able-bodied people take for granted.

Then there was the social adjustment. Disability evokes strong feelings in many of us, no doubt because it reminds us of our own vulnerability, fragility, and even mortality. These responses can be very hurtful even if they are unintentional, especially to someone like me, still anxious about my changed appearance. One particular incident soon after I returned to South Africa is etched in my memory. I turned a corner in the office where I was working and I startled a woman coming out of the bathroom. She looked at me in shock and terror as she noticed my appearance. I remember vividly feeling the sting of her reaction and how I cringed inside as I experienced her horror. On another occasion I had been shopping in a Cape Town supermarket with a friend. I tired of shopping and so I said to him, "I'll wait for you outside." I found a chair in front of the supermarket and before long, to my astonishment, a woman came up to me and took a coin out of her pocket and offered it to me because she thought I was a beggar. Of course I had no hands to receive it, so after some fumbling she took back the proffered coin and off she went. Incidents like these penetrate deeply into the soul of an affected person. And sometimes they also make us laugh. People with disabilities far more serious than mine, such as severe cerebral palsy, evoke even stronger feelings. While their bodies may twist unpredictably or they may speak with difficulty, inside there is a human being who is vulnerable to the pain of rejection and longing to be seen as more than the disability.

I had suddenly become a member of a minority that I had not anticipated joining, and I quickly developed a sense of solidarity with others like me. It also made me more sensitive to other minorities who experience discrimination. My disability could not be ignored. When I was introduced to someone, I could no longer shake hands. Instead I offered an arm or gave the person a gentle hug, but this too had the effect of calling attention to my disability. Bizarrely, from my point of view, some people insisted on shaking the metal hook. As an able-bodied person, like most people, I knew how to avoid drawing unwanted attention to myself, but now I had no such option; anonymity vanished completely. When I entered a room, some people stared at the hooks on my arms, while others self-consciously went to absurd lengths to look the other way. Then there were those who dealt with their discomfort by rushing to offer help I hadn't asked for and didn't need. I often recall one of the principles of my community that says, "Do not cumber others with services bred of your own presumption."

I began to examine my own preconceptions about people with disabilities. Had I been oblivious to their pain? Had I objectified them? As I looked deeper, I realized rather shamefacedly that my insensitivity had played out in my own family. My relationship with my older brother Peter, has always been a bit conflicted. He stuttered and I was an adolescent with a precocious religiosity and a somewhat inflated confidence in my own opinions. I was also blessed with a well-developed gift of speech, so in verbal combat I was able to fire the shots much faster than Peter who struggled. I now realize that I took unfair advantage of his disability, and that undoubtedly played a part in the distance between us. Of course the tables can be turned as well, and those of us with disabilities can use them to leverage special favors. At the end of a long day when I am tired, it is all too easy to say to a friend, "Would you do this for me?" when the "this" is something I could do for myself with a little extra effort. There are also things that I could do with some difficulty that I choose not to do, such as loading the dishwasher, helping with cooking, and carrying my luggage. I find myself thinking, "Well, disability has to have some advantages." Guilt can also be used as a weapon to punish people if they don't cater to our demands. Similarly the adulation of admiring people can go to our head in ways that are seductive but spiritually risky. These are the dangerous pitfalls of disability that encourage us to remain as victims and can be corrosive of our relationships with loved ones.

When people ask me how my hands operate, my normal answer is to say they operate by faith and hope, but actually they are connected to my shoulders. When I move my shoulder in a certain way, they open, and when I move in another way they don't. So, while they are quite coarse looking, they are actually very finely tuned instruments. In fact, I can type and I can drive a car. What I can and can't do is a bit unpredictable. For example, it's easier for me to drive or use my laptop or cell phone than it is to open the top button of my shirt. Just after I returned to South Africa, Archbishop Tutu invited me to dinner. I was still learning to be effective with my prostheses, so at that stage if I was holding a cup with the right one and then tried to do something with the left, there was a danger that it would fall. Sure enough, when Tutu poured coffee into my cup, it slipped, pouring coffee all over the archbishop. He asked me if I wanted to go home, but I said actually I would prefer another cup of coffee.

Each person's disability has its own uniqueness. This is most obvious concerning facilities. Some years ago I went to a meeting in Johannesburg that was held at a new conference center. The hosts looked unusually delighted to see me. I couldn't fathom their enthusiasm until it turned out that the new facility came replete with a disability suite. With great fanfare they marched me off to see it. When we got there and I looked around, it seemed quite ordinary—a bed, a chair, and a wardrobe, nothing particularly related to disability. Then they took me to the bathroom, and the one thing that was unusual about it was a hand-held shower! The designers obviously did not have me in mind. To their dismay I said, "Would you mind finding me another room?"

The United States is particularly challenging because, whereas more often other countries use door handles, the United States uses knobs that are impossible for me to turn. The first time I went to the United States after I was bombed I was in a hotel where I couldn't get in or out of my room without calling security. That was when I decided I would never again travel without a personal assistant. More recently, I was at a meeting in New York City at an expensively appointed set of offices in midtown Manhattan. As before, I was shown with great pride a bathroom that had been outfitted for disability. Unfortunately it too had a round doorknob. On that occasion, the door was refitted the very next day with a lever arrangement that I could use. When I go to a restaurant I often have to negotiate with the waiter to serve my tea in a tall narrow glass that I can grasp. What is striking is that the staff invariably discounts my experience that hot tea will not break the glass. No matter how patiently I assure them that it won't break, they doggedly insist that it will. It never has.

If the long months of convalescence had taught me the basics of living with disability, I soon acquired a postgraduate education when I undertook a long speaking tour. As it happened, I was more in demand than ever for engagements abroad. People knew what had happened to me and wanted to express their support in person. Then too, I was keen to express my thanks to all those who had accompanied me on my journey of recovery. Nevertheless, the endless talking about my bombing was very wearying. It isn't that it's retraumatizing; it becomes boring, actually. I found myself repeating the story over and over and inwardly saying, "Here we go again."

Politically, the ANC had recently been unbanned and formal negotiations between the white government and the liberation movement were under way. There was also a huge amount of violence with the white government stirring up trouble against and among rival political and ethnic groups as well as directly mounting its own violent repression. The apartheid regime had successfully destabilized the whole Southern Africa region and now began to do the same thing inside South Africa. In the face of the forthcoming elections the government wanted to keep the democratic forces fighting among themselves rather than mobilizing for votes. Some have suggested that the government was so naive as to believe that it could outmaneuver the forces for liberation and hold onto the substance of political power. No one knew the outcome. Was there going to be a blood bath? Was a peaceful change of government possible?

Foreign friends were anxious to hear my interpretation of these developments. So only eighteen months after my bombing I embarked on what proved to be an exhausting foreign tour of Norway, Sweden, the United Kingdom, the United States, and Canada. These trips were always grueling, but since I was still recovering my full strength and had no experience in managing travel in my new condition, it was a bit crazy on my part. If I arrived by train, for example, someone had to meet me on the platform because I could not move the luggage. Bathroom facilities were sometimes a problem. In truth, I myself couldn't always anticipate what kind of assistance I would need, and my hosts had little or no ability to do so. So we muddled through. I often had to reassure them, and they were sometimes frustrated if I seemed a little bit flippant. Then there were the endless receptions. Sometimes there weren't glasses that I could hold, and of course I couldn't manage finger foods. When I'm with close friends I ask people to put food in my mouth, but with strangers I didn't always feel comfortable doing that. All this was very new to me and sometimes stressful. I returned home somewhat chastened and with a much more realistic sense of what these trips entailed.

Not long after I left the Australian hospital I returned to Zimbabwe. People everywhere seemed to know me and expressed their delight to see me up and about. For example, while I was walking in the park with a friend, a policeman stopped me. "Don't you remember that I was one of your bodyguards when you were in the hospital?" he said. "How are you feeling now?" Virtually every single day I had similar experiences both with friends and total strangers. This made me feel profoundly a part of Zimbabwe and not just an exile waiting to return to South Africa. Then, soon after I arrived, I was dumbfounded to learn that I was to be awarded the Queen's Service Medal by the people of New Zealand in recognition of my efforts on behalf of the liberation of Southern Africa. As I said at the ceremony, this honor is usually reserved for captains of industry and retired army colonels, certainly not priests who join national liberation movements and defend the moral legitimacy of armed struggle! My comments evoked smiles, but no one moved to rescind it.

On the other hand, I soon discovered that disability was another planet for many people. I had occasion to meet some of my former comrades in the struggle. When I referred to myself as disabled they became extremely uncomfortable and said, "But you're not disabled!" Now what sort of nonsense was that? What they were really saying was that their conceptual framework simply couldn't encompass the idea of my disability. For them, I was a soldier injured in battle, and that was that. This was a notion they could fathom, whether or not it fit my reality. It didn't matter that I'd never fired a gun.

As I felt ready to go back to work, I decided to visit the bishop who had employed me as a parish priest in the Diocese of Bulawayo. I hadn't been able to assume my duties there because I was bombed two days before I was scheduled to begin. This particular bishop, a kind man, had come to see me in the hospital and prayed for my recovery. Now, seven months later, I turned up at his door. I said I was well now and thanked him for praying for me. Then I inquired about resuming my work. He looked extremely uncomfortable, and I wondered if it was because as a bishop he wasn't used to God answering his prayers. Finally he said, "But you are disabled. What can you do?" I replied, "Well, Father, I can do many things. For example, I can even drive a car," at which point he looked totally terrified. I think he thought he might end up on the same road with me. Then I said to him, "You know, Father, I think I can be more of a priest with no hands than I ever was with two hands," but the conversation went nowhere. This bishop wasn't a bad person, but he saw me as a liability. Archbishop Desmond Tutu, by contrast, invited me to work in the Diocese of Cape Town. He said with a twinkle in his eye, "You know, I've got one priest who is deaf; I have another who is blind; and now one with no hands. Wow! Come!" So one bishop saw me as a liability and the other saw me as an asset.

Other opportunities opened as well. While I was still in the hospital in Australia, I received a call from my friend Horst Kleinschmidt, a South African exiled in London. There he headed an organization called the International Defence and Aid Fund that provided legal help for South African political detainees. Because of his work he had his finger on the pulse of events in South Africa, including the prospect that white rule would soon come to an end. Horst had just made his first visit back to South Africa in many years, and he learned that a group of mental-health workers had begun discussing how best to provide emotional and psychological support in the future to people battered by apartheid. Plans were afoot to create a trauma center for victims of violence and torture at Cowley House, a Cape Town facility owned by the Anglican Church. Horst phoned to my hospital bed to say that he thought I would be uniquely qualified to work there. What was wonderful about the responses of both Horst and Archbishop Tutu was that far from diminishing me, they saw that what had happened to me had given me a new set of qualifications.

As I began preparing this memoir, I read a remarkable account of disability written by John Howard Griffin, a musician, writer, and mystic turned social activist who later became famous as the author of *Black Like Me*. His story reawakened in me an intensely private dimension of my healing journey that I do not find easy to talk about, and it caused me to reflect afresh on my own experience. Called *Scattered Shadows*, Griffin's book is a description of his gradual descent over a two-year period into total blindness and his utterly unexpected return to sight ten years later. The book mirrors my journey, not because they were identical—indeed they were often quite dissimilar—but because the richness was in the interplay between our differences and our commonalities. Both of us left home and traveled to a foreign country as teenagers on a quest for meaning, though Griffin, from the United States, initially sought his answers in music and a classical French education and I in theological training and the priesthood. He went to war as a young man, where he received the injury that caused his blindness, and he later became a pacifist, whereas I moved in the opposite direction, at least for a time. Our commonality was in our dedication to discerning God's will. His is a story of deep faith, though unlike me, he struggled mightily with doubt before finally converting to Roman Catholicism as a young adult.

Griffin's account of his emotional and spiritual struggle with disability, his extraordinary degree of self-awareness, and his ability to articulate with devastating clarity his sometimes contradictory feelings affected me deeply. In the memoir he sometimes lets others speak for him. While he was still able to see a little, he went on a visit to Tours where he met a blind, down-and-out street peddler. It was a profound encounter for both: Griffin had never before spoken with anyone about what it was like to be blind, and the peddler had never before felt valued for his blindness. The peddler's account of the painful loneliness of disability resonated deeply in me:

> I've lived in this quarter almost fifty years. Not a soul knows my name. . . . I have no name—only a condition. . . . I am the blind man. . . . When I was young like you, this craving for affection got so bad I even tried to go to prostitutes. Do you know why? Not because of sex, really, but because there, at least, I would be touched. . . . You can buy orgasm, but not those affectionate touches that give it meaning. So you buy only a deeper wretchedness. . . . I hated them for it.

This private internal dimension of my own healing was fundamentally a journey of the spirit, and I found solace in the wisdom of my faith tradition. I had once seen an icon of the Orthodox Church that depicted Christ with one leg shorter than the other. Dominant Western iconography always portrays Jesus with a perfect white male body—a physique that nobody has, except perhaps in Hollywood. Yet here he was with a serious imperfection like mine. The image was no doubt inspired by Isaiah's parable of the suffering servant:

See, my servant shall prosper; he shall be exalted and lifted up, and shall be very high. Just as there were many who were astonished at him—so marred was his appearance, beyond human semblance, and his form beyond that of mortals—so he shall startle many nations; kings shall shut their mouths because of him; for that which had not been told them they shall see, and that which they had not heard they shall contemplate.

The suffering servant of course prefigures the Jewish messiah, ugly to look at, reviled and rejected—a passage of Isaiah made famous by Handel's glorious alto solo "He was despised" in part II of "The Messiah":

He is despised and rejected of men; a man of sorrows, and acquainted with grief: and we hid as it were our faces from him; he was despised, and we esteemed him not.

As I reflected on these passages of scripture and allowed them to do their healing work, it began to dawn on me that disability is actually the norm of the human condition. Imperfection, incompleteness, brokenness—these are universal human experiences, and those of us with dramatic physical disabilities are mirrors for what is true of the whole human family. A few years later in my Healing of Memories work, the visible marks of my suffering created a bond with others who carried their own wounds, whether visible or invisible, and this bond became a bridge across cultures, religions, and geography. Pain is indeed transcendent.

There is a Christian martyr from the second century, St. Lawrence, who was commanded by Roman persecutors to produce the wealth of the church as tribute. Of course, they were expecting gold and silver. Instead, St. Lawrence brought the very old, the sick, the blind, and those who couldn't walk, and said, "Here, here is the treasure of the church." And so I began to understand that we who live with disability are the treasure of the human family. We are a sign that fragility, illness, and brokenness are inescapable parts of the human experience. In our need for assistance we personify interdependence. We awaken the gift of compassion in others, and we remind the human family that we need one another and cannot be fully human by ourselves. In many African languages there is a saying, "I am, because you are," or, to put it another way, a person is a person through other persons. In South Africa we speak about "ubuntu," which refers to a generosity of spirit as we travel a journey to wholeness together. As we who are

disabled demand a place in the sun, we are not just asking people to be nice to us; we are saying, "Actually, you can't be a real community without us." We don't ask for pity; we ask for justice. We say, "Don't just include us in your community. Instead, come, let's create one together." That's a very different concept.

Sometimes I ask myself why I survived the bombing when I had accompanied so many of my friends to the graveyard to say farewell. I believe the marks of my bombing bear witness to the horror of what we humans are capable of doing to one another, and they give the lie to those who would deny or minimize that. But more important, I think, is that we who bear the marks of war and torture also evoke loving responses in others, and these are also a sign—that justice, peace and gentleness, compassion and kindness are stronger than hatred, evil, and death. That is the message of redemption.

On April 27, 1991, in the Anglican Cathedral in Harare there was a mass of thanksgiving celebrating the first anniversary of my survival. In my address I said to the members of the congregation that it was only their support and that of others like them around the world that had enabled me to become a victor, and I concluded:

The people who sent me the letter bomb are more victims than I am. The bomb has deepened my faith, my compassion, my wholeness, and my commitment to the cause of justice and liberation in South Africa and Southern Africa. . . . And that is why I say to you, Congratulations! We have won! Victory is ours! *Makorokoto!*

PART II

FREEDOM FIGHTER

Holding my beloved stuffed bunny.

*Just after my ordination
at twenty-four.*

*The only picture of my family all together.
Back: Peter, Irene, Mother, Father, Ian, and me.
Front: Margaret, Barbara, and Helen.*

◇ 4 ◇

A Home-grown Faith

◇◇◇◇◇◇◇

WHETHER WE KNOW IT OR NOT, most of us have a set of principles that serves as a sort of moral compass. For me, that compass has always been the Christian gospel, which calls upon us to act in behalf of human dignity and justice, no matter what the consequences. As Christians we know that in the end good comes out of evil and life comes out of death. If we take that seriously, faith inspires political activity. One of my favorite quotations is from the Irish statesman Edmund Burke, who said, "All that is necessary for the triumph of evil is that good men do nothing." Consequently, the liberation struggle in South Africa was from the very beginning for me a matter of faith. Apartheid was a system that killed the souls of both white and black people in contravention of God's will. The courage to speak directly to the source of power and act on one's faith does not come easily or quickly. It is refined and tested over time, and it develops gradually by a process that begins in childhood. Scripture says, "When I was a child, I spoke as a child, I understood as a child, I thought as a child. But when I became a man, I put away childish things" (1 Cor 13:11). Faith is the journey of a lifetime.

I grew up in a little town in New Zealand called Hastings. My father was a flower gardener who worked for the City Council creating beauty in public places. He was well known to the community because people saw him working in the town gardens, and they enjoyed the flowers that he cultivated. My mother was a quiet, unassuming person who demonstrated her deep faith by her commitment to her family and the church. My parents' generation was shaped by a number of difficult events. The one we heard so much about as children was the Napier earthquake of 1931, which occurred on the very day that my mother started high school. The building fell down on her and she was pulled from the wreckage by someone who then went back to save others and was killed in doing so. Had it not been for his courageous action, none of us would be here. I always remember the look of fear on my mother's face when an earthquake took place, as they often did in our part of the world. My father would quietly comfort her by simply putting his hand on her arm.

Of course the other great events that shaped my mother and father's generation was growing up in the Great Depression and the Second World War. My father left to fight in the war soon after my parents were married. My great grandmother was reported to have said when my father came to say goodbye to my mother, "I can see on his face that he won't be coming back," much to the fury of my grandmother. How wonderful that she was wrong! Still, my mother once said to me, "Your father went to war, but the one who came back was not the one who left."

We were a large working-class family of limited means. I am the fifth of seven children, and since there were so many of us, life was a constant economic struggle for my parents. At the same time, I have many treasured memories of childhood. In the years after my father died, when we were grown up, my mother rejoiced in all our achievements and loved each of us uniquely, just as my father had done. Sometimes when I visited, one of my siblings would call and I would listen to how she responded when she heard the voice of one of her children. There was for each of us the same tenderness and joy. Both of our parents allowed us to be who we are. We were loved unconditionally, and they never put our lives in straitjackets. So we all seven became extraordinarily different people. I knew my mother was proud that I became a priest, but she was equally proud that Peter became an engineer, and Helen a health economist, and so for all of us. As we grew up, the family expanded. There was always room for spouses, lovers, friends, children, grandchildren, and in-laws. All were members of the family and all were embraced.

In New Zealand at that time seven was considered to be a very large family. None of my contemporaries came from such large families. Even so, I never experienced hunger and I always had a bed to sleep in, though I shared a room with two of my brothers. That, incidentally, prepared me well for my first year in a religious order where we also slept three or four people to a room. It was only after I finished my training for the priesthood that I finally had a room to myself. Being rather poor in an advanced welfare state meant that my parents received a small child allowance from the government for each of us. My father supplemented the family income by working weekends in local orchards picking fruit. My mother belonged to what was called a Christmas Club. She would put aside a few shillings at the local grocer each week so that there would be enough money to buy a nice Christmas dinner. New Zealand was a relatively egalitarian society, and the social distance between people of different means was less than it is in many other countries. For example, my father was a very keen lawn bowler and played in tournaments with people from a variety of backgrounds. My parents were devoted churchgoers and were leading figures in the congregation. People from different social strata mingled there and took leadership positions in the church. So I grew up with the sense of a fairly wide-reaching community, and this encouraged me to imagine a future full of possibilities and not to feel bound by our economic circumstances. I also was given a good public education, and though I chose not to take that route, I could have gone to a university in New Zealand.

I worked after school sweeping floors in shops and putting rubbish in tins to earn a little spending money, and for several years I delivered newspapers in the morning. Actually, I was so effective and solicitous as a newspaper boy that I earned enough Christmas tips to fly to Auckland to visit my uncle and cousin on a two-week holiday and had sufficient left over to pay a reserve paper boy while I was away. I was bright enough to be placed in the top academic stream in high school; many of my fellow students' parents worked in businesses or the professions and were much better off than my own. In fact, for a while I was embarrassed about my father's occupation. Ironically, in later years when I became more politically aware and my views moved increasingly to the left, I felt ashamed of my embarrassment. Then I thought, "How wonderful that I have these totally working-class credentials." How one's outlook changes!

Though my parents were dedicated churchgoers, my mother didn't talk much about her faith, and home devotions were not a regular part of our family life. We said grace before the evening meal, but we did not pray or read the Bible together as a family. People would have said of my mother that she did not in any way flaunt her faith but rather expressed it by seeking to live a Christian life. She was a steadfast and loving mother who taught us by example and allowed us room to be ourselves. She felt no need to hit us over the head with her faith. She lived her Christian life, but there was space and respect and reverence for whatever we, in our individual journeys, believed. Over the years I have come more and more to appreciate all that she gave us. As a priest who consistently works in interfaith and secular environments, I daily feel indebted to her for her teaching and example in this respect.

A few years ago my good friend Marion Keim Lees compiled a book that contains reflections by fifty well-known South Africans about the women who raised them.[1] It includes a letter that I wrote to my mother on the occasion of her ninetieth birthday, and I include an excerpt here:

Dear Mother,

It was good to speak to you on the phone again today. When you were eighty-nine, I did wonder if you would make it to your ninetieth—pretty amazing for someone who has had seven children and also endured your own share of ill health. I was overjoyed that you reached your ninetieth and that you were happy that you did. It seems only the other day that you were telling us that you hoped you would make it to the year 2000.

In the year before I left home and New Zealand to study for the priesthood and join a religious community, we had become more like equals. We could talk together almost as two adults. You and Dad never tried to influence us about our life choices but supported us in what we decided to do. I was seventeen when I left, and since that time I have only come for holidays. I remember when you came to Australia with Dad for my ordination as a priest. I know that this was also the fulfillment of a lifelong dream for you. Since 1973 my whole life has been spent in the countries of Southern Africa. You told a friend of yours that you knew I would not return to live in New Zealand or Australia because my life's work is in Africa. I felt that you understood and accepted the choices I have made.

As the years passed I found that you had begun to speak to me as if I were a child. When I asked you why, you said very honestly that it was because you didn't know me any more, so it was easier to return to a mother-child relationship. I knew the comment was true but I found it very painful. For a number of years I was not relaxed and did not relate easily when I visited. In recent years this has changed and the relationship has become once more open and easy.

Inevitably it was a deep shock to you when I was bombed in Zimbabwe in 1990 and lost an eye and both hands. I remember the first time we spoke on the phone a few days after the bombing. How wonderful it was for me, and I am sure very painful for you then and later when you visited me after I was transferred to hospital in Australia.

Over the last few years, as your physical health has deteriorated, I often ask you how you are doing. Unfailingly you have told me that you are wearing out, but always insisting that, "in myself I am fine," "emotionally

---

[1] *uMama: Recollections of South African Mothers and Grandmothers* (Cape Town: Umuzi, 2009).

and spiritually I am 100%." I know it is true. You have said that you have no fear of death.

A year ago, my close friend Ndukenhle, whom you also met, died of AIDS just before Christmas. I was greatly moved by your compassion and support for me in the midst of my grief.

I am often amazed that you retain an abiding interest in my own involvement with Healing of Memories.

One of the greatest privileges I have had has been to celebrate Mass in your home and give you Communion. Most humbling have been the occasions you have asked me to be a priest to you. I admire and sometimes envy you the depth and simplicity of your faith in God and the way you live out the Christian Gospel.

Thank you for the way you have loved me and each of your seven children unconditionally. This has given me deep emotional stability. Thank you for being proud of me. I hope I will be worthy of that pride. Thank you for being my Mother.

> With my prayers.
> Much love,
> Michael

My mother died at the age of ninety-three while I was preparing this memoir. She was to the very end a person who was cheerful and in good spirits, a woman of deep faith and a faithful follower of Jesus Christ. Her faith was simple and unshakeable, and she had her own personal and direct experience of God's presence. She wanted her memorial service to be a service of thanksgiving and it was.

As a boy I was certainly much more religious and devout than any of my other brothers and sisters apart from my older sister Irene who at different times entered two different convents, though she did not remain in either of them very long. One could say I did church "big time." At the age of twelve or thirteen I was an altar server at not one but two churches, one quite close to my home in the suburbs and another in town. In my high school years I went every Wednesday to an early morning mass where I would be the only young person, everyone else being middle aged or elderly. The priest in the downtown parish was my confessor and became my spiritual adviser. In the Anglican Church there is a saying with respect to confessing to God in the presence of a priest, "all may, none must, some should," so adopting a confessor as I did was an additional expression of my adolescent piety.

Alas, I didn't always have an age-appropriate sense of my limits, and I think I was sometimes quite obnoxious with my religiosity. It certainly caused some irritation in the church and even my family.

In the Anglican Church people are baptized as infants, and in those days they were confirmed when they were about thirteen or fourteen and were then able to receive communion. I remember the priest at my local church saying, "No, not this year. You need to wait another year to be confirmed," and my thinking impatiently, "No way." I then went back to see the same priest and explained to him why I thought I was ready. Though he demurred at first, he finally succumbed and I was confirmed. I knew I was being a bit willful, but I went ahead.

In another telling incident a Presbyterian theologian had caused great consternation in the church with some unorthodox views about the resurrection. I was only a schoolboy of fifteen or sixteen, but I went to a meeting at the Presbyterian church to discuss this potential heresy. In the midst of it I rose to enter the debate and make my own views known. It was a bit shocking, and the fact that I was not ejected forthwith was probably because I was in the company of good Christian people. I'm certain everyone there was thinking, "Who in the world is this precocious child?"

High school was a difficult time. I was already hoping to join a religious order, and I wasn't interested in the power trips that the adolescent boys played out. There was a great deal of fighting and aggression on the playground. I wasn't good at sports, nor was I interested in combat with other boys. In truth, I lived in a different world. What interested me was the church and the library, where I spent a lot of time reading about religion and literature. I was further isolated due to the influence of my sister Irene, who had become a committed pacifist. Later I also read the works of Gandhi and Martin Luther King. These ideas had a huge impact on me, which only grew stronger over my later years in seminary. In New Zealand secondary schools everyone was required to do military training. It was a bit ridiculous—adolescent boys in the public schools marching up and down in army uniforms with guns, playing soldier. In order to be exempt, one had to have a letter to the headmaster from one's parents. In my school the only children who did that were Jehovah's Witnesses. Not deterred, I announced to the school authorities that I was not going to do military training and that I had no intention of asking my father for a letter because he was a returned World War II soldier and I assumed he would have taken a dim view of my pacifism. My parents were not the sort who talked much about these things. My mother, for example, made one comment of disapproval and that was that. My father never mentioned it at all. I think they avoided knowing what they knew. The irony for my poor parents is that years later they discovered I was supporting the armed struggle, and I think that was as hard for them to stomach as my pacifism. It couldn't have been easy being my parents.

The school system shook a bit, but once again I got my way. The problem for me, though, was that on days of military training, I would be wearing my ordinary school garb, whereas the other boys would be running around in their military uniforms. Naturally they wanted to know why I wasn't wearing mine, and I made up excuses and lied. So I had the courage to take on the school authorities but not my peers. The gulf between them and me made high school quite unpleasant, which only reinforced the refuge I found in religion and literature. Because of my relatively narrow interests my academic results were mediocre, although I came out at the top of the school in English during my final year. Thankfully, by that time the ambient testosterone level among other boys had receded somewhat, and I felt more respect and acceptance from peers for my values and beliefs. Nevertheless, I remember quite well rejecting the view that schooldays are the best years of our life. I knew then that that wasn't true, and I still feel the same way today.

Adults often ask children what they want to be when they grow up. When I was only four years old I was already considering becoming a priest, though I must have had only the dimmest idea about what that entailed. It wouldn't be quite accurate to say that I never considered other careers, however. As a youth I had a stamp collection, and at one point I thought of running a stamp shop. In high school I applied for a job with the New Zealand court system, partly because it would have helped pay for my university education. Being practical, I always had a backup plan in case a career in the church didn't materialize. When I was quite small I also dreamed of becoming a clown. The circus fascinated me; I loved the humor and the excitement. Then too, in both the circus and the church there is a great deal of pageantry and drama, which appealed to me as a young boy. Humor has always been important to me. I think it's healthy to laugh at oneself and to see the funny side of things, something I inherited from my mother. In many societies a clown figure is the person who tells people things they may not want to hear, and that can be an important role for a priest as well. So I think it was appropriate that when I was ordained years later, my brother Peter congratulated me on having succeeded in accomplishing both at the same time. Despite what Peter said, I never actually made it to the circus, though some of my more secular friends might disagree.

Through Irene I became acquainted with what one might call the Catholic side of the Anglican Church. She was a parishioner in a parish in Auckland that was very strong in the Catholic or high church tradition. In the sixteenth century Henry VIII suppressed religious orders and decreed the dissolution of the monasteries, but by the nineteenth century with a wider Catholic revival the orders returned to the Anglican Church, albeit with very small numbers. I was fascinated by everything about the church, and I began to imagine myself not as an ordinary parish priest but as a member of one of these Anglican orders. I read lots of books about monks and nuns, and for a pious boy like me, they were enticing. In 1963 I read an article in the first issue of *Anglican World,* a glossy magazine of the Anglican Communion, about St. Michael's House, the Australian headquarters of the Society of the Sacred Mission (SSM). I wrote to the provincial in Australia expressing interest in coming for training. At least in my fantasy I was ready to leave home and join up then and there, but he wrote back saying, "Well, as you are only thirteen years of age, there is no need to worry too much about training at this age." So I had to defer my dream throughout high school but I certainly didn't give it up. Joining an order was my way of obeying the radical demands of following Christ and taking the gospel to its logical conclusion. My sense of identity and meaning were completely tied to the faith community and I had a highly romanticized notion of what it meant to be a member of an order. I also believed that a religious order would give me superior training for the priesthood. Putting flesh on the bones of my fantasy and coming to terms with the reality of living in a religious community of course came later.

Had I taken the traditional New Zealand path to the priesthood, my suitability for it would have been tested. If the church agreed, I might then have been sent to a theological college, though it's also quite possible I would have been expected to take a university degree before enrolling in seminary. Only after I was ordained a priest would I have been free to pursue joining a religious order. All of this could have taken years, and I was a boy in a hurry. I couldn't imagine a future apart from the priesthood, and I wasn't about to relinquish the power to make that decision to anyone else if I could help it. In many ways I was a perfect candidate for SSM. It had been founded in nineteenth-century England to provide a path to the priesthood for working-class boys who wouldn't be able to go to Oxford and Cambridge, and historically it provided quality theological training without a university education. SSM undertook the theological training of priests as one of its purposes—a mission that was complementary to but separate from the possibility of joining the order. Thus, at St. Michael's House there were young men who were in training to become parish priests and a few of us who intended to join the order. Not only would other Anglican orders have expected me to first complete university and theological training, some would not consider candidates before they were twenty-one years old at the earliest. SSM, on the other hand, was willing to take me at age seventeen.

Joining an order at my age would not have been at all exceptional if I had been a Roman Catholic. Still, for the most part the Anglican Church had taken the position that it was not wise to allow young boys to join an order before they had grown up a bit emotionally. It is, after all, a very serious commitment and entails lifelong vows of poverty, celibacy, and obedience. Some compared it to the British Army in that a person may join at the age of sixteen and may later regret it, though goodness knows, that doesn't involve a vow of celibacy! My attitude, though, was that I needed to get to this religious order as fast as possible and not waste time. My mother and father were accepting of my plans. As parents they let each of us be the people we wanted to be and accepted the choices we made. Several of my brothers and sisters had left home at age seventeen or eighteen and got on with independent lives. My local parish priest, on the other hand, was a bit shocked and intimated that maybe a year or two more growing up would be a good idea. But I was quite headstrong and besides, I was leaving home with my parents' support. Whether or not they thought this was a bit premature was another matter. If they did, they didn't say so. Though I continue to be glad I made the choice when I did, in retrospect I do agree that it is probably better if candidates have more life experience under their belt before they join a community.

So, I turned up at St. Michael's House, the SSM headquarters in the hills outside of Adelaide. I was seventeen years old, and it was four years after my initial inquiry. I had been accepted for training as a priest but with no commitment to join the order. Here I was, having left New Zealand, the country of my birth, for the first time. The adjustment was not easy. I had to learn to live in a house with seventy other people. Also, I had done more reading and perhaps more churchgoing than most of the other boys, many of whom were in their twenties. I suppose I was a naive seventeen year old; I thought I would find a depth of faith in the seminary and even in the community that wasn't always there. They, for their part, saw me as something of a young upstart and overly pious.

I was still determined to join an order, and so at the end of my first year I tried to negotiate a bargain. I would join the community as a novice on the condition that I would be able to return to New Zealand as a part of establishing a new order that I would found. My motivation had little or nothing to do with being homesick, even though I was. Rather, I saw myself as being the springboard for creating a new Anglican community. I was now all of eighteen years old, having just completed my first year of training for the priesthood, and to use a very descriptive Jewish word, I had quite a lot of chutzpah—a rather startling audacity for someone my age. Perhaps not surprisingly, the SSM powers-that-be said no. I could apply to become a novice, but there would be no conditions attached. So I applied and was accepted. The year was 1968, and I was beginning my second year of theological training while also becoming a novice member of the SSM community.

The year 1971 was momentous for two reasons. I became a professed member of the SSM, and I was ordained. Professed members dedicate their lives to the service of God, make a lifelong commitment to the order, and embrace the vows of poverty, celibacy, and obedience. In practice, this means that income and property belong to the community, members do not marry, and life decisions such as vocation are made only in consultation with the community. Though I was only twenty-two years old, I was ready. It is a decision I have never regretted.

Later that same year I was ordained a deacon. One must be twenty-four years old to be ordained a priest under canon law, and normally twenty-three in order to be ordained a deacon. However, there was an exception in church law that allowed deacons to be ordained younger, and so I was ordained under the exception. Though I had been trained in Australia, by a special arrangement between the bishop of Canberra and bishop of Waiapu in New Zealand, the ordination ceremony and mass took place in the local church in Hastings where I had grown up. What was wonderful about that was that all the members of my family, including my elderly maternal grandmother, were able to be present. Interestingly, the bishop of Waiapu, Paul Reeves, who ordained me eventually became governor general of New Zealand. He visited me in the hospital in Australia, and when I went back to New Zealand after being bombed I stayed with him at Government House.

The radical demands of joining a religious order are not for everyone. For me, religious faith is a quest for the meaning of being human. Joining an order is one way—not necessarily the best way and certainly not the only way—for a Christian to make sense of that. Professing the vows of poverty, celibacy, and obedience brings the freedom to travel the world lightly, unencumbered by possessions and family responsibilities and able to rely on the wisdom of the community in relation to important decisions. With respect to celibacy, as I have traveled my own journey and listened to other people, I have concluded that most human beings don't find it particularly easy to live with their sexuality, regardless of what it may be. I think it always brings its own temptations, struggles, and tensions.

Even within my order some individuals have had midlife crises and questioned their celibacy. Some have left the order to marry—two members, to my astonishment, at the age of eighty plus. Such crises are part of the human experience, and in some cases they may be less about sexuality than about loneliness and companionship. If one is married, one has to choose to be married every single day, and the same is true for celibacy. No matter how connected or intimate with a spouse we are, within most of us there is an existential loneliness born of the reality that at a deep level each of us travels our journey alone, and ultimately we die alone. The other side of that reality, though, is that, as a celibate, one gains the support and affection of one's Brothers in the community. In Matthew 19 we find the words, "And everyone who has left houses or brothers or sisters or father or mother or children or fields for my sake will receive a hundred times as much and will inherit eternal life." So even if one has forsaken a natural family, one gains another kind of family. In my own journey the circle of that family has grown larger year by year, so that it now encompasses the entire human family.

After my ordination as a deacon I returned to Australia and was sent for a curacy to Canberra, where I served as an assistant in a parish. Now I suddenly found myself living with just three other Brothers in a small house on the other side of town from the parish where I worked. The two years I spent there were a sort of extended honeymoon. Perhaps it was the first time I enjoyed to the fullest being a young person. It was the early 1970s and a time of "flower power." I was young and newly ordained. I rode to the parish on a small motorbike, my long hair poking out from underneath a helmet decorated with flowers and my religious habit streaming out behind me. I adored the parishioners, and they adored me. I really blossomed in every way. I loved the pastoral work and was extremely well received by the congregation. I got on very well with the parish priest, Jim Tregea, and he and his wife, Helen, have remained lifelong friends to this very day. They are absolutely wonderful.

By the middle of 1973 I had finally reached the magic age when I could be ordained a priest. In the months previous to my ordination I would sometimes bump into the bishop, who would ask me if I was old enough yet. My twenty-fourth birthday was June 2 and I was ordained on June 29. Both my parents and my young sister Margaret came from New Zealand for the ceremony. It was the first time my mother had ever left New Zealand. After my first mass someone commented that he had the impression that I had been celebrating mass all my life, and one member of SSM, Fr. Thomas Brown, wryly commented that it was probably true that I had been practicing for about twenty years before that day.

I knew that it was possible that the order would send me abroad, and after some reflection I requested to be sent to Japan. Not to be! Shortly thereafter the decision was made that I should go to South Africa. To this day I do not know who made that decision or why. I remember not sleeping that night for I knew instinctively that my life was about to change forever. Indeed, my faith and courage were to be tested in ways I could not possibly have imagined.

◇ 5 ◇

South Africa—Torn Apart

◇◇◇◇◇◇◇

AS THE LONG HOURS WENT BY on the flights from Canberra to Johannesburg I kept trying to quiet the anxiety rising inside me. It was September 1973, and I was only twenty-four years old. The farthest I had ever been from home was Australia. As the plane pushed on over the endless sea, my family, my friends, my religious community, and everything familiar receded in the distance. Except from books, South Africa was entirely unknown to me. Even the members of the SSM community there were mostly strangers. Then there was apartheid. I had been a member of the South Australia Committee Against Racism, and I saw South Africa as a challenge to put my faith into action. I didn't think it would be easy, but I imagined I would find other likeminded people who opposed the system and together we would make a witness for what I knew was right. In that sense South Africa presented an exciting opportunity for a young idealistic priest.

When the plane landed in Johannesburg, I was met by relatives of one of my high school teachers in New Zealand, a South African expatriate. It was a relief to be welcomed by warm and friendly people, even ones I did not know. They took me home, fed me, and gave me a chance to rest from the long flight. Already that first evening the reality that was apartheid South Africa intruded ominously into our dinner conversation. We began talking about the church and I inquired if black people were part of their congregation. "Oh, yes," they said, "and they are very good—they always sit at the back." Though it was said with a smile, I felt it like a slap in the face, and this was just a foretaste of what lay ahead.

When I arrived in Durban soon after, a city that was to be my home for the next three years, by law I went to live in a white suburb. The signs of apartheid confronted me everywhere. The day after I arrived,

I went to the post office to send my mother a letter telling her that I had arrived safely. There were two entrances, one marked "Whites only" and the other, "Non-whites." Along the streets benches were also marked "Whites only." Durban is a seaside city and so I went off to explore the beach. There I discovered that even the sea was divided by race. The most beautiful beaches were where white people could swim; there was another for people of Indian descent, still another for people of mixed race, and far, far away, one for Africans. There was a curfew. Africans couldn't be in the city after a certain hour or the authorities arrested them. Africans had to carry a passbook twenty-four hours a day saying what area of the country they had permission to be in. If they violated it, they ended up in prison.

One image stands out in my mind to this day. There were two elevators in the government building where I needed to sort out my student visa. One was marked "Whites only" and the other "Goods and Non-whites." So whites were implicitly people, whereas people of color were lumped with goods. I found this profoundly shocking. There was no escape; apartheid permeated every corner of ordinary life in South Africa, and it contradicted everything I knew to be the Christian message. It was so upsetting that, when not long after I arrived and my father became quite ill, I phoned my mother and asked, "Should I come home to assist you?" In fact I knew there was little or nothing for me to do at home in New Zealand, but I was driven by the urge to get out of this place while I still could. Inwardly I was saying, "What a terrible mistake I've made. This country is both bad and mad!"

It's not that I had been unaware of racism. When I started primary school, I had a dust up with another little boy in the school playground. When it was over, he said, "You're just treating me this way because I'm Maori." That memory imprinted on me, and later I realized that even at that age he had a consciousness of discrimination. In my own home, though, everyone was welcomed as an equal, and in my church African bishops visited from time to time and were treated with joy and accorded respect. My father was a great friend of the Maori bishop. I trained as a priest in Australia in the 1960s, a time of student rebellion and a world awakened to the injustices of the war in Vietnam, in which both Australia and New Zealand participated. In the church it was a time of the liberalizing influence of the Second Vatican Council, which also had an impact on Anglican religious communities. As a young novice I joined demonstrations against the Vietnam War, and movements for social justice, nonviolence, and antiracism were formative influences in my life. In St. Michael's House we were a multiracial community with students from the Solomon Islands and Papua New Guinea. Nevertheless, racist comments and jokes about Aboriginal people generally went unchallenged.

Nor was I uninformed about South Africa. In 1960, when I was eleven years old, the South Africans refused to accept Maori members of New Zealand's rugby team. There was a petition in my church—No Maoris, no tour. Unfortunately, the New Zealanders capitulated and the Maoris were excluded, though in 2010 the New Zealand Rugby Association finally issued an apology to the now-aging Maori members. Then, when I was fourteen or fifteen I had read *Naught for Your Comfort*, a book by Fr. Trevor Huddleston, an Anglican priest from Britain. He had been a parish priest in South Africa when the government began forcibly removing Africans from areas designated "whites only," and his book blew the whistle on what was happening in South Africa for the English-speaking world. So I had strong feelings about apartheid before I arrived in South Africa. Even so, nothing could have prepared me emotionally or spiritually for the reality.

When I look back I think I was actually extraordinarily naive. Whiteness began to feel like leprosy. Like Lady Macbeth, no matter how much I washed, the whiteness would not go away. I knew that despite myself I was participating in evil.

The SSM priory and university chaplaincy residence where I stayed was a pleasant, modern suburban home. A couple of other Brothers there were involved in the university. Soon after I arrived I began exploring the building and found an outside stairway that led to the maid's quarters. In contrast to the rest of the house it was quite spartan, and what struck me most was the bathroom. It had only cold water and a shower that was situated over a primitive toilet. In actuality, our domestic worker didn't live there; she came in by the day, cooked a meal, cleaned, and left, but there was an unmistakable social distance. In Canberra as a young priest we had had a lady who cooked our evening meal and she then sat and ate with us. Here the domestic worker kept separate and certainly didn't eat with us. I found this very difficult and I worried too that we weren't paying her enough. So issues of justice and injustice surfaced for me even at the SSM residence. Though in the overall scheme of things these were small matters, they took quite a toll on me emotionally, particularly since members of my religious community seemed unconcerned and unaware.

The SSM had gone to South Africa in 1902 and was very much involved in education for Africans. All that came to a halt in 1954 with the passing of the Bantu Education Act, which was designed explicitly to keep blacks in a subservient role by providing them with substandard education. Dr. H. F. Verwoerd, then the leader of the National Party in the all white parliament and later the prime minister, justified the act in these words:

> The Bantu must be guided to serve his own community in all respects. There is no place for him in the European community above the level of certain forms of labour. Within his own community, however, all doors are open. . . . Until now he has been subjected to a school system which drew him away from his own community and mislead him by showing him the green pastures of European society in which he was not allowed to graze.

In response to the Bantu Education Act, SSM made a principled decision to close its schools, but we continued our pastoral work in the country, mostly in rural settings. The SSM main priory in South Africa was in the Orange Free State, a rural area where vast tracts of land were owned by white farmers. Most black people, if they were employed at all, worked as farm laborers and were completely dependent on the whims of the farm owners, who could be quite brutal. It was an extremely conservative part of the country. While the Brothers were pastors to the black farm workers, their social life revolved around the white farm owners. I was a good deal younger than the other Brothers who lived there. They had spent their entire lives ministering to black people, but some of them couldn't say a whole sentence without racist poison coming out of their mouths. They would relax on the veranda sipping cocktails and gazing across the veldt toward the mountains of Lesotho rising in the distance. Meanwhile black people were not welcome to even sit on that veranda. On one occasion I prayed aloud during the early morning mass for someone who had been detained by the authorities. Afterward, one of the Brothers interrupted what is known in monasteries as the Greater Silence to whisper in my ear, "We don't have those sorts of prayers here." Their attitude is starkly revealed in a letter written some years later by one of them to Clement Mullenger, the SSM provincial in Southern Africa. The writer is complaining about my political activity:

> There will never be, in this life, the sort of utopia that people like Michael want to see. The poor, we shall always have with us. Society has been oppressive and exploitive since time began. Changes come and go. Change now should not be the keystone of our Christian discipleship; and it must come by education and

not by revolution. In the end justice will be seen to be a relative and not an absolute or universal blessing. Some will always be more equal than others. . . . I simply do not believe in revolution, nor ever did, nor ever will, and I don't think Jesus thought much of it as a way of bringing into being the just society. I think that Jesus had rather higher values in his heart and they are forgiveness, compassion and love.

He went on to say,

I admire the guts of those Brothers of mine who find that "integrity" is one of the things that they have had to lay at the foot of the cross. What more could a man give for love of the gospel?

A swirling mix of feelings rose inside me as I confronted the appalling reality that apartheid had thoroughly penetrated the mentality of my own community. Nothing like this characterized the SSM community I had left behind in Australia. I hardly knew which was worse—the injustice itself or the fact that everyone else was completely blind to it. The possibility that there was something here to be outraged about was simply not a part of their world. It was a difficult time for me; I was trapped in a nightmare and I was alone with my feelings. Beginning with this experience I became interested in the "elephants in the room," which in many societies cannot be spoken about because they are actually the "hot button" issues.

It's true that some of our older Brothers gave no indication of being racist, even though they certainly weren't politically active. In fact, at least one had offered prayers at ANC congresses in the capital of the Free State in years past when the ANC was still legal. However, as the conflict over apartheid wore on, even those Brothers retreated into the safety of silence. Of course it is also true that at the universities in Durban where I became chaplain I was engaging with bright and politically aware black students who were very different from the rural farm workers in the Free State. Nevertheless, over the years, as I spoke out more and more, most members of my community were ambivalent about me at best. In a wonderful irony of history, I am now, these many years later, our Society's provincial for Southern Africa and have overall responsibility for the work of our order there. Even religious orders evolve.

Our work in Durban, where I was assigned, was an exception to our rural ministry. There, SSM had taken over the chaplaincy at the University of Natal, so I too became a chaplain while simultaneously enrolled as an undergraduate student. I served at three different campuses, one for whites only, one for people of Indian descent, and a medical school open to African, Indian, and Colored students. It was a privileged position in that I could relate to students of all racial groups unlike most white South Africans, who only encountered people of other communities in a master/servant relationship. Similarly, had I been a chaplain only in the black community, it would have been easy to adopt a stereotypical view that all white people were the devil, but reality is thankfully more complicated. Some people regarded priests as a race apart—there were blacks and whites and priests—and though one might smile about that, it gave me a point of entry into people's lives that I otherwise would not have had. Since I appreciated that opportunity, I encouraged it by always wearing my religious habit on campus. To me that was also part of what it meant to be a member of a religious order.

Despite my best priestly efforts, apartheid still created suspicion and distance. Soon after I arrived in South Africa I met a young African priest who said to me, "You seem quite nice now, but I give you six months." He'd seen other people come from abroad and behave like normal human beings but within a short time take on the values and attitudes of the dominant white minority. I vowed that that would not be me. Another time I told a black medical student that I didn't believe in apartheid, to which he replied, "That's very nice, Father, but where are you going to sleep tonight?" Though I instinctively looked for companionship to other black students who were, after all, my own age, there was a painful barrier that was not of my making. In one memory that is still poignant to me, I invited some black students to join me for a meal at one of the few restaurants that would quietly and illegally allow people of different races to eat together. When we got there, my friends said, "Why are we here? Is this a meeting?" But for me it represented a desperate desire to relate simply as a human being to people of color and not to be trapped in a prison of whiteness. Had I not been expelled from South Africa later on, I would probably have gone quite mad. It was an insane society, and I felt deeply traumatized by it.

On the white campus some professors were relatively progressive and tried to open students' eyes. This was, after all, my first exposure to a university education, and the knowledge I acquired in my sociology class began to combine powerfully with my inherent sense of moral and religious outrage at the injustice of apartheid. I began to understand that violence didn't just come out of a gun. Structural violence and systemic violence were less obvious but more unrelenting than the naked force of the police. I could be against apartheid all I wished, but I was going to be against it from the side of those who benefited from the violence that kept it in power. I awakened to the possibility that one could intellectually analyze the system that we all, white and black, were trapped in. I also came to appreciate the power of language. Even though I was still a pacifist and preached nonviolence to people, black and white, I soon saw that when black people picked up arms it was called violence and terrorism, whereas when white people used violence against black people it was called the defense of law and order. The reality was that pacifist though I might be, the police and army would shoot and kill to protect my interests as a white person. Religion too was used as a soporific to keep people of color docile. Everything having to do with the government and apartheid was defined as politics, and priests told religious people, especially black religious people, "Good Christians don't have anything to do with politics," which really meant, "Don't fight injustice." This planted a contrary seed in my mind that gradually grew into a deep conviction that the gospel and liberation politics were completely intertwined.

Leaving aside the fact that people of color had no vote, the great myth of apartheid was that the races were separate but equal. Once we students made a protest at the mobile post office on campus that had separate windows for whites and people of color. The white man behind the window was indignant and said, "But I'm treating everybody equally." The reality of course was that the races were separate and extremely unequal. One thing that struck me visually about Durban and its surroundings was that white people took up a lot of space. They had large homes surrounded by beautiful gardens; their schools had ample playgrounds and expansive athletic fields; and the business district was mostly white territory, especially after dark. The casual observer might have been forgiven for thinking that white people were in the majority, but of course white people were less than 10 percent of the total population and yet owned more than 87 percent of the country's land. Africans were forced into crowded urban townships where they lived in tiny shacks with no green space, and most owned no land. Legally, blacks were relegated to separate rural "homelands" or Bantustans that occupied only 13 percent of the land, and that was of inferior quality. People of color were thus considered guests in the urban areas where they provided a source of cheap labor, and the myth that they were merely sojourners in white areas provided the legal underpinning for the pass laws. So, while black people were denied the rights of citizenship in the land where their ancestors had lived for generations, I, as a white foreigner, would be eligible for citizenship and the vote in five years. In short, apartheid was always about political oppression and economic exploitation.

However, I came to see that there was another even deeper dimension, and that was the denial of fundamental human dignity. I began to realize that whether white people appreciated it or not, everyone, white and black, oppressor and oppressed, was a prisoner of the system. A survey published in South Africa in the 1970s documented that the dominant feelings of white South Africans were guilt, fear, and anxiety, and that does not spell liberation. White people lived in fear of their black fellow citizens, and a few confided in me, saying, "One day they will attack us." On the other hand, it wouldn't be freedom if the tables were turned and we replaced white oppression with black oppression. Freedom, when it came, would have to be for all South Africans or it would be for nobody.

The other Brothers in our priory in Durban gradually drifted away from the university to other things. One was not much interested in the university and the other was having a love affair that preoccupied him and he eventually left the community, so I became more centrally involved with the chaplaincy. The white university in Durban was in the English liberal tradition and it had a history of a certain degree of protest against apartheid. That was very different from Afrikaans-speaking universities that tended to be more conservative and conformist. On the Durban campus there was a kaleidoscope from those who would politely say, "We're opposed to apartheid," to those who took courageous stands and refused to go to the army. A burning issue for some white students was conscription. Most white students would say, "I have to go to the army." They would never say, "I've decided to go to the army," so the question of moral responsibility was taken off the table. I used my role as chaplain to raise the issue of conscientious objection with these students. The government informants, who were everywhere, no doubt viewed me as a provocateur. I also brought motions in support of conscientious objectors before the synods of the Anglican Church, where they were certainly not universally well received. Pacifism is not strong in our tradition, and Anglicans have blessed most of the wars in history. My advocacy increased my visibility in the church—and not in a way that endeared me to many.

For the mainstream white Christian students I was much too radical, but my aim was to arouse them to see the relationship between their faith and issues of justice. My success could be gauged by the location of my office, which over the three years I was chaplain gradually migrated from the top floor of the Student Union, where almost no one came unless he or she had an appointment, to the main floor, which was in the midst of the ebb and flow of traffic. I saw that as a sign of the contribution I had made in the marketplace of ideas on campus.

Nelson Mandela had already been imprisoned for eleven years, and the apartheid government painted him as a terrorist extremist whose writings were banned in South Africa. My political awakening took a giant leap forward when on a visit to my parents in New Zealand in 1975 I went to the local public library and took out Mandela's book *No Easy Walk to Freedom.* Without realizing it I had unconsciously absorbed some of the racist propaganda that portrayed Mandela as a terrorist who would stop at nothing to annihilate white people. I remember being shocked at the gap between his nonracial values and how he was perceived by white South Africans. His moral vision for the country was deeply affecting, and I began to understand that the book was banned precisely because of its reasonableness, wisdom, and deep humanity.

I found myself becoming sympathetic to the politics of the ANC and its vision of a nonracial society. In late 1975 a law lecturer at the university who was the brother of a fellow student was arrested for being involved with the ANC and the Communist Party. During his trial I served as a pastor to his family and got to know his mother quite well. The "terrorist" act of which he was accused was printing pamphlets aimed at keeping the name and program of the ANC alive. It was another step in my political awakening, and my association with this so-called terrorist may have been an element contributing to my eventual expulsion from the country.

June 16, 1976, proved to be a turning point in South African history and in my personal journey. Two years previously the South African government had passed a law mandating Afrikaans as the language of instruction in all black schools. Students resented this law because Afrikaans was not their home language and because it was seen as the language of their oppressors. Beyond the language issue they were also protesting the inferior education they were receiving under the Bantu Education Act. On June 16 students in Soweto outside Johannesburg organized a protest march against the law, during which the police opened fire, killing twenty-three young people. The massacre was the match that ignited protests throughout the country during which hundreds of people were killed and more than a thousand injured. Thousands more were detained and some of the wounded were carried into police stations only to emerge in coffins. Students I knew were detained and tortured. These were the most violent and widespread black protests that South Africa had ever seen. Television had only come to South Africa the previous year, and the government at first did not appreciate the unique power of visual images, so for a few days images of the police shooting children were broadcast in South Africa and around the world. Before long, however, these were replaced by "talking heads" opining about the dangers to law and order.

There was increasing repression, and it became more obvious than ever that South Africa was a police state. It was said that black radio station commentators didn't have control over their own microphones and that they were assigned a white minder who would switch them off if need be. Once a week the government put out a gazette listing everything that had been banned during the previous week. There were bans on a whole range of publications from sex to politics to religion. In fact, the chaos increasingly provided a pretext to ban anything that the Dutch Reformed Church found offensive. The censorship that the government quickly moved to implement partly succeeded in its aim of keeping the white community uninformed about the violence directed at the black community. Because I was chaplain I had access to both white and black students, and I found myself in the position of communicating to the white community what was happening at a time when information was being suppressed.

The killing of schoolchildren was for me extremely traumatic, and though the immediate crisis abated, the protests and demonstrations continued over many months with children dying in the streets. I had already seriously curtailed my own studies in order to devote more time to the chaplaincy. It seemed somehow extraordinarily self-indulgent to be sitting in a classroom when the country was going up in flames. I immediately began speaking out against the repression from my position as chaplain at the university. However, if I were to live with myself I needed to find even more effective ways of struggling against racism and on behalf of justice, and an opportunity soon presented itself.

The month following the Soweto events the annual conference of the Anglican Student Federation took place. It brought together Anglican students of all race and language groups, black and white, English- and Afrikaans-speaking. By that time, despite the government's best efforts, stories of detention and torture were spreading in the student community. I had a rising profile among students because of my denunciation of the brutality of the government. Of course I was not alone; many others, including Desmond Tutu, who was the newly appointed bishop of Lesotho, had raised their voices, but I had a direct connection with the students by reason of the chaplaincy. Some of the activist students at the conference successfully mobilized an election campaign on my behalf and I was elected national university chaplain. It was an unusual position since the national chaplain was not appointed by the bishops of the church or elected by the other chaplains but was chosen by the students themselves. My outspokenness had increased my prominence at a crucial moment in the struggle, and the person who had previously held the position was quite taken aback to find himself usurped.

Using my newly acquired national platform I immediately began traveling to other university campuses throughout the country speaking against the killing, torture, and detention of students, and quite naturally I became much more visible. The government was certainly unhappy about the fuss I was raising, and so at the end of September I received unwelcome recognition in the form of a letter from the government that my student visa would not be renewed and I had fourteen days to leave the country. The government took the easy way out by not renewing my visa, since it could have just put me on a plane and deported me if it chose. In any case I responded by arranging to speak at as many mass meetings as I could, and during those two weeks I traveled to various campuses outside Durban denouncing the government's policies. Of course I acquired a bit more notoriety by characterizing my expulsion from the country as an example of the state's unwillingness to tolerate critics of its repressive policies.

Although the government no doubt hoped I would quietly retreat to Australia or New Zealand, that was not a choice I considered for a moment. Not long after I arrived in South Africa I came to the conclusion that I either had to go home or make it my home, and I committed myself to the liberation struggle. My expulsion and the notoriety that accompanied it were fairly upsetting for my community, some of whom would have said they were against apartheid, but that didn't remotely involve any political activity against the government. In fact, their dominant attitude was that becoming involved in direct political activity was a sign of adolescence. One who had reached maturity might discuss issues of justice with a gin and tonic but wouldn't actually do anything about it. It was extremely patronizing. That said, my order, to its credit, agreed that I should take up residence in Lesotho, a small country completely surrounded by South Africa that sheltered a community of South African exiles where SSM had a presence.

Although some in SSM were uncomfortable with what they no doubt regarded as my provocative behavior, the church was quite supportive of me. The archbishop and the bishop of Natal tried without success to get the government to reverse it's decision, and the bishop of Natal went so far as to issue a press statement that I had his full support. In a letter to the SSM provincial in Australia, Southern African Provincial David Wells, wrote:

> [Michael] has tremendous support [among] the clergy in the Durban area who sent him a letter saying that they firmly back him up. . . . One particular priest, who had opposed him at Synod, also wrote to say that, although he had disagreed with Michael in some particulars, on the whole he admired him for what he had been trying to do and felt ashamed, as a South African, that the Government had asked him to leave the country. Student organizations from six different Universities throughout the country have written to him that they do not want him to resign as National Chaplain even though he will have to act "in exile."

In the days immediately preceding my departure I drove to a little rural town called Modderpoort near the Lesotho border where our community had a small priory. Even before I was expelled members of my congregation had become quite anxious that I might be picked up, and we had talked about what the Brothers would do if that happened. So many people were being detained that there were organizations that provided a list of what one must have ready—a toothbrush, toothpaste, clean clothes, and so on. For some reason a tennis ball was at the top of the list. So we joked about whether I had my tennis ball ready.

The South African government was not happy about the growing exile community in Lesotho and carefully controlled its border. Crossing was extremely dangerous if a person aroused any suspicion and everyone was understandably nervous. When the deed was successfully accomplished, Fr. Wells wrote to his counterpart in Australia saying, no doubt with a sense of relief, "Today we delivered him safely into Lesotho."

The Brothers and I had devised a subterfuge to cross the border with as few problems as possible. I would not attempt to drive into Lesotho myself. Because SSM had a presence there and was seen as nonpolitical, we had a six-month pass that allowed the Brothers free passage back and forth between Modderpoort and Lesotho, which they did quite often. Proceeding according to plan, I packed up all my clothes and other belongings, including what no doubt would have been considered banned literature, and one of the Brothers loaded them into his car. He was able to drive across the border without arousing suspicion because the guards were used to seeing him carry goods back and forth. After he got to Lesotho he phoned to say it was all clear, whereupon another Brother and I drove to the border without any luggage. The guards said, "OK, show us everything you brought with you." I literally had only the clothes on my back. Even so, I was ordered into a room at the border post for questioning, and I became quite alarmed when the guard closed not only the door but the window blinds. He questioned me for some time about my intentions, but in the end he allowed me through. It was the last I would see of South Africa for sixteen years.

*At Lelapala Jesu Anglican Seminary in Lesotho,
with Bishop Philip Mokuku.*

◇ 6 ◇

A Crisis of Faith

◇◇◇◇◇◇◇

IT WAS NOT QUITE FOUR MONTHS after the Soweto uprising and, quite literally, all hell had broken loose. Tear gas, tanks, and the crackling of gunfire had exposed apartheid for what it really was, a system based on brutality and terror. It was a system that inverted the moral order: good was called evil, and evil was called good. Language was perverted in an effort to justify the unjustifiable. Black people had to keep silent just to survive, and white people went about their daily lives content with their comfortable existence and inured to injustice. I knew with every fiber of my being that what was considered normal was actually evil. In its reliance on terror, it was immoral, and in its attempt to warp the perception of reality, it was insane. The choice was to numb oneself or to scream to high heaven. In the end I did neither, though I often thought that if I couldn't scream, I would go crazy. I was fortunate in a way. The public platform that the university chaplaincy provided me was an outlet for my anger and righteous indignation. There, at least, I was able to name what I saw forthrightly: murder, kidnapping, torture. So in addition to whatever political value it may have had, speaking out probably helped me keep my sanity. It would be another twenty years before people who had suffered under apartheid, glued to their television screens, would be able to watch South Africa's Truth and Reconciliation Commission expose the suffering and acknowledge the evil that the country endured for so long.

I left South Africa in a state of relief and grief, relieved at no longer being trapped in such a vicious, crazy-making system, and grieved at having to abandon a country and a people I cared about so deeply. To return to SSM in Australia was out of the question. At the same time, the turbulence all around me was deeply unsettling. I had cast my lot with the liberation struggle, and I had no idea what the future would

61

bring. I arrived in Lesotho traumatized by the dehumanizing years I had lived under apartheid and the violence of the preceding four months. I was a refugee from a country that I loved but had known for only three short years. I had come to South Africa overflowing with earnestness and youthful idealism to preach the gospel of love and peace. The Bible says we are required to love God with our heart, our mind, our soul, and our strength and our neighbors as ourselves. But in South Africa I couldn't be a neighbor to a black person. I was locked into an oppressor-oppressed relationship. Over the course of the three years I lived there, my conviction about what it meant to be a Christian gradually eroded and finally collapsed in the face of the shooting of innocent children. I began to realize that my understanding of the gospel did not take account of the sheer magnitude of evil. It was perhaps adequate to another time and place, but it had little to offer unarmed protestors facing a lethal barrage of bullets. As a result I began more and more to question my pacifism. My faith had been my comfort in the midst of oppression. Now I could no longer even depend on it, and spiritually speaking, I felt the ground shifting under me. I had to rethink my relationship to the gospel at the very time I faced the upheaval of beginning life in yet another country I did not know. It required all my courage, but courage, after all, had carried me this far.

I knew that the answer to my spiritual crisis was somehow to be found in my commitment to the liberation struggle. In response to the government's repression South African young people had begun streaming into Lesotho to join the armed struggle or to seek a better education, and they swelled the ranks of the exile community. I spent much time talking with them, most of whom already were or would become militant members of the ANC. The ANC was extremely attractive to me as a Christian because of its stand on nonracialism. It echoed the affirmation in the 1955 Freedom Charter, "South Africa belongs to all who live in it, black and white." The first president of the ANC, John Dube, was a Christian minister, the son of a clergyman, and the founder of a Christian school. Indeed, from its very beginning in 1912, many leaders of the ANC were professed Christians and some were Christian ministers, and they seemed to have taken their Christianity more seriously than their white counterparts. As Archbishop Desmond Tutu has often remarked, black people read the Bible, took it to heart, and saw in it a gospel of justice and freedom.

Despite this, however, I still parted company with the ANC over the issue of the armed struggle. I had gone to South Africa as a committed pacifist. I had refused high school military training in the face of peer pressure and the unspoken disapproval of my parents, and I thought my father was wrong to fight against Nazism in World War II. I regarded violence as the very antithesis of the gospel message of peace and love. As a young student I had read not only Jesus of Nazareth but also Mahatma Gandhi and Martin Luther King Jr. So for me pacifism was both a tactic and a principle of the gospel, and I believed that nonviolent methods were the only morally defensible way to deal with conflict. I was convinced that if they were prayerfully applied, they would eventually win out no matter what the situation. After all, had Jesus not died on the cross and triumphed in the resurrection? So for me this was an issue that went to the very heart of my faith. As I preached nonviolence to students, black and white, however, I began to notice that the apartheid state was extremely happy for me to tell black people that they shouldn't use weapons to achieve their rights. Suggesting to white students that they shouldn't go to the army, however, was another matter altogether; the conversation itself was illegal. So the state believed in nonviolence for the oppressed but never hesitated to use violence to assert its own interests.

As I learned more about the ANC I discovered that in one way or another it had always been an inclusive organization. Its first president had said, "Tribally divided we are ruled over forever," so though it began as an exclusively African organization, it provided a home for all tribes throughout Southern Africa. Over the decades its vision expanded, and it began to embrace other racial groups as well. By the time of the Soweto uprising whites who espoused its values and platform could join, though for some time they could not be part of the top leadership. I was present at the 1985 Congress in Kabwe, Zambia, where the ANC decided that every level of leadership should be open to people of all races. This stunning achievement was most dramatically visible five years later in 1990 when negotiations began after the unbanning of the liberation organizations. On one side of the table sat the forces for democracy, a rainbow people of all colors and genders, and on the other side sat the representatives of apartheid South Africa, a dour band of all white men.

I began to see that I was taking the same path that the ANC itself had followed as an organization. My respect for it increased when I learned that it too had come to the armed struggle reluctantly. In its early years it relied on persuasion and petitions, but it became more and more militant as oppression intensified. In the 1950s the government passed the Bantu Education Act that deprived black people of even a minimally adequate education, enacted a myriad of laws including those that greatly restricted their freedom of movement, and began forcibly removing them from their homes in order to create distinct separation of the races. The ANC responded by organizing a Defiance Campaign against these unjust laws that transformed the ANC into a mass movement. It was not until after the 1960 Sharpeville massacre of people protesting the pass laws that the ANC made the decision to embrace the armed struggle. Even then the first armed attacks were acts of sabotage, carefully carried out so that there was no loss of human life. Of course as the struggle became more intense and bitter, so too did the violence, but violence was a tactic that the ANC moved to reluctantly in response to extreme provocation. Even so, the organization remained clear throughout its history that what was being struggled against was an oppressive system and not a particular race group.

I began to see that in order to solve my faith problem, I would have to act politically. The more I read the scriptures with new spectacles, the more clearly that emerged. It was not primarily about what happens when you die; it was good news for the here and now. So I began to read scripture not just with the eyes of what I had been taught in church but from the perspective of someone committed to the liberation of all people. At the heart of that struggle lay an understanding that is also at the heart of the gospel—self-sacrifice and a willingness to lay down one's life that others may be free.

The vast majority of South Africa's people would describe themselves as Christian, but in reality there is a kaleidoscope of religions—Muslims, Jews, Hindus, Buddhists, and people who subscribe to no particular faith. So I also reached the conclusion that the future of humanity is not a Christian future but an interfaith future, including deep reverence and respect for atheists, agnostics, and those practicing indigenous spiritualities. I have always been very religious but doubt has been a consistent part of my faith journey. I have come increasingly to respect doubt, because I think total certainty slides easily into fundamentalism. All fundamentalisms, no matter of what religion, are scary because in the end they end up being willing to kill other human beings in the name of their creed. Doubt brings a kind of humility and opens the door to respect for the perspective of the "other."

The first person who articulated an interfaith vision of humanity for me was another one of my lifetime heroes—Archbishop Trevor Huddleston. He was a Christian archbishop who led from the front on interfaith issues almost before its time had come. In the liberation struggle we were an interfaith bunch, not only of different religious faiths but also different worldviews. I worry that an increasing proportion of conflicts in the world today have a religious dimension. I think this gives an urgency to the need to bring up a new generation of young people and encourage them not so much to tolerate other religions but to revere and respect them and see the wealth of wisdom there to be experienced and enjoyed. I long ago began to have problems with a kind of Christian view that we are in the light and other religions are in darkness. I think that is a very strange view of who God is. So I have no less desire to be a Christian, but from a Christian vantage point I seek to be deeply respectful of other traditions and of the integrity and humanity of people who have no religious belief. We need to have some understanding of why a person would come to that conclusion. Another way to put it is that we don't worship a small tribal God and that God is not limited in the way God works with human beings. Let us demonstrate our faith by the way we live our lives and the way we love and care for others. Let that be the real witness that will draw people to our faith.

Many years ago I was startled when I read a Christian theologian from Latin America, Carlos Mesters. He asserts that the whole created order, including human beings, constitutes God's First Book. The Bible, he writes, is God's Second Book, and it is like a guide that helps to make sense of the First Book. The Latin Americans led many of us to see that we must always begin with the context of our individual lives. None of us comes to scripture objectively; we each come subjectively in the light of the person that we are, including our place in the world and all that is happening in it. This means that the same passage of scripture will mean different things to different people and even to us at different times as the context of our life changes.

Given the dominant role that religion plays in the life of South Africans, black and white, the struggle against apartheid was always in some respects a theological battle. Even as far back as the nineteenth century some white South African Christians were unwilling to sit at the Lord's table with black Christians, so theological apartheid actually preceded political apartheid. Once it became government policy, the state put itself forward as the earthly manifestation of God's will. God's interpreter in this case, as everyone knew, was the white Dutch Reformed Church, the primary apologist for the apartheid government, given force by its political arm, the National Party. People sardonically referred to it as "the National Party at prayer." When protestors were detained and brought to trial for political acts, magistrates placed heavy reliance on one particular verse of scripture, Romans 13, verse 1:

Let every person be subject to the governing authorities. For there is no authority except from God, and those that exist have been instituted by God. Therefore whoever resists the authorities resists what God has appointed, and those who resist will incur judgment.

The scripture that was the bedrock of my faith was being twisted into an ideological weapon in the service of evil. And while there was undoubtedly an element of cynicism in this on the part of the government, what was I to make of the fact that millions of white South Africans had accepted it as God's wisdom as expressed in the scriptures? Black people, in turn, were encouraged by clergy, white and black, to be docile and accepting and not to worry that they were oppressed because a future awaited them in heaven.

This government not only declared war on its own people, but it exported it to the whole region. Throughout the states of Southern Africa the regime hunted us down like wild animals. What was our crime? We dared to believe that God had created us all equal, with an equal right to a place in the sun. We dared to believe in our common humanity, and we strove to live accordingly. For this crime a death sentence was passed on all of us. The regime financed, supplied, and trained bandits that made Mozambique the poorest country in the world and left Angola with more amputees than any other country in the world at the time—all in the name of Christianity. The same people who shot children at home or partied in Angola while bodies burned alongside them went to church and took communion at the Lord's table and were assured of a place in heaven. I wondered if we were going to the same heaven.

In South Africa there are many different churches. The white Dutch Reformed Church was virtually synonymous with apartheid, but on the other side of the spectrum were churches that consistently said apartheid was wrong and evil. Those who looked closely would notice that the churches were themselves sites of struggle. That struggle went on not only between the churches but within them. In 1985 a group of progressive theologians issued what was called the Kairos Document. It analyzed three kinds of theology in South Africa. One was state theology, which blessed the state and everything it did. Then there was church theology, which gave reconciliation primacy over justice. It condemned all forms of violence as if they had the same moral content. Church theology often spoke against apartheid but would not act against it. Then there was prophetic theology, which was really a theology of liberation. It emphasized action more than words, and it engaged and participated in the struggle for liberation. It sought to give hope to the poor. It was not neutral; it was a theology of action and partisanship. As the years progressed, particularly through the 1980s in churches that were traditionally very conservative, some people began to be forced by the reality of the scale of oppression to question the interpretation of the faith by their churches. Individual people of conscience reflected on their life experience and realized that for the sake of their own humanity they needed to struggle for justice. They couldn't keep silent any longer. All three types of theology played themselves out within a single church and sometimes within a single individual. During the 1980s the churches that made up the South African Council of Churches, together with the Roman Catholic Church, became increasingly active in their opposition to apartheid, and by the same token some individual Christians were fearless participants in the liberation movement while others were supporters of the apartheid regime.

My own faith crisis separated me from many in my community and from the loudest voices in the Anglican Church. That is not to say that it separated me from all individual Anglicans; some would have supported me strongly. My decision to join a religious order had meant that the Brothers in my community became family for me, and yet in South Africa I felt quite separate from most of them because of their passive acceptance of apartheid. Not that they didn't do what the situation required of them, such as helping me escape safely to Lesotho, but most of them supported me out of a sense of filial obligation rather than a deeply shared commitment to what I saw as the central meaning of the gospel.

Originally it was my pacifism that separated me from most other Anglicans; now my advocacy of the armed struggle would soon do so. While the church has historically blessed or condoned most wars, in South Africa it had taken a somewhat ambiguous position. On the one hand, it was outspoken in condemning apartheid as contrary to God's will, but at the same time it saw all violence as a sin. So there was a tendency to equate the violence of the liberation movement and the violence of the state as equally sinful. As so often happens, this approach tended implicitly to favor the power structure. For example, the church never took a firm position advocating conscientious objection among white youth conscripted into the South African army, though individual clergy and lay people certainly did so. In fact, the church provided pastors as chaplains to the army, whereas it never did this formally for the armed wing of the liberation movements. Such chaplaincy as there was for the liberation organizations came from people like myself who did so on our own initiative. I came to understand that there could be no middle way in the struggle to end apartheid; the church needed to take sides clearly and decisively, and this too put me well outside the church's framework.

In the end the Soweto uprising was the turning point for me. How could I advocate nonviolence in the face of the gunning down of schoolchildren? I reluctantly decided that pacifism was untenable and that people did have a right to defend themselves in the face of overwhelming force. To preach otherwise was to invite black South Africans to be complicit in their own deaths. It was not an easy decision. I suddenly came face to face with a God who always takes the side of the poor and oppressed. I was seized by the fervent belief that within our context the liberation movement was the human embodiment of the gospel message of love and justice. The armed struggle was one important means for realizing this, and therefore it was morally legitimate and justified. This was a fundamental shift and in the years to come I would pour my energy wholeheartedly into the struggle for liberation. While that struggle was in some ways all encompassing, it remains true that for me, ever and always, my political work was an expression of my deep faith in God's will for the human family.

◇ 7 ◇

Lesotho—Living in Exile

◇◇◇◇◇◇◇

MY SUDDEN DEPARTURE from South Africa meant that I had no time to make plans for my future. Fortunately, Desmond Tutu came to my aid. He had recently been named bishop of Lesotho, and he helped me to enroll at the National University of Lesotho to complete my bachelor's degree, which had been interrupted by the violence in South Africa. I eventually finished my degree in English and sociology there and obtained a teaching qualification as well.

I initially camped at the residence of another SSM Brother living in Lesotho, but when I became a student, I moved into university housing. That provided me with a welcome opportunity to get to know other students. Bishop Tutu also facilitated my appointment as assistant to Fr. Donald Nestor, the Anglican chaplain at the university. The following year I succeeded him as university chaplain. I inherited another responsibility from Fr. Nestor, the training of a few young men studying for the Anglican priesthood at Lelapa La Jesu, a tiny seminary that was connected to a larger Roman Catholic seminary nearby. By this time I had moved into the quarters of the Anglican chaplaincy, which, as I increased my political activity, became a place where students and members of the ANC congregated. One of those students was Michael Worsnip, whose testimony before the South African Truth and Reconciliation Commission accompanies this chapter. In it he describes his own days as a student at the university and his experience of my role as chaplain.

Though I embraced fellow African students as brothers and sisters, at the beginning the feeling was not always wholeheartedly recipro-cated. I was, after all, white and from New Zealand in an overwhelm-ingly black African environment. Then too, I had a rather complicated, multidimensional status. I was a student, a chaplain at the university, and the national chaplain for Anglican students for the whole of the Province of Southern Africa. I sometimes felt called upon to prove myself to African students, and since new ones kept arriving the issue never quite went away. On one particularly memorable occasion I had just returned from an international youth conference in Eastern Europe, where I had represented ANC youth. Soon after I returned I rose at an ANC meeting to give my report, and afterward I had a dust-up with a fellow student, Tito Mboweni. Years later Mboweni was to become the post-apartheid governor of South Africa's Reserve Bank. He asked me, "How can you, a white man, be representing the ANC youth? Wasn't there any black person they could have sent to represent them?" I remember looking at him calmly and replying, "Well, Tito, the ANC is a nonracial organization, you know. Black people, white people, everybody in the liberation struggle is welcome. It's a parliament of the people of South Africa." Tito looked doubtful, but it was the beginning of a long friendship and many lively discussions about nonracialism, not in the abstract, but in its very practical dimensions. Between the two of us we embodied it, contentiousness and all. Many years later, in one of life's ironic twists, it was my old friend Tito that I had phoned at the precise moment when the bomb went off. He recalls the phone suddenly going dead and wondering if something terrible had happened to me.

Despite the difficulties, Lesotho liberated me. Even though I was one of only two white students at the university, I felt free to be myself. This was in contrast to South Africa where every aspect of my existence was controlled by race. The university was in a small town called Roma, some distance from Maseru, the capital. The South African exile community had grown by leaps and bounds after the Soweto uprising as more and more young people left the country to join the armed struggle or in search of a good education, which was itself seen as an important contribution to the struggle. Since Zimbabwe's independence was still four years in the offing, there were many Zimbabwean students as well. Maseru was home to a substantial international community with many connections to the university. Some were professors, others worked for international aid agencies, and there was a large group of South African refugees, some of whom were ANC operatives. It was quite a radical campus, fairly bubbling with intellectual and political ferment, and filled with books, political tracts, posters, and a fair amount of student fervor. I made friendships of a lifetime with Basotho, Zimbabwean, and South African students. I was fortunate to be able to be a student among other students even though I was also white, a priest, and a chaplain in an almost totally African student body. It was an exciting time and those were very good years indeed. Recently my friend Tito was reminiscing about those days. Shaking his head he said, "We were an argumentative bunch then. We were struggling to solve very difficult, complex issues, often with very simple answers." Then he grinned and added, "Sometimes despite ourselves we managed to come up with the kind of complex answers the situations demanded." From his later experience heading the Reserve Bank, he certainly had reason to know how complex the problems can be.

I became very active in student politics and was elected vice president of the Student Representative Council. At one stage there was a controversy about campus food. We organized student demonstrations, which were unheard of in Lesotho, a country steeped in a tradition of deference to authority. The upshot was that the entire Student Representative Council was expelled, though eventually the expulsions were rescinded. The university went so far as to write to my parents in New Zealand, which needless to say caused a bit of a stir at home. Of course I was in quite an unusual position, one that must have given the university authorities fits, because while I had been expelled as a student, I was also chaplain and living in the Anglican chaplaincy on campus. I declined to vacate it, and ever creative as I was, my line ran, "The vice president has left, but the chaplain remains." As a result the university tried to enlist the help of Bishop Tutu to deal with me, but he was out of the country at the time. When he returned and was reading through his most recent mail, he discovered that I had been forgiven for he knew not what. It was not until he read his earlier correspondence that he discovered what sin I had committed. It was not the last time that Bishop Tutu would be shaking his head over my activities.

My relationship with the church in Southern Africa, which was never a honeymoon, got off to quite a rocky start in Lesotho. I had begun referring to myself as the national chaplain-in-exile. It was, of course, more a gesture of political solidarity than it was an ecclesiastical title, especially since I had been elected by students and not appointed by the church hierarchy. The South African bishops saw my claiming the exile part of the title as a provocation, and it caused great fury among them. Administratively speaking, the problem was that the Anglican Province of Southern Africa included South Africa, Lesotho, Mozambique, and Swaziland. Because of this, all the issues of apartheid played themselves out within the whole of the province, and the South African bishops thought they were entitled to weigh in on this matter. But the reality is that some were already angry about my outspoken denunciations of the government before I left South Africa. They obviously felt I should have just resigned and gone away, preferably as far as possible. I received quite a stern letter from the liaison bishop to chaplains, who was also the bishop of Pretoria, complaining about my using the title national chaplain-in-exile. He also criticized my public statements expressing solidarity with the liberation struggle on the grounds that they were insufficiently couched in explicitly Christian language and thus could be seen as simply humanistic or, God forbid, Marxist. In my reply I declined to accept his advice, pointing out that there was no denying that I was still the national chaplain and that, though I was a priest in the Province of Southern Africa, I was undeniably in exile from the country I came to serve and to which my order had sent me. Some of my close comrades were not Christians, let alone Anglicans, and I countered that the prophetic word of God could indeed come through humanists and Marxists. I said that expressing the gospel message in exclusively Christian language risked inviting some students to reject it as irrelevant. Since the church was not prepared to move against me at that point, the matter subsided with some muttering.

The events set off by the Soweto uprising continued to reverberate in South Africa throughout 1977, the year after I went into exile. Steve Biko, the much-revered Black Consciousness leader, was murdered in detention, and important leaders of the resistance movement in South Africa such as Winnie Mandela and Mamphela Ramphele were put under house arrest and effectively silenced by being prevented from speaking publicly. The same year the Annual Conference of Anglican Students was held in Morija, Lesotho. It was the first time it had met outside of South Africa, a deliberate decision made so that I would be able to attend. The church leaders no doubt perceived this as a provocative act on the part of the Anglican students, and it was compounded further by the very partisan position I took at the conference. I said that while I didn't think it was morally legitimate to go to the army to defend apartheid, I did think it was morally legitimate to take up arms against it. The news of my position was reported in South Africa, of course, and caused much outrage and consternation. I suppose it's true that in this and other matters I had a certain disregard for church diplomacy, but in my view diplomacy was often used to justify morally indefensible positions. So what I saw as my Christian duty in speaking truth to power, others regarded as troublemaking. All of this caused increasing discomfort within the church hierarchy and members of my community in South Africa. Whereas previously in my community I had been seen as merely "out in front" of other

Brothers, now there were moves made to expel me, though at that point they came to nothing.

As time went on I grew more and more convinced that the ANC's vision for South Africa embodied the gospel message of liberation. Whereas many well-meaning Christians saw the church as a sort of middle way between the apartheid regime and the ANC, for me there was no tenable middle and the ANC's platform *was* the Christian way. I also came to the conclusion that solitary prophets, as important as they could be, were not a sufficient threat to the status quo and that it was only when people organized themselves in a disciplined way that they could wield enough power to challenge an unjust system. In fact, the state sometimes congratulated itself that it allowed a few people to speak out; in that way it tried to confer a little legitimacy on itself in the eyes of the international community. Needless to say, it more often silenced people, especially black people, if it thought it could get away with it. For all these reasons, I felt it was important not to act solely as an individual but rather to become part of the liberation movement.

I therefore made a formal application to join the ANC. Joining involved far more than signing a piece of paper at the end of a political rally. The ANC operated in an exceedingly dangerous environment. The white government in South Africa felt itself under siege by rising protests in the country; acts of sabotage by the liberation movement; the independence of Mozambique and Angola, with a Marxist government in Mozambique and civil war in Angola; and the approaching independence of Zimbabwe. Agents of South Africa were everywhere, penetrating ANC structures and passing information to the apartheid government, often with lethal consequences. We heard regularly of comrades meeting unexplained "accidents" and outright assassination and we learned to be careful of revealing even seemingly innocuous information to bystanders.

Lesotho had obtained its independence from the British in 1966. Its government was initially quite autocratic and had been historically aligned with South African interests. Because of this it continued to be unpopular with the students. In many ways, though, it had little choice, since it was a landlocked country completely surrounded by South Africa and economically utterly dependent on it. For many years it refused entry to South African exiles, but beginning in 1973 it quietly began opening its doors. It gradually became more sympathetic to the ANC and, at considerable risk to itself, began to distance itself as far as it could from the apartheid regime, although it remained disliked by many of its own citizens. The apartheid state had become very adept at trying to block direct communication between resistance forces in South Africa and the ANC in exile. So by the time I arrived there was an "underground railroad" from Lesotho that smuggled people and information in and out of South Africa, usually under the cover of night in remote rural areas. ANC activities in Lesotho were directed by Chris Hani, a leader of the South African Communist Party and the eventual chief of staff of Umkhonto we Sizwe, the military wing of the ANC. Even though I was at the university and not directly involved in these underground activities, after I joined the ANC I, like all members, was answerable to its command structure and for a time I reported directly to Chris Hani.

Accountability within the ranks of the ANC was mandatory because of the high stakes involved, and it maintained a tight organization that demanded strict discipline. Applicants for membership were carefully screened. There were other key members of the ANC who were white, but there was some skepticism about me, not least because I was from New Zealand. I knew that do-gooders often came to South Africa and supported the antiapartheid movement while they were there, but they were careful to hang onto their passports and when events threatened to boil over, they fled. I made up my mind I would not be one of them. If I were truly committed to fighting for a free South Africa I couldn't keep my passport in my back pocket and think, "When the going gets tough, I'll run away." The commitment had to be irrevocable or not at all. The leadership of the ANC agreed and my application was accepted. Years later, in 1990, I gave an interview to Hilda Bernstein for her book, *The Rift*, about the South African exile experience. In it I quoted what I said to the ANC in my application:

> I am asking to join the ANC, by which I understand I am taking citizenship in the country we are still fighting for. . . . I will live with the implications of what I am saying. And if I walk this road with these people, I will continue to walk that road as long as we need to walk. Forever.

Two months after I gave that interview to Hilda in Zimbabwe, I was bombed.

As time went by my involvement with the ANC deepened. Operatives elsewhere in the country were careful to remain underground so as not to attract attention. We at the university, on the other hand, formed an above-ground chapter on campus, at the time one of the few visible units of the ANC anywhere, and for a while I headed it. We made no effort to hide our message, and we fulfilled a useful function in keeping the voice of liberation going out to South Africans and the student world, particularly in Lesotho and to a lesser extent in all the front-line states of Southern Africa. The Anglican chaplaincy became a discreet focal point for political agitation. People came and went freely at most hours of the day and night. Some of them were people I knew and some of them weren't. The process we were engaged in had a momentum of its own, and I made little effort to keep track of it all. There was a feeling of excitement, even romanticism, in the air that is no doubt akin to movement politics everywhere. Since much of my energy during this time went into political activity that was not necessarily expressed in spiritual language, others may have seen me primarily as an ANC operative. If the truth be told, at times I saw myself that way as well. Nonetheless, I continued to serve as chaplain to the university in the midst of my political engagement, and I never lost sight of the reality that the bedrock of my commitment to the struggle was the gospel message of liberation.

Back in South Africa conscription of white males was mandatory, and most young men not wanting to go to the army simply left the country. The government passed new legislation instituting truly draconian penalties for refusing military service and making it illegal to even discuss the possibility with young white males, but in fact the number of young men who stayed in the country and courageously refused service increased. Their importance far outweighed their relatively small numbers because their principled stand gave the lie to the government's efforts to characterize the conflict as purely racial and military service as normative. The government also depicted the struggle as a battle between Christendom and godless communism, so with the ANC's support I began to use my position as a priest and a member of the ANC to challenge this misuse of religion and to build support among the faith community.

One of my first acts was to write an article entitled "Christianity and the Just War" in *Sechaba*, the ANC journal published in Dar es Salaam. I articulated some of the arguments from a faith perspective for supporting the armed struggle. While there is no doubt that nonviolence is the morally superior way, and it is the preferred option whenever possible, there is nevertheless a long history within the Christian tradition of just war theory. St. Thomas Aquinas developed the theory, not as an attempt to bless war, but as an attempt to say that if there is to be war, there still needs to be a form of morality. Just war theory provides a sort of checklist that must be exhausted in order to conclude that a war is permissible. In the *Sechaba* article I took apart the theory point by point and demonstrated how in my view the liberation struggle met its criteria. I emphasized that just war theory was not created to make it easy to justify killing; on the contrary, it was to provide as many moral safeguards as possible and to make sure that war is used only as a last resort. Nonviolence becomes most problematic when the oppressor in no way recognizes the humanity of the oppressed. If we look at the nonviolent resistance of the Jewish people in the Second World War, we see that those measures did not prevent them from going to the gas chambers. In the face of that kind of fascism is it really desirable that people should not resist violence? For me, similarly, in South Africa the state itself was fundamentally violent. The state used structural and institutional as well as naked violence to retain power. I argued therefore that it was morally legitimate and justifiable under such circumstances to resist.

The interesting thing about the South African experience is that the majority spent fifty years traveling on a nonviolent road before finally opting for arms. But in the face of their nonviolence the regime ever and always increased its own violence. At the same time it is important that violence should never be romanticized. The option of the armed struggle was costly for our humanity. In the South African context the refusal of the regime to negotiate a just settlement eventually made an armed option inevitable. I think the resort to arms must always be the last option, certainly not the first. I further outlined some of these views in an article I wrote for the World Council of Churches Programme to Combat Racism entitled "Why I Joined the African National Congress—The Option for Life." It described the dehumanization that apartheid imposed on whites and blacks alike and explained why, as a Christian, I felt I had no option but to support the armed struggle. This latter article was read widely by progressive Christians the world over and was no doubt one of the first steps in bringing my views to the attention of the international faith community.

The World Council of Churches Programme to Combat Racism was launched in 1969 at a workshop attended by Oliver Tambo and Bishop Trevor Huddleston, so it had from the first a focus on Southern Africa. The following year the program set up the Special Fund, which made generous grants for humanitarian purposes to the liberation movements in Southern Africa, primarily the ANC and SWAPO (South West Africa People's Organization). This became the subject of intense controversy especially in Europe and the United States, whose governments were frequently supportive of the status quo. For example, an October 2, 1978, article in *Time* magazine was titled "Going 'Beyond Charity': Should Christian Cash Be Given to

Terrorists?" In November of that same year the archbishop of Cape Town wrote in *Seek,* a church publication:

> We did in 1970 and still do . . . reject the apparently uncon-
> ditional support for, and identification of the Church with
> particular political movements, or governments for that matter.
> Such unconditional support . . . makes the supporters of that
> programme responsible for whatever such movements do which
> is inconsistent with Christian faith and ethics.

In response, Fr. John Osmers and I wrote an open letter to the archbishop and sent copies to all the bishops of the province. After cataloging the many ways that the church colluded with apartheid, we pointed out that the Anglican Church seemed to have no problem in licensing priests as paid officers of the South African army who are bound by all the discipline and regulations of the military and for whose actions the church is then presumably responsible.

My increasing prominence as a priest and member of the ANC and my identification with the armed struggle eventually became the source of some conflict with Bishop Tutu. I had gone to him to discuss the possibility of either going to teach at the ANC's Solomon Mahlangu Freedom College in Morogoro, Tanzania, or of joining Umkhonto we Sizwe. He admonished me about the dangers of over-identification—a position I did then and still do find problematic. I think I was simply too radical for him and he criticized me for getting "carried away." It may have been partly a question of style. When I became part of the liberation struggle I had to learn to fight to survive and to fight for the integrity of my ideas. This was also true in the church and in my community, and this at times made me unnecessarily and inappropriately combative. Especially in an overwhelmingly black movement I was in one sense swimming within a broad stream, and in another sense, as a white person in a black movement, I was swimming against the stream. That created its own inner tension that may have emerged from time to time in a certain feistiness on my part. Over the years Bishop Tutu has continued to speak about how obstreperous and difficult I was as a priest in Lesotho, but I think some of what he regards as my unmanageability was related to our fundamental difference over the role of the religious and the political. For me they were and are inseparable. There was also another dimension. I'm not sure how much either he or I realized that I had been traumatized by the racism and violence I witnessed during the years I spent in South Africa under apartheid.

None of this, however, should be taken to imply that Bishop Tutu was not a vigorous and outspoken critic of the apartheid regime. He is truly one of the giants of the liberation struggle, and he also often couched his criticism of the regime in explicitly religious language. Our difference has to do with his conviction that, as a Christian, one must leave the door ajar to all sides, whereas I felt called upon to serve a God who unambiguously chooses sides. There are historical precedents for religious leaders doing just that. To take one modern case, Pope John Paul II decreed that priests should not be involved in politics, except of course in his home country of Poland where he was an outspoken partisan. He himself wasn't able to escape the intersection of religion and politics; in the end he was a Polish Catholic. Years later, as I struggled to heal from being bombed and adjust to a permanent major disability, I knew in my heart that what had happened to me was a consequence of how I had lived out my faith in the political sphere. While I regretted the outcome, I in no way regretted the choice.

Not long after our conversation Bishop Tutu left Lesotho to become the general secretary of the South African Council of Churches. Since I now had earned a teaching qualification at the University of Lesotho, I decided to follow up on my wish to teach at the ANC school in Morogoro. It would have been an exciting opportunity, for the school, which was just getting started, had a twofold mission. One was to provide a quality education for the young exiles streaming out of South Africa in the wake of the Soweto uprising, and the other was to serve as a pilot for what revolutionary education would look like once the ANC became the government of the nonracial South Africa we were fighting for. Though I had been accepted to teach there, when it came to the ears of Oliver Tambo, the president of the ANC, he took a different view. He said that the work in Lesotho was of strategic importance and that other people could teach in the ANC school but that it would be far harder to replace me in Lesotho. The problem was that I had already said to Bishop Phillip Mokuku, Bishop Tutu's successor, that I had prayed about this, that the Holy Spirit had led me to decide that this is what I should do, and that therefore I would be leaving the chaplaincy at the university. Both he and the director of SSM had approved of my doing so. This put me in the position of having to come back to the bishop and say that I would be continuing in the chaplaincy at the university after all, whereupon he looked at me and said with a wry smile that perhaps the Holy Spirit's name was Oliver Tambo.

Our political activity predictably attracted the attention of the South African press. On one occasion a reporter from a South

African newspaper interviewed me and then wrote a completely scurrilous article suggesting that the Anglican chaplaincy was virtually a bomb factory. It was quite scary because it endangered not only the chaplaincy but a kindergarten housed at the Anglican church nearby. Later I became the subject of an article entitled "Priest Who Is an ANC Propagandist," which appeared in *The Citizen*, a right-wing newspaper that was the English-speaking voice of the National Party. The article was in some ways unintentionally complimentary in that it suggested that I was the propaganda voice of the ANC to the churches and gave me a far more prominent role than in fact I played. Another article went so far as to compare me to Fr. Camilo Torres Restrepo, a Roman Catholic priest and Latin American revolutionary, who tried to reconcile Catholic theology and Marxist revolutionary thought. His example would have been perhaps an unfortunate one to follow since he was killed in 1966 on his first combat operation in Colombia. The apartheid regime was especially irked by white people like me who were involved in the struggle and therefore were seen as race traitors in addition to being political operatives. On top of that, I, a white priest, was unmasking apartheid's claim of moral legitimacy based on faith.

All this attention from the South Africa press was flattering to my ego, however unwarranted, but the danger in it was that it created a climate for assassination, since it softened public opinion so that people would say, "Who is this man really?" I suspect that I was most likely already on a death list by this time, and this had to be taken seriously because the apartheid state was on a rampage throughout Southern Africa. The clandestine underground organizing going on in Lesotho was certainly known to the South African security apparatus. That and my support for the ANC along with others at the university was used by the apartheid state to whip up fear and buttress its own position. Lesotho was painted as a hotbed of godless communism. It was a dangerous situation, and it finally boiled over while I was out of the country.

In the dead of night on December 10, 1982, while I was on leave visiting my family in New Zealand, the South African National Defence Force launched a helicopter raid into Lesotho. About one hundred South African soldiers were dropped into Maseru and a rein of terror ensued as they stormed from door to door, firing weapons, detonating fire bombs, and bursting into homes, climbing through broken windows, and shooting many people in their beds. In all, thirty South African exiles and twelve Lesotho citizens, men, women, and children, were massacred. Houses were set on fire and blown up and young children who had seen their parents killed before their eyes had to be pulled from the bloody, burning wreckage. The entire exile community was thoroughly traumatized.

For me, seven thousand miles away in New Zealand, this news was surreal. Not that it was a total surprise. We lived with danger on a daily basis, and we were prepared for assassination attempts. All of us knew people who had been killed or maimed by car or letter bombs, but most of us were unprepared for a massive assault like this. The sheer brutality of the blood bath was horrifying. I was on a speaking tour when I received the news. I felt numb with shock and disbelief that was soon followed by anger and grief, and I took a vow on that day that my own life would be dedicated to ending apartheid and creating a society in which little children could go to bed at night and wake up safe.

For what seemed like ages, but was actually only a few hours, I had to live with the anxiety of not knowing. Had any of the people I knew and loved been killed? I dared to hope they had not because the news said that the raid had targeted Maseru, the capital, and spared Roma, where most of the university community lived. Eventually the communication system of the ANC proved itself even in this crisis, and I received a telex from ANC headquarters in Lusaka with a list of those who had been killed. While I knew several of the victims, thankfully there was no one who was a close friend. Because I was widely known in New Zealand as a spokesperson for the liberation movement, the national media contacted me immediately, and that same evening I appeared on national television and made a statement denouncing the massacre. I was not at home when the word of the massacre reached New Zealand, but my parents had long since resigned themselves to the dangerous life I was leading. I'm sure they must have felt considerable anxiety at the news but, if so, they didn't express it, and certainly no one in my family suggested that I should not return to Lesotho. As it turned out, however, others in the church were of a different frame of mind.

Over the years my membership in the ANC had made members of my community and the hierarchy of the church extremely uncomfortable. So, in a convergence of interests, they conspired to use the widespread fear engendered by the massacre as the means to get rid of me. A letter was sent to me under the signature of Bishop Mokuku reflecting the decision of the church senate that I should not return. Fortunately for me and not for them I had already left New Zealand, and the letter did not catch up with me. When I arrived in Lesotho in mid January I was met at the airport by Bishop Donald Nestor, the suffragan bishop, and Fr. Clement Mullenger, the SSM provincial for Southern Africa. They informed me that I was effectively persona non grata and that they had every intention of seeing that I was expelled from the country. By meeting me at the airport they intended to head off my return to the university in Roma, because they knew there would be considerable support among the students once I returned. What seemed inhumane was that I was expected to abandon my personal possessions and was not even to be allowed a farewell to friends and colleagues at the university who had been my family. It is not clear where they expected I would spend the night since the Brothers at our SSM priory had decided that I was unwelcome and that they would not sleep under the same roof with me. It was one thing to be banned by the church and quite another to be rejected by my fellow religious.

The church authorities argued that I was one of the targets of the massacre and that if I were to remain in Lesotho the South African troops would return and there would be further bloodshed. It struck me that they didn't seem to mind if I was killed, but they were quite concerned that some of them might be. They were worried they would become collateral damage. To be fair, there was fear and terror in the country after the raid. The soldiers had deliberately spewed bullets and firebombs recklessly to terrorize the population and to discourage support of the ANC community, and they partly succeeded. Because of the constant worry about infiltration by spies, people became suspicious of one another. In a sense the only decent thing was to be dead. Some people wondered if the invading forces had deliberately spared certain others. Why would they spare anyone unless that person was a spy? Since I had been out of the country, some people might have imagined that I had been tipped off. So in the minds of some, I no doubt did represent a danger. But the fact is that we all lived with danger every day, and this was hardly a new thought. The fear was understandable and real, but I think the analysis that turned me rather than the apartheid regime into the problem was faulty. They were blaming the victim.

For the most part the argument that my presence was a threat to others was merely a pretext for efforts to get rid of me that predated the Lesotho massacre. Earlier that year an open letter, possibly instigated by the South African Security Police, was written to Archbishop Russell in Cape Town calling for disciplinary action against me because of my membership in the ANC. In that instance the archbishop rejected the request on the grounds that the church accepted the legitimacy of Christians serving in either the South African army or joining the liberation movements.

Contrary to the bishop's orders, I went back to the chaplaincy house at Roma that very night and told the priest who had been serving in my absence that I would be saying mass the next day, which happened to be Sunday. When I told the student congregation what had happened, this set in motion quite a bustle of activity on my behalf. Thus began a long and highly contentious process in which it became clear that the decision of the church and the attitude of the SSM Brothers were based on their disapproval of my membership in the ANC. At the same time the church had no problem with priests or seminary instructors who supported the South African government, a fact that I pointed out whenever the opportunity presented itself.

The diocese had in fact ignored the procedures of canon law in summarily dismissing me. I refused to accept that, and so I appealed the decision, first to the diocese and later to Archbishop Philip Russell in Cape Town, and this process ground on for many months. The church increasingly saw the issue as one of disobedience to its authority, whereas my position was that it had misused its authority. However, the heart of the conflict, for which the administrative issues were only a cover, was that I answered to a God who unmistakably sided with the poor and oppressed, and I was implicitly critical of a church that made compromises. This the church hierarchy found intolerable. Stressful as this process was, it provided me with time to travel to Lusaka to consult with the ANC and to wind down my responsibilities at the university and the seminary in an orderly way. Most important of all, I was able to maintain my sense of integrity to myself and to my faith.

To return in the midst of the trauma and suspicion that followed the massacre was dreadful enough, but to once again be faced with expulsion from a country that was my home and the university community where I had good friends was deeply unsettling. There is a bond that forms among those who live daily with danger and depend utterly on one another for survival that is not easily ruptured. The disapprobation of the church senate and the bishop was not a surprise. I was used to finding myself in conflict with the church, though this was particularly heavy handed. However, being shunned by members of my own community compounded the sense of estrangement I had felt from them for a long time. For example, in a letter to the provincial, Fr. Clement Mullinger, one of the Brothers wrote:

It seems to me and others that this matter has gone far enough and that if it is allow to continue the consequences for the Society may be very hard to bear. . . . Brothers are very angry. . . .

Michael by his actions shows no desire to be at one with his brothers. He is right in this situation and everybody else in the Province is wrong. He wants us to take sides and so alienate part of the body of Christ to whom we are sent to minister. I do not question his "Christian" right to kill in the name of Christ. . . . I do question his obedience to Society authority; he seems to have an allegiance to a political party that is stronger than his professed promises to religion. . . . If he wants to live and work in this way, let him not pretend to himself and others that he is part of a Society, or that he has tacit Society backing.

And he concluded with a quotation from the SSM Constitution:

Let none, especially those who are young in discipline, imagine that a miscellaneous activity neglectful of imposed rules for the sake of fancied usefulness, can be anything but vanity.

Another Brother wrote an even more scathing personal attack:

I feel raped, sullied, utterly bewildered by Michael's attack on the integrity of the brothers who are already bowed down with the pain of apartheid and who are not in a position to see the glory that shall be revealed by their patient suffering. . . . Things can never be so clearly black and white as people like Michael think. What naivety, what pomposity he displays in his holier than thou attitude. All my life I have shriveled in the face of bullies. That is the effect Michael has on me now. He is clever, accomplished, and very cunning, and never forgets a word of what we in our incompetence keep on trying to articulate. But we don't speak the same language and we are not clever. . . . Using the word "heresy" in connection with apartheid is about as appropriate as to say that smoking is a heresy.

For me, this was a contest for the very soul of my community. To whom is our ultimate allegiance? To the discipline of the Society or to God, who sides unequivocally with the poor and dispossessed? As I reflected on the uncertainty in which I found myself, I knew that my allegiance to the liberation struggle was unshakable, and that steadied me and gave me courage. When I joined the ANC I said that I would not be found wanting. My friends and colleagues had sacrificed their lives; my commitment to continue the struggle was the least that I could offer their memory. For me, the priesthood too was not in question, but I was less sure about my community.

The Brothers sent a resolution to Fr. Edmund Wheat, the SSM director in the United Kingdom, saying that I should not be allowed to set foot again on the African continent and that my political activities and attitudes "constitute a threat to the life and work of this Province." Fr. Mullenger, the SSM provincial, said that my membership in the ANC meant that I should leave the order. I began to think that perhaps he was right. I would have to consider whether I could continue as a member of the order, especially when the Brothers had ostracized me in the way that they had. Perhaps I should leave.

Some time later I wrote a rebuttal to the Brothers that, after expressing my pain at their rejection, concluded:

> Perhaps the greatest indictment on us as a Society is that we don't constitute a threat to the life and work of the apartheid state. . . . [Rather than prohibiting me] or anyone else from setting foot on the continent of Africa, would it not be a greater blessing to send those of us back where we came from, be we young or old, who continue to speak or act in a racist manner? . . .
>
> You all know in your hearts that your attempt to drive me out of SSM and out of Africa is both unchristian and unjust. . . . Nor will our ostrich-like actions prevent the inexorable process which will eventually lead to the overthrow of the apartheid state and the creation of a non-racial democracy in South Africa.

In response to my having been banned by the church and denounced as a terrorist by my order, I agreed to go to the United Kingdom to consult with Fr. Wheat in person about what I should do next. There had been talk for some time of my enrolling for a master's degree in the United Kingdom, and the church no doubt hoped I would do exactly that and stay out of sight and out of trouble. Not long after I arrived in the United Kingdom, word came that the archbishop in Cape Town had rejected my appeal, and so with that I had no choice but to abandon any hope of returning to live in Lesotho for the foreseeable future.

Today, of course, many people in the world have come to the realization that the apartheid government was the real terrorist. We in SSM have also traveled our own journey in the intervening years. In

1985, only two years after I was banished from Lesotho, the Society closed the Southern African Province. That was the right decision at the time, as the province had become a sad group of men who had lost the plot. It was agreed that two or three would remain as individuals. Later, we joined forces with the Australians to form a new Southern Province, and that revitalized our presence in Southern Africa. Eventually the Brothers there decided we should become an independent province once more. By this time all but two of us were black Africans, almost all from Lesotho. Ironically I was elected as the first SSM provincial or head of the province, which I still am at the time of writing. Although I do not live with the Brothers of the community in Lesotho, I visit frequently. The responsibility of all of us is to seek to know and do God's will. Part of my responsibility is to give overall pastoral care and to seek to articulate directions, having listened to the common mind. We have agreed that Healing of Memories is part of our mission in Southern Africa, so this means that my full-time work is part of the fulfillment of our Society's mission statement. Often, before I undertake Healing of Memories work, especially in a new country or situation that I know is characterized by great pain, I call upon my Brothers in the community to support me in their prayers. Their love and support sustains me.

Michael Worsnip's Testimony before the Truth and Reconciliation Commission regarding Fr. Michael's Role in Lesotho

I met Michael in 1979 when I left South Africa to go to Lesotho as a war resister because I had come to the conclusion that I could not serve in the SADF [South Africa Defence Force] in any capacity whatsoever. [Michael's] house was a meeting point for South African refugees and all of us discovered each other there. It was a most remarkable place to be. For people like me who had lived in a fairly closed white society, it was the first time on a person to person level I was able to meet, debate, converse, and disagree with, on an eyeball-to-eyeball level, fellow black South Africans. And for me it was a conversion experience; once I had gone through that, there was no turning back. I was not the only person for whom it was an important place. It was a house of peace. I want to emphasize that I never saw weapons there—ever! It was a house of protest; it was a house of debate where people met in real terms and could discuss and disagree, but it was a house of peace and sometimes also a house of prayer. That is the context in which I met Michael.

The only violence I personally encountered while living in Lesotho was the two raids that happened from South Africa into Lesotho in 1982 and 1985. The level of terror which those raids caused, killing and maiming civilians inside Lesotho, is beyond description. The country and all of us living in it felt raped by the aggression and senseless killing. Michael's name was probably on a list for one of those raids; he just happened to have been out of the country at the time. There were times in Lesotho when everybody was scared, particularly South Africans living in that society, and Michael was quite clearly a particular target of the Apartheid State. Because unlike many others in the Church, Michael would make no compromise. He was a target because he was white, and because he, as a very committed and very public Christian, supported the armed struggle against apartheid. This was not something which the Apartheid State could really overlook because his being itself challenged many of the myths which apartheid had constructed.

The first myth was that it was a struggle for the racial survival of whites against blacks. The ANC was portrayed as an all black organization and no white in their right mind would want to join it because it was out to destroy them. That was the first myth. The second myth was that the ANC was a Marxist/atheist organization. To have a priest of the Anglican Church publicly being a member of it and functioning as its chaplain could not be condoned. And that, despite the fact that in the history of the ANC many priests, and religious people of many different faiths, have belonged to the ANC. The ANC was also identified almost entirely with Umkhonto we Sizwe [the armed wing of the ANC]. In other words, the only picture that was given to the South African public was of an organization with only one goal—violence, terror, and destruction. Michael, while not a member of Umkhonto we Sizwe but wholeheartedly supporting the armed struggle, exposed some of the contradictions with this kind of presentation, and I think his effectiveness in communicating this message must have been an enormous threat to the state and that in itself must have made him a target.

My wish is to see the Government of the Day express remorse and sorrow not only for what they did to Michael, but also what they did to us all, how they damaged the entire nation, both physically and psychologically.

◇ 8 ◇

Zimbabwe—
The Struggle Is Everything

◇◇◇◇◇◇◇

AFTER LEAVING LESOTHO my stay in Manchester gave me time to reflect on all that had transpired. It was clear that the church's line that I was a magnet for attacks that endangered others was in the main a ruse to get rid of me. The church simply could not abide the partisan position that I had taken as a member of the ANC. Of course this was the same hierarchy that willingly provided chaplains to the same South African army that had carried out the Lesotho massacre. Exiling me was a political decision.

The Anglican hierarchy and my SSM Brothers no doubt thought I had been safely placed under a sort of ecclesiastical house arrest in the United Kingdom, albeit with university study privileges, all under the watchful eye of Fr. Edmund Wheat, the SSM director. They did not count on the disposition of Fr. Wheat, who was cut from an entirely different cloth. He took the situation seriously, but he was not above poking fun at what he saw as the pomposity of the bishops. He supported my stand that my highest obedience was to God as revealed to my own conscience and that this position was borne out in the SSM constitution. He and members of my order in Australia were quite unhappy with the attitude of the Brothers in Southern Africa. He did not insist that I undertake a master's degree at the University in Manchester, which I was disinclined to do. Instead, we agreed that I would live at the priory in Manchester for nine months, and in consultation with him I would decide what to do next. He did not assign me a job, and so effectively I was free to work full time for the ANC.

I began to write articles in the secular and church press that were intended to mobilize public support for the struggle, and I also wrote for ANC and South African Communist Party publications. The ANC arranged speaking engagements for me in Britain, Holland, and Sweden, and the personal connections I made on these tours continued to be valuable to me and to the ANC over the coming years. Piet Meiring, who is now a member of our board at the Institute for Healing of Memories, remembers meeting me in London at that time. Piet, an open-minded cleric and a professor of theology, was at that time a strategically placed member of the Dutch Reformed Church who was interested in investigating the role that Communist theory played in the thinking of the ANC leadership. Piet and I made a connection then that has endured through the years.

When I had applied for membership in the ANC, I vowed that my commitment was irrevocable. Now that the archbishop had rejected my appeal and I was effectively banished from Lesotho, how would I live out that commitment? While I was useful to the ANC as a publicist and advocate in the United Kingdom, Africa was where my heart was. Had I stayed in Europe, even working for the ANC, I would have felt sidelined from the struggle and that was something I simply could not bear. I had to find a way to return to Southern Africa.

Zimbabwe was the obvious choice. After a protracted war with the white supremacist regime of Ian Smith, the country was at last majority ruled and had become independent in 1980. It shared a long border with South Africa and the new government headed by Robert Mugabe sheltered a community of South African exiles. The Mugabe government had inherited what was then the most developed country in the region apart from South Africa. The University of Zimbabwe was a first-class institution, and Adrian Hastings, who was professor of religious studies there, was one of the foremost historians of the church in Africa. I applied and was accepted to study church history under him, and I did a course in Marxist philosophy as well. To be accepted as Professor Hastings's student was something of a coup, and so with the blessing of Fr. Wheat and the Society, I left Manchester at the end of 1983 to begin work on a one-year master's degree in Harare, Zimbabwe's capital city.

Professor Hastings was a fortunate choice for me since he was quite a free thinker with a long and distinguished career, and like me, did not shy away from controversy. He came from an affluent English family, was brought up a Roman Catholic, and was educated at Oxford and in Rome. He was ordained a priest, joined a religious order, and was sent to Africa. He eventually left the order and moved to Masaka,

Uganda, because he preferred to serve as an ordinary diocesan priest under what was then the only black African Catholic bishop. He was a staunch critic of colonialism and attracted considerable notoriety by accusing the Portuguese of atrocities during Mozambique's war of independence. He was active in ecumenical circles, particularly with the Anglican Church, and was an active supporter of the reforms of the Second Vatican Council. He opposed the church's ban on artificial contraception, and he began advocating for an end to the requirement for celibacy of clergy, particularly in Africa where he saw it as an impediment to recruiting young men for the priesthood. In 1979, only a few years before I began studying with him, Professor Hastings took his own advocacy seriously and married without seeking ecclesiastical permission or resigning from the priesthood.

It was a great joy to find myself back in Southern Africa in the midst of a small South African exile community. I immediately became part of ANC structures in Harare and was involved in producing an ANC magazine in addition to taking classes and working on my dissertation. I chose to examine the role of the Anglican Church during the struggle for majority rule against the white supremacist Ian Smith regime. Though I made no effort to hide my partisanship, I undertook quite a scholarly effort with meticulous documentation of the pronouncements and letters of the church and its leaders. What I found was a mixed bag. Several important Anglican bishops were little better than outright apologists for the Ian Smith regime, saying such things as, "'one man one vote' is not in itself a Christian or an Anglican principle." Many others equivocated with a wishy-washy neutrality that in effect supported the status quo. There were a few, however, who positioned themselves as outspoken critics of the white government and staunch champions of the oppressed. I needed to do little editorializing of my own—the record spoke for itself. What I did was name names and lay out the truth for all to see.

My dissertation, titled "Neutrality or Co-option? Anglican Church and State from 1964 until Independence of Zimbabwe," was published in Zimbabwe in 1986. I dedicated it to "all those people of faith and hope who gave their lives to liberate Zimbabwe, and to all those who are living and dying to create a human society in South Africa." The foreword was written by the president of Zimbabwe, Canaan Banana, himself a Methodist clergyman, and it was hard hitting. In it he said:

> With a few notable exceptions . . . church leaders dined and wined with the devil. . . . No doubt this study will be viewed by some as an explosion, the author as a mischief-maker who

dared to tread in the Holy of holies to excavate the "sacred" confidentials that should belong in the museum of the privileged few, but for many it will be an eye-opener.

The dissertation did indeed cause quite a stir, but because, unlike South Africa, power had already passed to the black majority, I did not find myself in any jeopardy. Another thing in my favor was that Zimbabwe lies in a separate Anglican jurisdiction from South Africa and Lesotho, so I was beyond the reach of the bishops from either of those countries. Even so, the local church bookshop refused to have a copy on the premises. When asked by an inquirer whether she had read the book, the woman who ran the shop said, "Of course not, and I never will."

Peter Hatendi, bishop of the Diocese of Harare, expressed interest in having me serve full time as a priest in his diocese. Diocesan bishops are sometimes a bit hesitant to employ priests who are members of religious orders because they effectively answer to two masters, the bishop and the head of the order, and this can create divided loyalties. In support of my application Fr. Wheat flew out from England to meet with Bishop Hatendi, and they readily reached an agreement. I was delighted. I relished serving a parish, and remaining in Zimbabwe freed me to work discreetly for the ANC.

During 1985, the first year after completing my studies, I was not assigned a parish. Instead I assisted a little with the chaplaincy at the university and also worked directly with the bishop in the diocese. He gave me very significant responsibilities, and I became his trusted favorite. He made me his examining chaplain, a position that involved advising him about the suitability of candidates for ordination. I undertook other important administrative duties in his behalf as well, such as becoming a member of the liaison structure with other Zimbabwean dioceses. Toward the end of that year he appointed me a rector of St. Michael's Parish in Mbare, a nearby township. St. Michael's was a large urban church that had fallen on hard times. I was delighted to be living and working in a township setting, and I was able to continue my work with the ANC.

I used a liberatory bottom-up model of engaging with the parishioners rather than the top-down approach that is all too common among clergy who see themselves as providing leadership to a congregation incapable of setting its own course and in need of firm clerical direction. I soon noticed that on a given Sunday only about a quarter of the congregation came forward for the Eucharist. As this continued week after week I began to inquire gently why this was so. I learned that a goodly number had either been forbidden to take the sacrament by the priest or were living under a self-imposed ban because they or their children had not been married in the church or had children out of wedlock. This was a poor congregation, and a church wedding in their mind entailed an expensive wedding dress, flowers, and a fancy reception that many could not possibly afford. Upon learning this I assured the congregation that all that was required for Christian marriage was a wedding ring and two people with a commitment to live their lives together in love and faithfulness. The result was that I soon had a queue for weddings that often entailed a beaming couple, their children, and the grandparents. The parishioners responded with rapidly increasing enthusiasm to this new style of pastoral care. Attendance quadrupled in six months and involvement by the congregation grew noticeably. Bishop Hatendi, for his part, said he was not sure whether this huge increase meant that the people were following me or Jesus.

It was during my tenure in Mbare that I first met Helen Clark, who later became the prime minister of New Zealand. She was a member of parliament and had come to Southern Africa on a fact-finding trip. While in Harare she learned that there was a young New Zealand priest who was working at a church nearby and she came to call. We hit it off immediately and had much to talk about. Of course there was a bond because we were both New Zealanders. She was a welcome connection to my homeland and to the New Zealand antiapartheid movement, and I, in turn, provided her with fresh insights into what it was like to live in the thick of the struggle. We became lifelong friends, and whenever I returned to New Zealand I went to see her. During her tenure as prime minister she became a patron of the Institute for Healing of Memories, which she has continued in her present role as administrator of the United Nations Development Program.

Imagine my distress when only a few months into my tenure in Mbare I read in a diocesan newsletter that the bishop had appointed me to run a seminary! I had been at St. Michael's for less than a year; the church was coming to life again, and now I was being moved. But the most astonishing thing was that I had neither been consulted in advance nor informed after the fact. Instead I was left to find out by reading about it. I went to the bishop immediately and told him that I should have been consulted before this change was made and that since I was a member of a religious order, the head of my order also had to be involved. The bishop's response was, "When you became a priest in my diocese, you gave up the right of consultation." I said I did not wish to give up that right and in any case I was in no position to waive it for the head of my order. Needless to say, Bishop Hatendi did not take kindly to what he saw as my cheekiness, and this set off a protracted and fairly dramatic conflict between the two of us. My fall from grace was nothing short of spectacular. I went from being his blue-eyed boy to persona non grata overnight. This time, however, I had the full support of my community. In fact, Fr. Wheat wrote me that he favored my staying in the parish and said that I had had my full share of running what he referred to as "tin pot theological colleges," which was an oblique reference to the little seminary in Lesotho that I had been responsible for. He wrote to the bishop on my behalf, thinking that this would smooth things over, but he couldn't have been more wrong. The conflict went on and on and during it the bishop removed my license as a priest in his diocese. He even went so far as to use his influence to try to have me expelled from the country. Since I had official connections that were at least as powerful as his, including my friendship with President Banana, these efforts went nowhere.

As I look back now, I think the bishop's motive for assigning me to run the seminary was actually an expression of his confidence in my ability, though it is possible I had shined perhaps a little too much as a priest at St. Michael's. He was used to running the diocese as an autocrat, and I think he felt personally stung by my response, especially coming from someone who had been his favorite. Parish priests who are not members of religious orders have nowhere to go if they fall out with the bishop, and so they are inclined to accept his authority without question. A priest owes the bishop what is called canonical obedience. Although the colonial church was quite hierarchical, the church in the immediate postcolonial period was even more so and exercised power in a way that churches elsewhere would not attempt to do. The issues on the ground often involved power and the abuse of authority that were mystified by the term *obedience*. So it was not unusual for bishops to interpret canonical obedience as an absolute. If they said "jump off a cliff," they expected the priest to jump. Bishop Hatendi was completely unprepared to deal with my questioning his decision or the dual authority he had with the head of my order, even though he had signed off on the agreement at the beginning.

Removing my license as a priest was a very serious matter, though it applied only to the Diocese of Harare. In time I secured licenses for the other three Zimbabwe dioceses, so I was not estranged from the church as a whole. I made efforts over several years to have my license reinstated, all to no avail. Perhaps the most painful moment for me was when I asked for a special dispensation to say a requiem mass for my father, who died in 1987. The bishop was unmoved and unwilling. However, at the time of my bombing he turned up in my hospital room to wish me well, and I took the opportunity to ask once again to be reinstated. There was no immediate reply, but not long thereafter a letter arrived containing the license. I must say it was necessary to go to extraordinary lengths to get it back.

Having fallen out with the bishop, I was without a job, and my future was once again uncertain. Since the struggle was my life, leaving Zimbabwe would have been a devastating blow. This time, however, I had the full support of my community to remain. Fortunately I found a position with the Lutheran World Federation, where I worked for the next three years. It turned out to be particularly desirable job because the Lutherans were engaged in quite a prophetic ministry, and so it provided me with a platform from which to continue my activism within the faith community. I headed a very interesting program called the Development of Theology. People in the church often talk about the theology of development, but this program turned the issue on its head and focused on how theology itself needs to develop in response to the social and political conditions around it. This was a period in which the ruling party in Zimbabwe described itself as Marxist, so the issue of Marxist-Christian dialogue became an important part of our discussions. Since this topic was related to an aspect of my master's degree, I was primed for the work.

Zimbabwe at this time was a place of intense intellectual debate taking place against a backdrop of tremendous social change. The civil war against the white supremacist Ian Smith regime had taken a terrible toll and was only a few years in the past; secret agents of the South African government were in the country and seizing every opportunity to stir up trouble. In a region of Zimbabwe called Matabeleland, the new black government led by Robert Mugabe carried out a brutal repression with strong ethnic overtones out of sight of people in the urban centers. The conflict there included a massacre of black Zimbabweans who had supported a rival liberation movement. With the benefit of hindsight the seeds of Zimbabwe's present plight under Mugabe's despotic rule were being sown then. At the time, however, the Mugabe government was doing many wonderful things to develop the country and enjoyed the gratitude of a majority of the population. Many people in the urban centers knew little of what was going on in Matabeleland, and for those who did, it evoked deep ambivalence and pain that they dealt with mostly by ignoring it. We in the Lutheran Federation felt it was our responsibility to help church leaders grapple with the crushing problems that communities faced. The Development of Theology Program therefore organized a series of workshops to address this and other urgent problems such as the hunger and starvation occurring particularly in the rural areas and the destabilization of the country instigated by South Africa.

Pastors and lay leaders were confronting daily the human toll of conflict, hunger, and destabilization, and they did not always know how to respond. I recall one pastor, for example, seeking the group's guidance about what to say to a young mother who, desperate for food to offer her hungry children, waded each week across a dangerous river to obtain food available on the other side. On one of these trips she slipped and fell and her young child drowned. What does one say to this young mother to help her with her grief and guilt? And what is to be said of the British colonial system that had so impoverished parts of this rich country that these tragedies occurred? We struggled mightily with these issues. As if that were not enough, in the 1980s AIDS was beginning to rear its head, and I organized workshops where we discussed how the church should respond. Of course we had no idea then of the magnitude of the disaster about to befall us.

Our philosophy was to seek community answers to community questions in the light of faith. We understood theology to be a living organism that had to grow and change in response to the conditions in which people lived. That was, after all, Jesus' way. His teachings were so often prompted by what people brought to him; he did not bring sermons to them. We asked participants to respond to each topic from their own personal experiences illuminated by their faith. Then we tried to discern as a group what the Christian response should be; the path was often far from clear. My role was simply to help church leaders discern what it meant to follow Jesus' example in the challenging world in which we all lived. We provided a safe place where participants could think critically, speak freely, and deal with despair, as well as search for hope. Our discussions were often very rich and sometimes heated, and a fair amount of criticism emerged about the way power was used both in the government and the church. We encouraged each person to contribute, and we learned through experience to trust the process. I believe we made a modest contribution in helping church leaders cope with extraordinary problems.

About this same time I was approached by Zimbabwe intelligence officers who told me that they had information that I had been placed on a South African hit list and targeted for assassination. From then on armed police were stationed outside my front and back doors, and I had to explain to friends and visitors why the armed guards were there. Their visible presence was a reminder of the dangers we all faced. I remember saying, "This is a sign from the South African government that what we're doing really matters, and our work is not in vain. So even though we feel frightened, we can also feel encouraged." This unwelcome recognition was flattering and ominous at one and the same time. The regime was certainly exaggerating the danger I was to them, but there was no denying that assassinations were part of the era in which we lived. There was comfort in knowing that this was a just struggle and that we were fighting an evil system.

My understanding of God, faith, and belief went through its own evolution during the time I worked for the Lutheran World Federation. I was born and brought up an Anglican and had adopted some fairly narrow views of other churches. Now I was working for the Lutheran Church and with people from many different denominations. It was eye opening in the way that going to another country for the first time can be. Even more important, being part of the liberation movement meant being comrades with Jews, Hindus, Muslims, and people who didn't believe in God at all. I often found I had more in common with them than with Anglicans who had placed themselves on the other side of the freedom struggle. I sometimes tried to play down that I was a priest, but I discovered that many comrades expected and wanted me to be a priest to them. Interestingly, it wasn't just Christians who said this, but also those of other faiths and nonbelievers as well, and this touched me very much. I learned to give expression to my faith in ways that people of other traditions could relate to, and this in turn subtly reshaped my own spirituality. The scriptural imperatives of social justice took on increasing urgency for me, and more and more I saw a God who welcomes all members of the human family. So my faith developed not so much from reading books as from working in the trenches and living with the danger. It was an interfaith vision of the world and a respect for people who themselves were not at all religious but were willing to sacrifice their lives for the freedom of others. My view of scripture began to change to the perspective of someone in a liberation movement, and I began to read the Bible with new spectacles. I suppose this amounts to a form of liberation theology, but I arrived at it not by reading books but in the crucible of the struggle. I admire thinkers who have written about these matters, but systematic theology of that sort is not me.

The Zimbabwe government had courageously given shelter to the exile movement at considerable risk to itself and its citizens. Bombings, assassinations, and unexplained accidents were a daily presence throughout Southern Africa and beyond, as the South African government reacted to increasing internal and international pressure by upping the ante against the ANC. The Lutheran World Federation felt a need to respond to this reality, and so I began coordinating its program called Church and Liberation that was designed to mobilize support in the faith community for the liberation struggle in Southern Africa. It was a popular education program using videos, films, and community theater to raise people's awareness of the struggle going on across their border, and we organized demonstrations outside the South African mission in Zimbabwe. Sr. Janice McLaughlin, a Maryknoll Sister, and I worked together on many cases involving South Africa's destabilization campaign, including one where the South Africans planted a bomb in a television set and the explosion killed innocent people in an apartment building. While I was by no means the only person under threat from the South African government, our program certainly increased my visibility to the South Africans and may have marked me more firmly for assassination.

At the same time, I was involved in meetings between the ANC and visiting white South Africans. The World Council of Churches sponsored some of those meetings, which took place in both Lusaka and Harare. They included representatives from South Africa, especially progressive church leaders like Beyers Naudé, Frank Chikane, and Charles Villa-Vicencio. The South African government, especially in the late 1980s, was quietly beginning to consider negotiating with the ANC. From time to time delegations of white South Africans representing churches, academics, or civil society would appear in Zimbabwe. The ANC always welcomed these delegations as part of its commitment to nonracialism and to building as broad a base of support as possible. The meetings did, after all, provide an opportunity to demystify the ANC, particularly to the white population, and show that we were not all bogeymen with horns. These gatherings were not usually secret, as some were at the highest level of government, but they were discreet and certainly not advertised. There was one meeting organized by the London-based Catholic Institute for International Relations that took place in Harare and was supposed to be secret. I was not officially included in the meeting, but the problem was that the house where the South Africans were staying was only two doors away from mine, and the location where I lived was advertised by the presence of an armed guard. Some of the South Africans were old friends that I did not have the opportunity to see very often for obvious reasons. So people sneaked back and forth through the lane behind my house to visit me, hoping not to be detected. As one person commented, "It was quite a hilarious cloak-and-dagger affair—actually far more cloak than dagger."

Progressive churches were part of the nucleus of a highly effective antiapartheid movement in nearly every country. They brought huge pressure particularly on Western governments that in many cases were all too willing to go to bed with the apartheid regime. My dual role as priest and ANC activist meant that I often had a unique role to play in framing the liberation struggle not just as a political question or even as a human rights issue but as a matter of faith. My experience was that both church people and nonbelievers responded to this message, and my talks often brought people into the churches who would not normally have been there. Some churches in the developed world generously funded the liberation organizations, and their emissaries often visited us in Zimbabwe. In my work with the Lutheran World Federation I was often called upon to meet these visitors and also to do a fair amount of traveling.

For example, just before I moved to Zimbabwe, I was part of an important joint six-week-long tour of Canada organized by the ANC and SWAPO, its partner liberation organization, in what was then called Southwest Africa and is now Namibia. Southwest Africa had been a German colony, and after World War I it became a League of Nations mandate administered by South Africa. The founding of the United Nations initiated a protracted struggle between South Africa and the international community and South Africa's occupation was eventually declared illegal. South Africa nevertheless continued to hold the country in defiance of UN resolutions. Because of this history the struggle for the independence of Southwest Africa and the struggle to end apartheid were inextricably linked. We went to twenty Canadian cities and visited many churches and community organizations, and we received a lot of publicity. I believe we made a serious impact on public opinion in Canada.

Since I was from the southern hemisphere I also had a special role to play in countries of the south, a little bit in Australia, but especially in my home country of New Zealand. In 1979 I made an extensive speaking trip there on behalf of the ANC. I benefited from the credibility I gained from my unique position. I was not an outsider; to the contrary, I was a New Zealand homeboy, and at the same time I could speak firsthand about the reality of apartheid. The fact that I had been expelled from South Africa for criticizing the government made a dramatic impact on New Zealanders, as did my description of life in the exile community. In 1981 the New Zealand Rugby Association organized a tour by the South African team, the Springboks. Earlier Springbok tours had met with some resistance, including one when I was still a boy, but by this time sentiment had crystallized. The tour sparked huge controversy but it went ahead. Opinion was highly polarized, and marriages even broke up over it. There were massive demonstrations around the country, and demonstrators succeeded in preventing two of the scheduled matches. In fact, for a time New Zealand became home to the largest antiapartheid movement in the world outside of South Africa itself.

In 1982, the year after the Springbok tour, I was back in New Zealand where I made an extensive tour of the North Island, speaking every day in yet another tiny town, mobilizing public opinion. Toward the end of that trip the Maseru massacre occurred, which brought massive publicity and the opportunity to further educate the public. I developed a following with the public, who kept track of me and would have known, for example, that I was later expelled from Lesotho for my outspoken support of the ANC. The New Zealand antiapartheid movement was eager to promote my speaking engagements and facilitated my meeting important leaders, such as the heads of the two main political parties, the prime minister, the governor general, and members of parliament. Analysts later wrote that I was one of the people who helped shape national policy toward South Africa, particularly the decision to break diplomatic relations with Pretoria in 1984 after the Labour Party came to power. It was easy to see these tours as purely political, and sometimes I felt that way myself, but the conviction in my voice that stirred my listeners arose directly from my deeply held faith in a God who stands for liberation.

My high profile nationally created some difficulties with my family, some of whom were perhaps irked that my time in New Zealand was taken up with political work, and I spent little time with them. The media would sometimes seek them out and question them about me, much to their dismay. No other member of my family had such a public persona in New Zealand, and there was quite a range of opinions among them with respect to my activities, not all of them unreservedly favorable. Here too my priorities arose from my faith. With the vow of celibacy I had embraced a different set of priorities—not that I rejected my natural family, but my first obligation was to a wider family.

In September 1987, soon after I joined the Lutheran World Federation, a very significant international conference on the status of children in South Africa was held in Harare. I was seconded by the Federation to help organize it. Huge numbers of South African children were being detained by the apartheid state. Earlier that year South African Minister of Law and Order Adriaan Vlok acknowledged that in excess of fourteen hundred children were being held for more than thirty days without trial, virtually all having been arrested in antiapartheid protests. What he didn't say was that prison conditions were overcrowded and barbaric and that many were tortured and killed. The conference brought about an extraordinary engagement of representatives from civil society in South Africa, the ANC in exile, representatives of the United Nations, and human rights activists from around the world, and it really helped to shine a bright light on what was happening to children in South Africa. The international pressure that it generated led to the release of many of these children and increased the pressure from governments and the United Nations on the apartheid state at a crucial time when we now know it was beginning to consider negotiating with the ANC. Organizing this conference had deep meaning for me because it brought me full circle. It was the detention, torture, and killing of children that had led me to denounce the government in South Africa eleven years previously, and that in turn was why the government had expelled me. Now I had an opportunity to help bring this issue before the world community.

In late 1989, three years after joining the Lutheran World Federation, my contract came up for renewal and questions were raised by the Lutheran Church of Zimbabwe, which was one of the constituent churches of the Federation. The Development of Theology program had provided a safe space for people to talk freely and some raised awkward questions about justice and injustice within the church itself. It was not that I had taken a position about these issues, but as the person who presided, I had created a framework for these discussions to take place. Church officials were unhappy about this, and since they were the host church in Zimbabwe, they had a good deal of power over the Federation's programs there; they demanded that my contract not be renewed. It was a little like the Vatican closing down liberation theology in Latin America. It wasn't because the theology was offering a critique of the societies but because it was offering a critique of the church. So my contract was not renewed.

Though I was certainly disappointed, by this time I had learned that there were often consequences for speaking unwelcome truths. Then too, I was not without options. Though my license as a priest in the Diocese of Harare had been revoked, I still had licenses for the other Zimbabwe dioceses, and I soon secured a position as a priest in Bulawayo, Zimbabwe's second largest city. In many ways I was looking forward to becoming a parish priest again.

February 2, 1990, was a historic day for South Africa and the world. On that day President F. W. de Klerk suddenly announced in parliament that he was unbanning the ANC. Nelson Mandela was released from prison nine days later, on February 11. The backdrop for this was that the struggle for liberation had been growing exponentially both in South Africa and the world. Apartheid had become an issue for the whole human family, and finally the pressure on the apartheid state had become so great that it said, "We will talk." I always feel terribly sad that the ANC had been saying to the government since 1912, "Let's talk," and now it was 1990. Some people estimate that by the late 1980s we had lost a million lives in Southern Africa as a direct consequence of the actions of the apartheid state. So it was in that context that Nelson Mandela was released and the ANC was unbanned. Though rumors of negotiations had been afloat for some time, the news caught almost everyone by surprise. There was jubilation everywhere but after the momentary euphoria, calmer heads in the ANC and the antiapartheid movement internationally prevailed. What was the government up to?

Before taking up my position in Bulawayo I embarked on a long-promised trip to Canada at the invitation of the Canadian churches, and I also visited Cuba. The Canadians, like the rest of the world, wanted to know the significance of these startling developments. Was this the end of the beginning or the beginning of the end? No one had answers to those questions, and after my bombing, the Canadians made a film entitled "Apartheid Has Not Ended." I remember while I was there saying to them somewhat presciently, "The curtain is going up on the last act of the apartheid drama, but we don't know how long it will take or how costly it will be." I was soon to find out the cost personally, for I never got to take up my new position in Bulawayo. Instead, I was bombed, and that changed my life forever.

PART III

BECOMING A HEALER

With Nelson Mandela, standing outside his former cell on Robben Island on the fifth anniversary of his release from prison.

Returning to South Africa—
Forging a New Identity

◇◇◇◇◇◇

I OFTEN SAY THAT MY LIFE JOURNEY mirrors that of the nation, and that was especially true for the timing of my bombing. As I lay bloody and bandaged in my hospital bed in Harare, six days later an event took place thirteen hundred miles away in Cape Town that changed the course of history. There, on May 4, 1990, at Groote Schuur, the president's official residence, the government of South Africa and the ANC signed a document that set in motion negotiations that eventually gave rise to the democratic country that we had struggled for so long. Both for me and for South Africa a long road of healing lay ahead.

People sometimes ask how the bombing changed me, and then they provide their own answers. Most people say they find me softer and gentler, less contentious and easier to get along with. While it's true that others often see us more clearly than we see ourselves, I do sometimes want to say, "Well actually, I'm still the same person." I don't find the changes quite as remarkable as other people do. Still, it's true that I've been maimed, I've escaped death by a hair's breadth, and I live with a serious disability. Being through something like that leaves nothing untouched. Going down the road of bitterness means getting mired in hatred and anger. It's true that if I hadn't been bombed, my life would be immeasurably easier in some ways. But while I'm the same person I always was, it's impossible to overstate the gifts that have come my way through the Healing of Memories work I do, and it was the bombing that made that possible.

There are reasons why others saw me as a bit combative. Surviving in the liberation struggle meant toughening up. Because I'm white, some other white people thought of me as a race traitor and resented me because they saw my choices as a judgment on those they failed to make. I had to endure their animosity and the vicious things some of them wrote and said about me. Then there were occasions when black people weren't quite sure if I was for real. That meant at times a project of having to prove myself to the very people I was risking my life with and in some cases those I had grown to love and care about.

One has to develop a thick skin to deal with the slights and hurts coming from all directions. I suppose I had to put away some of the feelings, so my life then was something of a "head" journey, whereas since the bombing it's been more of a "heart" journey—a project to reclaim the gentleness that I had to leave behind. Another way to put it is that I had to become tough to survive. Che Guevara once said that revolutionaries have to learn how to endure without losing tenderness, and that is an admonition I cling to. So, yes, I'm sure I have softened since I was bombed, and I identify with other people's brokenness in a way I could not possible have done had I not been broken myself.

Then too, the changes in me have to be seen through the lens of history. It's not true that I'd changed as much as circumstances had changed. For example, many white people in South Africa believed that the Chris Hani who was committed to negotiations and reconciliation was a different person from the chief of staff of Umkhonto we Sizwe. But in fact it was simply a different time. Negotiations began at practically the same moment I was bombed. Slaying the monster was the issue of the 1970s and 1980s, whereas the 1990s were about healing and reconciliation. There is a key passage in chapter 12 of the book of Revelation that says, "And there was war in heaven: Michael and his angels fought against the dragon; and the dragon and his angels fought." That's a passage about good and evil. So what was the form of that battle for us in Southern Africa? It was the struggle against apartheid. Scripture also says, "For we wrestle not against flesh and blood, but against principalities, against powers, against the rulers of the darkness of this world, and against spiritual wickedness in high places" (Eph 6:12), and this points to the systemic character of evil. At times during the struggle there were calls for healing and reconciliation, not infrequently from the churches and sometimes from people with a vested interest in maintaining the status quo. There was a value to these calls in that they pointed the way toward the eventual outcome, but at the time they were premature and a diversion. The people who made these proposals emphasized the interpersonal nature of reconciliation, but the evil was structural, and first we needed to dismantle the institutions of apartheid.

Now was quite a different era; we had a democratic space in which to work, and healing and reconciliation were on the table in a fundamental way. By the time I had recovered from my injuries, the old trenches were gone. The theater of struggle had been ceded to people like my friend Glenda Wildschut, a nurse practitioner, who dreamed of founding a trauma center that would provide mental-health services for people who had previously been embattled and on the run. So as the drama of the struggle wound down, it was replaced by nation building and the quieter work of healing from the damage we had done to one another. This transition was reflected in my own life as well, as I moved from freedom fighter to healer. The stories presented at the human rights hearings of the Truth and Reconciliation Commission, for example, were quite varied. Some were told with anger, but many others were softly spoken, the speaker perhaps stifling a sob or lapsing into a long silence while struggling to regain control over a deeply felt emotion. Healing work is like this. It requires quiet, focused attention, and it rewards us with the satisfaction that comes from witnessing the transformation of pain and sometimes bitterness into a measure of peace and hope.

In Ecclesiastes 3 we find the words, "To everything there is a season. . . . There is a time to love, and a time to hate; a time to build up and a time to tear down." Although I wasn't yet sure what lay ahead, the bombing was like a refining fire that gradually brought me clarity—I would find a way to use my visible brokenness as a tool for healing others. As my friend Horst Kleinschmidt had told me, I was now equipped in new ways, however costly, for this new battle. The loving support I had received from friends around the world was a privilege that was not available to others who were equally deserving. With privilege comes responsibility; I would express my gratitude by walking the same path with others that was walked with me. That gratitude fuels my work to this day. As I travel the world I minister to some of the poorest of the poor, and for them, privilege is a foreign continent.

Of course these ideas initially lacked concreteness, and it remained to sort out their practical implications. When I returned to Zimbabwe from my convalescence in Australia I learned that the parish position in Bulawayo that I had accepted before my bombing was no longer available. Meanwhile, momentous changes were taking place in South Africa with the release of Nelson Mandela, the unbanning of the ANC, and the start of negotiations. I decided to see the changes for myself and I therefore arranged a visit in mid 1991. It was a bit mind-boggling to contemplate returning after all these years. The pace of events had left us breathless.

The ANC had always spoken about the four pillars of the struggle: the armed struggle itself, the underground organization in South Africa, the mass mobilization of the population, and international solidarity. Different leaders had their favorites, but increasingly the ANC began to see that all of them contributed to building pressure on the regime. Some people may have imagined that an armed guerilla movement in the country would eventually be able to seize power, and I think some of us thought the armed struggle would deliver more than in the end it actually did. The ANC literature in the mid 1980s, with the rise of the United Democratic Front (UDF) within South Africa, began to speak of the possibility of making the country ungovernable. Perhaps a general insurrection would sweep the government out of power, as happened in Egypt in 2011. I'm not sure how realistic all this was, and there may have been a certain degree of naivete about it. In fact, the ANC was always open to negotiations beginning with its founding in 1912, and it initiated many clandestine contacts with key figures in civil society and the apartheid government over the years, especially in the 1980s. Nevertheless, I personally was prepared for a much more protracted struggle than proved to be the case. Since I was an admirer of the Cuban revolution and had been to Cuba several times, I had a fantasy of tanks eventually rolling into Pretoria and crowds throwing flowers at the guerilla fighters, rather as they did with Fidel and Che when they triumphantly rode into Havana. I'm not sure any of us took our fantasies too seriously, but they were there and they helped keep up our morale.

The timing of my bombing, originally so inexplicable, soon became significant as a straw in the wind. Far from ushering in a respite from apartheid repression, an unprecedented wave of violence and loss of life threatened to consume the country during the period of negotiations. We lost thousands of lives during this period, including our beloved leader Chris Hani, who was assassinated just a year before the election. The country almost became unhinged, and his murder threatened to derail the whole negotiation process. While much of the violence can be laid at the hands of the government directly, there were endless stories of "black on black" violence. Massacres occurred in the dead of night when gangs of men living in hostels far away from their families descended on hapless township residents with spears and firearms. Most of the attackers were poor, uneducated men from distant rural areas who needed to support their families and migrated to more urban regions in search of work in the mines because there was no work at home. They were exploited by the apartheid system as a source of cheap labor under very dangerous conditions and now they were again being exploited to do the government's dirty work. Naturally these attacks provoked retaliation. It is true that there were rival political groups within the black community, but there is excellent evidence that the government manipulated genuine disagreements to foment violence. It stands accused of directly aiding and abetting what came to be known as a destabilizing third force, in some cases by sharing intelligence information with rival black groups and in other instances by providing direct material support. So the apartheid government negotiated in the daytime and killed at night. The government's hope, of course, was that the resulting chaos and animosity would make it impossible for the majority black community to pull itself together and present a united front in the negotiations. There were times when we thought that the government might succeed, but in the end wiser heads prevailed, thanks to the steady and calming presence of Nelson Mandela and other senior figures in the ANC. An interim constitution was eventually drawn up, an orderly election process was put in place, and at the last minute everyone agreed to participate. On April 27, 1994, what seemed like a miracle took place—South Africa became a democratic majority-ruled country on the basis of "one person one vote" for the first time in its history. For me, though, the common use of the word *miracle* belies the scale of suffering and sacrifice stretching back centuries all the way to slavery and beyond that finally delivered election day.

In 1991 the thought of returning was a bit unnerving. I had mixed feelings, not having set foot in South Africa since 1976. Although it would be good to be back, it would not be easy at a time when the country was being torn apart by violence. I had no idea who had sent me the letter bomb; perhaps they would be lying in wait when I returned. Given the violence that was already engulfing the country, it was not an unrealistic thought. Friends in Zimbabwe said to me, "Why are you returning to South Africa? Are you crazy? Those people tried to kill you. Stay here with us." Despite my own doubts, my response was to say, "Ah, but I am only in Zimbabwe because of the struggle. The time has come to be part of building a new country. Also, because of how I've been able to respond to the bombing, I think I have a part to play in healing the nation. It's time to go." I had to experience for myself the dramatic events unfolding. Remaining in Zimbabwe out of reach and listening to news reports from just over the border was much too frustrating. Besides, at the practical level one of my aims was to reestablish personal connections that would be vital in obtaining work when I returned permanently.

I arranged a three-week trip. My visa application was at first denied, and I was told that in order to be admitted to the country as a member of the ANC I required indemnity. The negotiations had stipulated that it should have been granted automatically, but the South Africans played cat and mouse with me anyway. Since I am a priest, not a lawyer, it was clear to me that they were forgiving me for their sins, not my own. Finally indemnity was granted, which theoretically meant that they were not supposed to arrest me when I landed at the Johannesburg airport. I was not so sure, although the ANC mission in Johannesburg confidently reassured me. As I sat in my airplane seat heading toward Johannesburg with my still-new prostheses resting in my lap, a swirl of thoughts and feelings chased themselves through my head. It was only a year since my bombing and a few months since my return to Zimbabwe from Australia, and I felt vulnerable traveling with my disability. Even though a young Zimbabwean, Cosmas Mulonda, accompanied me to help with the things I could not do for myself, I still felt dependent on the kindness of other people. I was a bit like a stranger in this country for which I had sacrificed so much. Would I recognize it after so long? Then too, most of my closest friends and comrades were with me in exile. Though I had kept in touch with friends who remained in South Africa, I had not seen some of them for many years. An odd mix of anticipation and loneliness pervaded me. Arriving at the Johannesburg airport, I was not arrested, and we were met by an old friend, Fr. Kingston Erson, a priest of the Community of the Resurrection and like me originally from New Zealand. As I disembarked amid the bustling throng of travelers, there was no parade, no admiring crowds, and no one threw flower petals. Though I really didn't expect flowers, I wryly thought to myself, "This isn't the way it was supposed to be." Still, I was thrilled to be back.

I had arranged to visit three cities on this trip, Johannesburg, Durban, and Cape Town, and my arrival in Durban was rather nicer than Johannesburg. My friend Phyllis Naidoo, who had been at my bedside after I was bombed, met us at the airport. Phyllis had organized a number of comrades to come to the airport and greet me. Of course they had never known me without hands, and though Phyllis would certainly have told them, it must have come as a bit of a shock to see me in my present condition. That did not deter the warmth of their reception, and they said simply, "Welcome home, Michael! How wonderful it is to have you back." It was deeply satisfying to hear them affirm that I was indeed home.

I had been invited to attend the ANC congress that was held in Durban from July 2 to July 6. It was a historic gathering, since it was the first congress to be held in South Africa since the ANC was unbanned. Nelson Mandela, who had been released from prison only fifteen months previously, was elected its president. There was much work to do as the ANC scrambled to transform itself practically overnight from a liberation movement into a political party ready to govern. Even though the outcome of negotiations with the apartheid regime was not yet clear, the congress symbolically represented the triumph of the struggle for democratic rule. For all of us present, and many comrades who were not, it was difficult to believe that the ANC was about to govern South Africa and that we were giving assent to policies that would shape the new democratic country we had fought for. The immensity of the responsibility did not outweigh the joy, and many of us wept.

Afterward I went to Cape Town and was invited to have dinner with Desmond Tutu, who had by then become the Anglican archbishop. I took Cosmas with me and I insisted that he must wear a tie to dinner at the archbishop's residence, so I felt a bit sheepish when we arrived and found the good archbishop wearing a track suit. It was at that same dinner that, still a bit awkward at manipulating my prostheses, I spilled coffee on Tutu, who was very gracious about it. He encouraged me to come back to South Africa and assured me of his support. We agreed that I would be licensed as a priest in the Diocese of Cape Town. A potential stumbling block, however, was that he had instituted a new requirement that his priests could not be members of political parties. It was a shadow of the old controversy that had existed between us when I had joined the ANC in exile. Of course circumstances were now very different, but apart from my personal desire not to relinquish my membership in the ANC, it provided the legal means for my return. Improbable as it might seem, I was not yet legally a citizen of South Africa. My New Zealand passport would not have provided the basis for my permanent return, especially since the apartheid government, which was still in power, was not fond of me and might have taken the opportunity to refuse me entry. On the other hand, the negotiations had provided for ANC members to be admitted to the country. I pointed this out to Tutu, but he was unwilling to make a formal exception. Nevertheless, there was an unspoken understanding between us that if I kept my head down, the issue would not be raised. In fact, the archbishop was very, very good to me after I returned, and he invited me to many events that were attended by only a small circle of people closest to him.

Ironically, for a time it appeared that I was in danger of not being able to vote in the 1994 election because I had not yet obtained my

South African citizenship. However, there was another option and that was to apply for permanent residence status. Since permanent residents were allowed to vote, I was able to cast my ballot. In the end, in order to become a full citizen Steve Kahanowitz at the Legal Resources Centre had to press my case with the new minister of home affairs, Mangosuthu Buthelezi.

I returned to Zimbabwe at the end of my visit feeling more certain than ever of my decision to move back to South Africa. To complicate matters I unexpectedly received an offer of a social justice position with the Zimbabwe Council of Churches. Though I was briefly a little tempted, in the end I decided not to accept it; my heart was in South Africa. However, I was committed to what proved to be a long and exhausting speaking tour to Norway, Sweden, Canada, and the United States. When it was completed, I moved back to South Africa.

I had applied for a church job in Durban, but they seemed to think that I was "too hot." I eventually secured a position as director of the Theology Exchange Programme (TEP), an organization that facilitated exchanges for theological study between South Africa and countries of the global South. Its goal was to provide opportunities for church people to learn from one another's experiences of faith and liberation, in particular South Africans and Latin Americans. Because of my own history I was a perfect fit for the job, but unfortunately other factors intervened. It turned out to be an organization with quite a lot of internal conflict. The fatal aspect for me was that the director who was my immediate predecessor remained a member of the staff. He was a gifted man and in some ways the skills we brought to the table complemented each other. Regrettably though, I felt he was unable to relinquish his investment in leading the program. His institutional knowledge made me feel boxed in, so that I was not able to make my own mark. Because I was a priest in the diocese, I went to Archbishop Tutu and said, "This is not working." His response was, "If you tell me you get up every morning and dread going to work, then it's a sign you should move on," and he supported me in that. The timing was actually quite fortuitous, because in the meanwhile discussions about founding a trauma center had been moving forward.

The group of mental-health workers involved in the planning were progressive professionals who had situated themselves in the struggle for liberation. They were not afraid of politics, and indeed some of them had provided counseling to comrades on the run and their families, and they were used to working in fairly nontraditional ways. They knew firsthand the effects of violence and had dreamed of one day forming a trauma treatment center. Clinically trained professionals in South Africa at the time were overwhelmingly white, and many of them had either supported apartheid or looked the other way. They were therefore viewed with understandable suspicion by the very people who needed their services most. Barry Bekebeke, who later worked for us at the Trauma Centre for Survivors of Violence and Torture, was a school student during the apartheid years and he once said to me, "The police would just pick you up and do all kinds of things to you, beating you up and threatening you and your family. All the professionals in my area were white, so there was a perception that they wouldn't really understand what happened to you. Even if you tried to tell the doctor that treated you after you've been beaten, 'This is what happened really,' he'd just dismiss you as a liar." For reasons like this, having the appropriate political credentials was almost a mandatory requirement for anyone who was going to be involved in a counseling center for returning exiles or people who had been in detention.

The planning group approached the Anglican Church with its idea to locate the Trauma Centre in Cowley House, a building owned by the church. It was the perfect setting because the building itself had the sort of struggle credentials that would inspire confidence in people who might otherwise have been intimidated about coming for counseling. A charming old building surrounding a lovely courtyard on Chapel Street, it was built in 1898 as a home for the Anglican Fathers of the Society of St. John the Evangelist (SSJE), and they lived there until 1978. By that time the apartheid government had already incarcerated large numbers of political prisoners on Robben Island, a rocky islet about five miles offshore of Cape Town's harbor. Many of the present leaders of South Africa, including Nelson Mandela, spent decades imprisoned there along with countless others who are less well known. In the early years family members of prisoners would arrive in Cape Town from all over the country and as far away as Namibia to visit their loved ones on Robben Island. Usually they knew no one in Cape Town and had only a tiny bit of money, so they ended up sleeping under miserable conditions in train stations or on the streets. In 1978, soon after SSJE departed, the Anglican Church made Cowley House available as a place where these family members could stay and be taken care of before embarking for the island to see their relatives. When they returned to the mainland most stayed there another night or two before departing for their homes. Cowley House became a magnet for progressive people wishing to support these families. Accommodations were crowded and very simple, but visitors were treated with dignity and respect and for many people of color this may have been the first time in their lives that they were served by a caring white person. Their visits to see relatives were often fraught with emotion, and so it was also a place of compassion and solace. It would thus have been known by any South African who had relatives imprisoned on the island. With the unbanning of the ANC in 1990 political prisoners were rapidly released from Robben Island, and Cowley House now took on a different role as a reception center where prisoners were reunited with their families. Its little courtyard, piled high with parcels, crowded with a bustling throng of families and the cries of small children, was a place where people waited expectantly for a father, a son, or a brother that in some cases they hadn't seen for decades. So it was transformed once again, this time into a much happier place of greetings and reunions. Some returning prisoners needed help reintegrating into the hustle and bustle of an urban society, especially those who had been locked up on the island for a very long time, and so counseling was also a part, even if a small part, of what went on there during this new phase.

A number of people on the planning team, including Tom Winslow from the United States, had been involved in supporting Cowley House in its earlier mission. The Anglican Church had all along been a party to the discussions about founding a trauma center, and so Archbishop Tutu agreed immediately to make Cowley House available. Once assured of a home, plans were quickly concluded. Unfortunately, the crowds of people over the years had taken a bit of a toll on the old structure, but for those of us who were veterans of the struggle it indeed felt like home. When it became known that my position as director of TEP was not working out, the possibility that I might become chaplain at the Trauma Centre took on new immediacy. There was a bit of "to-ing" and "fro-ing" about my appointment because, as one person remarked, "How would children cope with someone who has no hands?" I think most people recognized the reality that black children at least, especially those from traumatized families, already knew far too well the horrors of apartheid violence. I had quite a lot of support within the diocese and the planning committee, and so I was hired. Officially, I remained a priest in the Diocese of Cape Town and was seconded to the Trauma Centre.

Tom Winslow and I walked through the doors of the Trauma Centre for Victims of Violence and Torture, later changed to Trauma Centre for Survivors of Violence and Torture, on opening day in July 1993. It had already been a turbulent year. Three months earlier Chris Hani, some would argue the most popular person in South Africa after Nelson Mandela, had been assassinated and the country had almost exploded. Horrific violence threatened to engulf the nation and everyone was much on edge. Only a few days later the liberation movement suffered another huge loss when Oliver Tambo, the national chairperson of the ANC, died of a stroke. What a time to be founding a trauma center! Everyone felt the weight of responsibility.

Tom and I were the first two staff members. Tom was not a trained counselor, but he was very good at organizing and raising money and he set up the center and functioned as our development officer. Bea Abrahams, who was a therapist, soon became the director. Initially Tom and I were the management committee since we were the only two staff members, but Bea joined us as soon as she signed on and we gradually added others. The remainder of the little informal planning group gradually morphed into the board of directors with Glenda Wildschut as its chair. Glenda later served on the Truth and Reconciliation Commission and still later became the first board chair of the Institute for Healing of Memories. The Danes were very generous to us, as they had been to the liberation movement during the years of struggle. I believe our first support came from the Rehabilitation and Research Centre for Torture Victims (RCT) in Copenhagen plus the Danish government and embassy, and so we were blessed with considerable startup funding. It was a mixed blessing because, while it allowed us to hire much-needed staff, we expanded too rapidly. We went from three to thirty persons in only eighteen months. It proved to be impossible to assimilate so many new people and build a cohesive group with common loyalties in such a short time. The structures were simply not in place, and the result was much unnecessary conflict.

For my part, joining the Trauma Centre was the culmination of a major life transition from freedom fighter to healer. The thing that struck me on my return to South Africa was that we were a damaged nation—damaged by what we had done to one another, damaged by what was done to us, and damaged by what we failed to do—and everyone had a story to tell about our experience of the apartheid years. It seemed to me that if we didn't deal with what we had inside of us, we wouldn't create a very nice society. I came to the conclusion that we needed to proceed into the future based on two pillars. One pillar was dealing with the social and economic legacy of apartheid, the need for water and electricity, for shelter, education, jobs, and health care. And the other pillar was dealing with the psychological and spiritual effects of the journey the nation had traveled. These two pillars were interconnected and intertwined, so even if basic needs were met, people would still be angry, frustrated, and bitter unless we dealt with what we had inside.

At the same time no one, including me, knew what the chaplain of a trauma center was supposed to do. There was no job description to speak of, and none of us had any real clarity about it. As I look back I can see that at the very beginning I was floundering, trying to figure out what my role was, but once I found my footing I had enormous freedom to create whatever I liked. In those days very little was known about helping people heal from torture, and RCT was in the forefront of investigating and systematizing the treatment of torture victims. Founded by Danish physician Inge Genefke, it was an outgrowth of Amnesty International's first medical group. So while it is true that I was unclear about my role as chaplain in the broader sense, we were all moving into uncharted territory together. This too contributed to the difficulty of building cohesion among the staff because each person had his or her own ideas. Nevertheless, from the perspective of fund raising, we were fortunate to be in the forefront of what was then a new movement. In November 1995, only two years after we began, RCT and its sister organization IRCT, the International Rehabilitation Council for Torture Victims, joined with us in sponsoring an international conference in Cape Town on treating survivors of torture. It drew physicians, mental-health providers, and healers of all sorts from many different countries, particularly from Africa. The exchange of ideas among this heterogeneous group of healers was very rich, and the conference helped to put the Cape Town Trauma Centre on the map globally.

As the first two years passed there was increasingly unpleasant conflict among the staff. It was quite ironic that though we were a trauma center we continued to inflict trauma on one another. Particularly difficult was a struggle at the top. Bea was the director, but Tom had set up the center, and so of course he had quite a bit of institutional memory and contacts in the community. The original idea was that he would get us going and then leave when a director took over, but that didn't happen, and he retained a good deal of power. In an odd way it was similar to the problems I had encountered as director of TEP. The enormous changes that were taking place with respect to South Africa's position in the world also were a major factor in stirring competition among the staff. After years of sanctions South Africa suddenly became the world's darling. The country was flooded with foreigners from the developed world, most of whom would not have dreamed of setting foot in South Africa under apartheid. They brought with them a whirlwind of new ideas and opportunities, some welcome and some unwelcome, but nevertheless exciting. For some of our staff who had been isolated from the world community by sanctions and from the professional community in South Africa by reason of race, it was a bit breathtaking to discover a world out there that suddenly felt tantalizingly within reach.

More time at staff meetings was spent discussing overseas trips than any other single topic, and it stirred up conflict, not only among the staff but also among board members who needed funding to go to conferences. This was a point of resentment toward me in particular. People across the world who knew me were hungry to hear my take on the dramatic events unfolding in South Africa, and a continuous flood of invitations came my way, often as the keynote speaker at conferences. My travel never cost the Trauma Centre anything, whereas other staff had to submit scholarly or clinical papers and, if accepted, then apply for travel money. At one point the discord was so intense that people would send vitriolic emails from one office to another rather than sitting down and having a cup of tea together to work out the conflict.

For the most part I was left to do my own thing and was simply the odd one out. It was not so much a matter of my international travel or my disability as it was that I was not a trained clinician and the chaplaincy project was my own patch. It would be a mistake, though, to think that no one was interested in my ideas. Indeed, some like our director, Bea Abrahams, and our board chair, Glenda Wildschut, were engaged from the beginning and were highly supportive. So while I would say I was not the focus of the conflict, I like everyone else inevitably became a participant. I think we represented the unfortunate tendency of traumatized people to pass on their trauma to others. We were so busy taking care of others that we were inattentive to ourselves. Most of us were undoubtedly effective with the people who came to see us, but we weren't able to learn the lessons for ourselves. We made many attempts to work through our difficulties; it wasn't that people simply didn't bother. We even hired outside facilitators to try to resolve the conflicts, but none of them was really successful.

Despite all this the experience was very valuable for me. As so often happens it was a matter of learning what one finds beneficial and what one decides to jettison. For one thing, the whole discourse of the psychiatrists, psychologists, and social workers was new to me. I was unfamiliar with the clinical vocabulary and was forever asking, "What does 'this' or 'that' mean?" I came from a theological background and the church is no stranger to the need for healing, but we express our ideas in God-talk. The clinical constructs seemed like "psychobabble" to me, though of course we church people have our own theological jargon. When I look back though, I think I could have been more creative in highlighting the spiritual dimension of my work. It would have been possible to do so without undermining the interfaith commitment that we had. I sometimes regret I didn't make more use of the little chapel at Cowley House, for example. I guess I was walking gingerly in the context of the Trauma Centre and being careful not to impose anything overtly religious.

There was also an unfortunate tendency sometimes to foist on people expectations that arose from theory rather than accepting their lived experience at face value. I remember a discussion that occurred many years later that illustrates the point. I was speaking with a person who had lost a loved one in the bombing of the World Trade Towers and was now a member of a wonderful peace-building organization called 9/11 Families for Peaceful Tomorrows. This woman spoke movingly about how she had felt alienated from well-meaning friends who insisted that she must be angrier at the loss of her loved one than she actually was. What she felt instead was sadness and regret at what she saw as her country's role in provoking such resentment in the world. The same disconnect can happen between a client and a psychotherapist who proceeds too rigidly from theory.

At any rate, as I learned more about the clinical approach I drew two conclusions. The first was that there was a danger of "over pathologizing" people. As much as it was clear that some traumatized people were struggling and in need of long-term clinical intervention, it was equally true that the majority of people who had also gone through terrible experiences were leading quite functional lives. That is not to say they were free of distress; indeed, many of them labored under a heavy burden of unfinished business. My other conclusion was that we had "over expertised" the response to human pain. My point is not to devalue the role of the expert but to say that we had undervalued the wisdom of the ages, that is, the perspective of the great faith traditions and the insights of ancient cultures.

What trauma survivors were looking for was often quite simple. For example, a woman requested to see me, and after I had listened to her particularly painful story I said, "I'll refer you to one of our psychologists or psychiatrists." She looked at me and said, "Well, actually I've talked to them already." When I asked, "So why have you come to me?" she answered, "Because you know pain." So I continued to see her. Of course many clinicians on our staff had been part of the struggle and certainly knew pain, but theirs was not visible like mine, and for the most part their training would not have allowed them to show it to their clients. The fact that I too had suffered was much more important to this woman than clinical expertise. Experiences like this one helped me realize that I had rich resources of my own, and over the next few months a plan gradually took shape that eventually became a Healing of Memories workshop.

◇ 10 ◇

Breaking the Chain of History

◇◇◇◇◇◇◇

MY BOMBING WAS ONLY TWO YEARS behind me and the memory was quite fresh. I was still deepening my reflection on what had helped me recover in body and spirit, especially in relation to where we South Africans were in our collective journey. So the nation's experience and my own were in a constant creative interplay in my heart and mind as I tried to imagine what my contribution might be. Arriving in South Africa as a young priest in my early twenties, I eventually came to see that helping to free all South Africans from the shackles of apartheid would be the fulfillment of the vows I had taken to my order and to God. For more than two decades, that had meant supporting the liberation movement in whatever way I was able. Now we had achieved one part of that goal. We were politically free, and that was a precondition for everything else. But as a people we were, and in many ways still are, imprisoned by the memories of the past. During the days of struggle we had a slogan, "Don't mourn, mobilize." It may have been good politics, but it was bad psychology. We still have a lot of grieving to do as a nation. I've noticed since 1994 that when someone dies there is a huge outpouring of grief. Sometimes it seems a little disproportionate, but I think people are grieving for all those who died without ever seeing victory, for the lost opportunities, and for the cost of what we endured during the struggle. Similarly, I believe that the huge amount of violence in our country now reflects pent-up anger that did not dare to find expression during the apartheid years. What we are trying to do with Healing of Memories work is to break the chain of history—a chain that in so many countries means that the oppressed in one generation become the oppressors of the next. That was true of the Afrikaners in South Africa who survived the concentration camps invented by the British at the beginning of the twentieth century, and I believe it is also true of the relationship between the Jewish people and the Palestinians in Israel. The oppressed who still think of themselves as victims eventually become the victimizers of others and justify their actions because of their continued victimhood. These were the thoughts that were going through my mind as I reflected on what sort of healing process we might devise.

It turned out to be an advantage that neither I nor anyone else knew what the chaplain of a trauma center should do, so I was free to explore the possibilities without any preconceptions. I had read about healing ventures in a religious context, and I drew on my own past experience at the Lutheran World Federation as well. There the workshops I led were aimed at discerning a collective wisdom that would help people weighed down by poverty and AIDS and traumatized by the devastation of war. Despite my skepticism about "psychobabble," our work at the Trauma Centre had given me a deeper understanding of the emotional needs of survivors of violence and torture. I saw that we needed to focus on how the journey of the nation had affected the journey of the individual. The healing ministry of the Linn family was a creative influence on my thinking. They led retreats that featured storytelling, prayer, and liturgy in a Christian context. Their Christocentric approach would have been of limited value for a country with a diversity of religious and cultural traditions, like South Africa, but their work pointed me in the direction of a nonclinical healing process that was experiential and practical where spirituality was a key component.

In the year since I had returned to South Africa I discovered that everyone regardless of who they were, rich or poor, white or black, had a story to tell about the apartheid years. They were tales mainly of anger, hurt, and loss, but sometimes touching stories of gentleness and caring across the lines of conflict. What was particularly striking was that while many people were eager talk to anyone who would lend an ear, others were reticent, and this was often but not always along racial lines. Many whites avoided the topic, no doubt hoping it would go away. As I listened I thought how blessed I was that so many people knew I had been bombed and were able to accompany me through their prayers and encouragement. They were vital to my recovery. As I examined more carefully what that had meant to me, I realized that two elements were at the heart of the matter. One was having the dreadfulness of what had happened to me acknowledged and understood. The messages I received were full of expressions of shock and horror. The other was that I felt my well-wishers' presence there with me. They were people of different faiths, different ideologies, and different worldviews—and none of that mattered. What mattered was that they were accompanying me in my suffering. The children's drawings plastered on the walls of my room were a vivid reminder of their presence. At this point I knew that whatever healing experience we created had to be a collective process wherein acknowledgment, accompaniment, storytelling, and an underlying spirituality would be critical elements. Also, I had long been interested in the power of creative liturgy as a means of enacting our human journey. Although it had not completely crystallized in my mind, I began to think of it as a workshop for healing memories.

Having arrived at a broad concept, I decided to present my ideas to some of my colleagues. The year was 1994, just before our first democratic election. There was already serious talk of forming a Truth and Reconciliation Commission (TRC), although the Government of National Unity did not actually pass it into law until the following year. The first hearings began in 1996. Meanwhile, an interfaith group called the Religious Response to the Truth and Reconciliation Commission had grown out of a large interfaith meeting convened by the Western Cape Council of Churches and a few other likeminded NGOs interested in peace building. The Religious Response organized itself into various working groups that were intended to engage the TRC process, each with a distinctive mission. The Lobbying and Networking Working Group, for example, played an important role in influencing the parameters that guided the formation of the TRC and the criteria by which its commissioners were chosen. As chaplain of the Trauma Centre I was a founding member of the Counseling Working Group, whose mission was to organize support for survivors of human rights violations. Exactly what that meant was left to us to decide. At the very first meeting I said that I thought we needed a parallel process to the TRC and that that might even become more important than the commission itself. By law only those who had suffered "gross human rights violations" were eligible to appear before the commission. These were defined as murder, attempted murder, abduction, torture, and "severe ill treatment," whereas literally millions of others had suffered terrible though less drastic violations. I sought the members' participation in creating a plan to make Healing of Memories workshops widely available. We envisioned the workshops as providing a healing experience for those unable to testify before the TRC, either because their injuries did not rise to the level of "gross violations" or for myriad other reasons. However, we did subsequently also offer Healing of Memories workshops to those in the Western Cape who gave evidence to the TRC, and many people availed themselves of the opportunity.

We provided survivors of abuse with an opportunity to tell their stories and be recognized and honored for their sacrifices and suffering, and in this respect the process mirrored the experience of those who appeared before the TRC. As it turned out, Healing of Memories outlived both the TRC and the Religious Response. The TRC issued its final report and ceased formal operations in November 1998 and the Religious Response changed its name to the Centre for Ubuntu and continued to do important work, especially during the years immediately after hearings of the TRC. For example, it organized community forums where urgent discussions of reconciliation, reparations, and forgiveness could be continued among members of the public who might otherwise rarely have encountered one another. Unlike the TRC hearings, the forums were highly interactive and were the site of sometimes heated exchanges and touching scenes of reconciliation, such as when Ma Irene Mxinwa, whose son was shot and killed by the security police in the 1980s, lit a candle for Wilhelm Verwoerd, the grandson of the state president who was one of the architects of apartheid. Despite its good work, by the year 2000 funding for the Centre for Ubuntu had begun to dry up and it ceased operations, generously bequeathing its few remaining resources to the Institute for Healing of Memories.

As the plan for Healing of Memories workshops took shape, we agreed to begin with ourselves. I managed to persuade several members of the Counseling Working Group and a few others to come together for our very first workshop at a small conference center in Stellenbosch. We began at 9 a.m. and were finished by lunchtime. We allowed two hours for storytelling and I laugh now when I remember being worried that we had allowed too much time and people would lose interest. In reality a number of people expressed amazement at what they had heard themselves saying and indicated they could have used far more time, so this certainly confirmed that storytelling was the heart of the experience. That marked the beginning, and before long Healing of Memories workshops became the central mission of the chaplaincy project and the counseling working group.

Not long after, we had a second workshop that involved some of the folks at St. George's Cathedral, and later still another very powerful interfaith workshop where we had Jewish, Muslim, and Christian participants come together. Two members of the original Counseling Working Group, Christo Thesnaar and Rashied Omar, remain members of the board of the Institute for Healing of Memories to this day, and both have had distinguished careers on behalf of reconciliation across racial and religious lines in South Africa and elsewhere in the world.

Most of the people who came to those early workshops were from civil society organizations that partnered with the Trauma Centre. Many of them were themselves caregivers who had their own traumas that they had not touched while they were busy helping others, so these were important workshops with people much in need of healing. The Trauma Centre also referred its own clients who had been in exile or tortured in prison. We tweaked the workshops in ways small and large based on what we learned from each experience. For example, not long after I arrived in South Africa I attended a workshop where we were asked to draw our biographies. From that it struck me that asking people to draw their life story would open up their emotions in a powerful way, so we incorporated drawing into the workshops early on. We soon learned that we needed much more time than we had allowed originally, and so workshops became weekend residential experiences.

Since the workshops were conceived in parallel to the Truth and Reconciliation Commission, originally we began on the first night with a PowerPoint presentation that was intended to educate people about the impending TRC. We did that perhaps two or three times, but on the third occasion a participant said, "You've developed this extraordinarily experiential workshop, but you begin as if we're in a classroom!" That took me a bit aback, but the minute I heard it, I knew he had touched something important. Beginnings set the tone for what follows, and so instead of a lesson, we needed to begin with something that would put people in touch with memories and open up their feelings. I drew upon my experience at the Lutheran World Federation where we had worked with community theater groups, and I hit on that as a solution. We decided to commission a small theater group to make a short dramatic presentation. The name of the group, Mina Nawe, means "me and you" in Zulu, and this reflects our philosophy that healing comes from caring and compassionate connections among people. The direction we gave the theater team was, "Go out into the community and talk to people about their experiences of the apartheid years and then come back and create a drama based on what you've heard." The drama they created proved to be so evocative that many participants wept, and we used it for many years thereafter. Even when participants had experiences different from those depicted in the drama, we discovered that feelings are transcendent and that people were still moved by what they saw.

When we work in other countries now, we open the workshop whenever possible with a short dramatic piece, a film clip, or photographs that capture that country's experience. Endings also matter a great deal, and by the third workshop we had introduced a ceremony that celebrates the communal experience we have just shared and looks ahead to the future. So, whereas our first workshop was mainly about telling stories, we added more elements that enriched the process and gave a sense of a journey unfolding. After a while we said to ourselves, "This is the model. We're happy with it. It works!" The workshops are not inflexible, but the broad outline we created in those early days has served us well in a variety of contexts ever since. Put very simply, a Healing of Memories workshop is at heart a weekend-long journey that moves from pain to hope.

Soon after I started work at the Trauma Centre I hired two individuals for the chaplaincy program who remained with me for many years and made very significant contributions. One was Shanti Mather, who became my personal assistant and took over virtually every aspect of our administration. I could not have gotten along without her, for she held things together when I was out of the office traveling, as I was a great deal. She got her baptism by fire right at the beginning, for two weeks after she joined the staff I disappeared for several weeks to lead Healing of Memories workshops in the four corners of the country. Shanti, who barely knew her way around, was a self-starter and had things organized by the time I got back. Later on, after we founded the Institute for Healing of Memories, we no longer had the Trauma Centre to keep track of our funds, and so she took over the role of money manager. That was something of a relief, since we were perpetually in the dark about how much money we had. Shanti and Tom Winslow, who was responsible for budgets at the Trauma Centre, had what might charitably be called a difficult relationship, because Tom rarely produced the figures on time, if at all, and Shanti was often hot under the collar. All told, Shanti was with us for more than ten years, and she knew nearly as much about the organization as I did.

The other person who joined us was Barry Bekebeke, a young man who had recently graduated in social work from the University of the Western Cape. Barry was hired to assist with the development of Healing of Memories workshops, and he was someone who knew trauma firsthand. In November 1985, about the same time I had left my post as priest at St. Michael's Parish in Mbare, Zimbabwe, he was involved in a protest in his home township, Paballelo, just outside of Upington in the Northern Cape. During a demonstration that involved hundreds of township residents a policeman was killed. In the ensuing chaos the police seized twenty-six people and charged them with murder. That twenty-six individuals could be charged with the murder of a single person under apartheid South Africa law was a patent absurdity, and the judge distinguished himself with his rigidity and bias. After a trial that dragged on for almost two years, twenty-five of the twenty-six, including Barry, were convicted and fourteen were sentenced to death, including Barry's brother. Barry was not among the fourteen, and he and several others were eventually released on parole, though their convictions for murder still stood. Because of its unfairness the trial came to epitomize the racism and excesses of apartheid in the eyes of the world, and the Upington Twenty-six became an international cause célèbre. Observers and journalists came from around the world to attend the trial and its appeals. After a legal battle that did not end until 1991, all fourteen death sentences and twenty-one of the murder convictions, including Barry's, were vacated by the appeal court, and in the end all but one person was freed that year. Barry has said that when he came to work at the chaplaincy project one of his first tasks as a participant in a Healing of Memories workshop was to work through his feelings about those terrible years. He was a very skilled natural facilitator and soon became a lead facilitator as well. Barry related with great sensitivity to workshop participants out of a deep appreciation of the kind of suffering that black people had experienced during the apartheid years, especially those who had been activists in the struggle. He was also a skilled linguist and spoke four or five languages extremely well. That was a huge asset as we moved through different linguistic communities in South Africa. I led the early workshops, but when I was out of the country, Barry led them. Together we trained other facilitators, and we were blessed because they proved to be an extraordinary group who remained with us for many years.

Our facilitators have always been volunteers, and this has greatly increased our reach even though, as a small organization, we operate on a modest budget. In the first years of democracy, issues of healing and reconciliation were on everyone's mind, and people lived and breathed the changes that were taking place. Many people saw becoming a Healing of Memories volunteer as an opportunity to help create a new society. While that ardor has understandably cooled a bit with the passage of time, as late as 2007 when we interviewed facilitators as part of an evaluation of our work, some said that part of the satisfaction of facilitating Healing of Memories workshops was that they were helping to build their country.

An invitation soon came to the chaplaincy project from the South African Council of Churches to partner in offering Healing of Memories workshops throughout the country. It was a demanding schedule; Barry traveled with me regularly while Shanti kept watch over the office in Cape Town. While we had a roster of well-trained facilitators in our home province, the Western Cape, developing facilitators in other provinces proved to be a bit dicey. Unless we returned on a regular basis we could not provide adequate training. People had a tendency to assume that if they came to one workshop and thereafter we gave them a few hours training, they could happily run these workshops by themselves. But of course that's not the case; there is a rather steep learning curve on the path to becoming a good facilitator. Nevertheless, by the end of 1997 we had offered workshops and in some cases trained facilitators in every province except KwaZulu-Natal.

One troubling aspect of these workshops was the near total absence of white people. Here we were, working with the South African Council of Churches, which included multiracial denominations with many large, mainly white congregations, yet most white people seemed to feel little imperative as Christians or South Africans to seek reconciliation with black people. Black people who came to our workshops displayed an astonishing openness to healing old wounds and would say, "We're willing to reconcile, but we have no one to reconcile with." This is a problem that continues to bedevil our work. Even though we employed a white pastor to reach out to white congregations his efforts met with limited success. Unfortunately, many white people have little sense that they too were damaged by apartheid, so they feel no need for healing. In the white community there continues to be massive denial of responsibility for what happened, and we have not been able to break through that denial to the degree we would like. Still, we continue to chip away at it. When I am tempted to get discouraged, I think of the German experience, where it is now members of the second or third generation who are willing to look directly into the horror of Nazism and the Holocaust and take some personal responsibility even though most of them were not even alive when the events occurred. Young people are now beginning to ask questions of their parents and grandparents about their role during those years. Perhaps South Africa too will have to await a new generation of white people before reconciliation based on acknowledgment of responsibility becomes possible. I have included with this chapter comments by two courageous individuals, each of whom is committed to encouraging his or her respective communities to assume responsibility for a dark history. "Confronting Germany's Past," by my friend Karin Penno-Burmeister, brings to life her important work as the director of a concentration camp memorial in Germany. The other essay by Christo Thesnaar, our board member and a minister in the Dutch Reformed tradition, describes in personal terms his own journey of dealing with guilt and shame. Both make the point that these emotions can be poisonous and destructive or life-giving and redemptive depending on the manner with which we engage them.

During those first years of offering workshops in South Africa I was also much in demand to speak internationally, because people were keenly interested in what everyone saw as the new South Africa. After the Truth and Reconciliation Commission had begun its hearings in April 1996, revelations of atrocities were widely publicized abroad, as were some remarkable stories of reconciliation that occurred during the commission's hearings. People were full of questions: "What is the attitude in the country toward the TRC?" "Do white people support it?" "What about divisions within the black community?" "What changes are occurring, if any, on the ground?" There were also personal questions: "Has the TRC identified the person who bombed you?" "How would you feel if it did?" And then there were the impossible ones: "What can be done about the vast inequalities in wealth and privilege?" "How long do you think it will take to achieve real equality?" "Is reconciliation possible?" It was challenging and exciting to try to convey to a foreign audience a little of the deep hope in the country and yet to temper it with a sense of what was realistically possible. Looking back now from my present vantage point, I am sad to say that I was excessively optimistic and naive. I could not have foreseen then that in 2011 our young democracy would be laboring under such a heavy burden of corruption, racism, and inequality of wealth and opportunity.

Many of the people I spoke to abroad had been movers and shakers in the antiapartheid movements in their home countries, and they felt a personal stake in the transformation unfolding in South Africa. There was a sense, often articulated by Archbishop Tutu, that we owed a debt of gratitude to those who had supported us through the years, so in that spirit I tried to honor as many requests as I could. Naturally I also talked about the Healing of Memories work that we were beginning and this broadened the network of support for the chaplaincy project and later for the Institute for Healing of Memories.

Although I thought that the medical complications from my bombing were behind me, that proved not to be the case. In 1997 I undertook a trip to Cuba, Canada, and the United States. While in Cuba I developed a persistent runny nose. The Cubans decided I had a mild case of the flu, so I decided to keep to my schedule. Soon after I arrived in Canada, however, I had a seizure and ended up in the hospital.

I was diagnosed with bacterial meningitis, a very dangerous infection, and doctors discovered a tiny opening in my skull that remained from the damage of the bombing. Bacteria were eventually able to penetrate it and the runny nose that had plagued me was actually excess fluid draining away from the infection in my brain. The Canadians filled me with antibiotics and took good care of me, so before long the infection was cured. However, they advised me that I would need more brain surgery or the infection would almost certainly recur. This was not good news. For seven years I had got on with my life, and now I was being taken back again, not exactly in the sense of reliving the trauma itself, but back to the impact it had had on my life. I had believed I was finished with all that. Now I thought, "Here we go again," and I felt sad and depressed.

When I was strong enough I cancelled most of my trip to the United States and returned to South Africa by way of Australia where I consulted with doctors and made arrangements to have the necessary surgery there. A short time later, Shanti recalls seeing me off at the Cape Town airport with a group of my friends and feeling extremely worried about me and fearful that she might never see me again. In truth, I too wondered if the surgery might be fatal. A bit dramatic perhaps, but not completely unrealistic given the seriousness of bacterial meningitis. Certainly I felt that I had been taken back to the reality of the bombing. In fact, the surgery went well. After a few weeks recuperation in Australia, that was thankfully the end of the matter, and I returned to my normal active life.

The year 1998 was a pivotal one for the Healing of Memories program, because for the first time we offered a Healing of Memories workshop outside South Africa—at the Riverside Church in New York City. Riverside had a reputation for its social justice witness and its progressive multiracial and international congregation. Martin Luther King Jr.'s famous speech against the war in Vietnam was delivered from its pulpit. During apartheid, nearly every prominent leader of the ANC had preached there, and it was the "home away from home" for many South African exiles residing in New York City. On the day of Nelson Mandela's release from prison I am told that the church overflowed as thousands of New Yorkers and South African exiles spontaneously headed uptown and crowded into its ample nave to celebrate with speeches, the beat of South African music, and much dancing in the aisles. Riverside was also prominent on Nelson Mandela's agenda when he toured the United States after his release from prison. Not long after, a member of the congregation, Dr. Ruby Sprott, led a group from Riverside on a tour of South Africa and it paid a visit to the Trauma Centre. This led to the invitation to give the workshop at Riverside.

What was striking about the makeup of the workshop was that even though it was sponsored by the church, the participants were from a wide range of backgrounds and nationalities, including Africans. Somehow the word got out in the New York City grapevine and people came. While most were members of Riverside, some had never even been inside the church before. There were Christians, Jews, Buddhists, and people from no religious background whatever. What they had in common was a commitment to social justice, and that drew them to the Riverside workshop. As is always true in Healing of Memories workshops, people worked on whatever pain was in their hearts, but what was striking as a common theme was unfinished business from the U.S. civil rights movement. In our small groups people spoke of their joys and disappointments, their hopes and their resentments from that struggle. This was an activist group, and for quite a few of them this was the first time they had had an opportunity to work through their pain in relation to the movement, as distinct from a political analysis. We set up a little altar and people were encouraged to place a treasured object there. Several people brought a memento from the civil rights days and shared from the heart what it meant to them. I was told by church members that participants in the workshop continued to talk about the impact that the workshop had on them for weeks afterward, and the positive reverberations continue to echo to this day. Of the people present that weekend, two presently serve on the board of directors of the newly incorporated Institute for Healing of Memories—North America, one on the advisory board, one volunteers regularly as a facilitator for our workshops in the New York area, and one, Steve Karakashian, is a coauthor of this memoir.

The success of the Riverside workshop and a subsequent one that we did later that year in Rwanda convinced me that we had devised a process that worked well regardless of culture and context and was not restricted to the content of apartheid. As word traveled through the international community about the Healing of Memories workshops, invitations to offer them in other countries began to flow in. Until now I had hesitated, uncertain how transferable the process was. Now I began to envision Healing of Memories work on a wider scale and to question whether the Trauma Centre was the best locus for our expanded mission. For some time we had taken on a life of our own apart from the Trauma Centre. My foreign speaking engagements had given the chaplaincy project an international constituency that set it apart from the center's other programs, all of which operated solely in the Western Cape. Despite this, I might well have thought, "We have settled in here; let's just continue as a part of the Trauma Centre," had it not become such an unpleasant, factionalized place to work. In the end I decided that we needed our own separate organization, and we made plans to leave. We managed the transition very well despite the conflicts that were raging around us. Nomfundo Walaza had become the director after Bea Abrahams left. She and I had a cordial relationship, and we both worked very hard to make our parting harmonious. In the end we left the Trauma Centre with its blessing and support, which even included arranging to take along our office furniture. The chaplaincy project had always had a significant amount of independent funding from the Scandinavian countries and from the archbishop of Melbourne's Relief and Development Fund. Some of our donors questioned our move, but in the end nearly all of them agreed to shift their support to the new Institute for Healing of Memories. Judging from the fact that their funding continued over many years, I don't think they regretted it, and over time others who knew me from the struggle years joined in funding us.

From the beginning most of our international funders have been Christian churches and agencies, and since I am an Anglican priest, we have always had a special relationship with the Anglican Church. The church has exercised a vital presence in the life of South Africa, often but not exclusively in the person of Archbishop Desmond Tutu. It was influential in setting up the Trauma Centre, and while Cowley House is leased to the Trauma Centre, it remains Anglican property. Archbishop Tutu more than anyone personified the Truth and Reconciliation Commission, not only because he was its chairperson, but also because he was its moral compass. My community, the SSM, made a grant that helped create the Institute as a separate organization and has continued as a mainstay. For all of these reasons I thought it was in our interest to have a sponsoring but not controlling link with the Anglican Church. I remain a priest in the Diocese of Cape Town seconded full time to the Institute for Healing of Memories. So there is a clear structural relationship through my person as director. Consequently, we made an arrangement whereby the archbishop of Cape Town would have the right to nominate a member of our board. This gave us our independence and yet recognized that we were part of the Anglican extended family. Some might say we are a faith-based NGO that from the beginning worked in a secular and interfaith environment. In that spirit we also joined the interfaith World Conference of Religion and Peace and a network of secular organizations doing trauma work, while at the same time we became associate members of the Western Province Council of Churches and the South African Council of Churches.

That said, I sometimes think we could have been, and maybe should have been, more deliberate in opening ourselves to interfaith work. In truth, I didn't worry much about that at the time. Christianity was my home base, and while I have always believed that every faith tradition brings riches to the table, the pressures of starting a new organization from the ground up required that I use the resources that were readily available to me. The organizer of our two international conferences was a Muslim woman, and one of our board members, Rashied Omar, is a Muslim imam committed to interfaith dialogue. Nevertheless, we still haven't done enough to reach out to other faiths, especially in transcending the Christian/Muslim divide. We have had Muslims come to workshops, but it's been a small minority, and it's fair to say that we really haven't made an impact in the Islamic community in South Africa. It probably would require an intentional decision to reach out to other communities in order to enrich us as an organization. We've done much better in establishing ecumenical relationships within the Christian community. Nevertheless, over the years and in many different countries we have worked well with individuals and organizations representing many different faith traditions while still maintaining our Christian identity.

Confronting Germany's Past

by Karin Penno-Burmeister

I am the Director of the Concentration Camp Memorial and Community Center in Ladelund, Germany. I was born in 1956, and my parents were young National Socialists, so I am a member of what is known as "the Second Generation." I knew nothing about National Socialism growing up and I first learned about it when my school class went to the Dachau Concentration Camp. We young people were not prepared for what we saw and it was very upsetting. When we went home our parents did not want to talk about it and many were angry about being asked.

After the war many people tried not to remember, no doubt because they wanted to avoid their responsibility and guilt, although in later years some people have been willing to accept it. It is now more than sixty years later, and a few elderly Germans are beginning to speak about the actions that they were involved in, but this is rare. The victims who survived the camps also did not speak publicly for a very long time, perhaps because nobody was listening or because they thought no one would believe them. Some may also have wanted to live normal lives and did not want to bear the mark of these terrible experiences.

As it turned out, I went into a profession where I could deal with the shame and guilt of my family history. Remembering the crimes of National Socialism has become the theme of my life, my family, and my identity. At the Ladelund Concentration Camp Memorial we have succeeded in bringing together elderly people who are former supporters of National Socialism and the families and children of people who died in the concentration camps, and they now regard each other as friends. Some even invite each other to birthdays and weddings.

The history of Germany illuminates the issue of shame. On the one hand, shame can be very dangerous and destructive. I think fascism in Germany came about because Germans felt so much shame about losing the First World War, and the international community contributed to this. So the country began looking for a strong leader who would show the world that Germany was a strong and powerful nation. This became a very dangerous situation, and in the end it produced an absolutely criminal ideology. On the other hand, shame creates an opportunity that can lead us to change. Many children of former perpetrators are open to feeling shame. Not that we feel personally responsible, as we were only children and we are quite clear about this. But we do feel a broader sense of shame because our parents were National Socialists or supported Hitler, or more simply because we are Germans and these things happened in our country. So we have been motivated by our collective sense of shame and this can be a very good thing. It is a sign that we have a new moral outlook and that we intend to live differently than our parents' generation. We must accept this sort of shame and ask it to help us rather than fear that it will destroy us.

Most of the elderly people who come to the concentration camp memorial were children during National Socialism. The oldest were adolescents or young adults. They come hesitantly, after suppressing their personal memories for decades. Now at the end of their lives they are looking backward and taking stock. For some, a bitter realization lingers that the ideals, the energy, the enthusiasm of their youth were abused and led astray in the service of an unjust ideology. Some of them battle with this awareness by attempts to justify what happened through denial, political polemics, or an appeal to finally close the book on history. One of the most powerful weapons against taking responsibility is the claim to victimhood. Of course many of these people were indeed victims of terrible things such as nightly bombings, and the older ones may have been involved in direct combat or were prisoners of war. The younger ones remember being refugees or homeless. These things did happen, but they are sometimes brought forward to justify the unjustifiable. For some, it is simply unspeakable that they took part in this unprecedented crime against humanity.

Nevertheless, those who dare to enter the memorial site can sense the importance of facing these memories, no matter how painful, because it opens a dialogue between the older and younger generation that is important for the future. And this is the beginning of liberation from a lifelong struggle with shame and guilt—not in suppressing, but in remembering; not in justification, but admission; not in weighing one against the other, but in the willingness to mourn and be sorry; not in bitter retreat into protective arguments, but in asking for forgiveness.

There are lessons for the young people too who come to our memorial center—that we are responsible for all that we do and also for what we do not do. I ask them if they believe that something like the concentration camps could ever occur again. Often they say that they cannot imagine this—that it could never happen again. Then I provide examples of other places in the world where inhumanity, cruelty, and racism still exist. We try to explore together these human problems. We talk about small happenings in every day life, such as on the school bus, the hate toward people who do not look like us, the fear of minorities, the discrimination against foreigners—all of these contain the spirit of National Socialism even if they are in themselves small things. We speak about how we can recognize these and then develop the courage to act whenever we recognize them. It is only through this undertaking that we can safeguard our world.

Dealing with Guilt and Shame

by Christo Thesnaar

I have struggled with my identity as a white Afrikaans-speaking South African male because of the injustices that were done to my black fellow South Africans under apartheid and the fact that the Afrikaans Dutch Reformed Church that I was so involved with was instrumental in supporting it. I could have dealt with my guilt and shame about this in many ways. For example, I could have simply blamed the white Afrikaners who went to the army, or who were in the police service or in the government that made the laws, or those who led the white Afrikaner church that theologically supported it. I could have easily justified myself by explaining that I resisted going to the army. I also could add that I grew up in the former Transkei homeland that was nominally independent and that therefore I did not live directly under apartheid. I could point out that I had black friends, and

I could also honestly say that I personally did not violate the rights of any other human being in this country.

But as I listened intently to the painful stories of my black fellow South Africans in Healing of Memories workshops, I began to realize that I could not hide behind these excuses. The truth is that I benefited immensely from the apartheid system in many ways, including my education, health care, housing, and freedom to travel. I began to accept that this made me as responsible for what was done under apartheid as those who were guilty of gross human rights violations, and so I had to make decisions about how to deal with my responsibility in a constructive way.

I think there are many positive things about shame and guilt, but they can also be very destructive emotions. Shame rips the heart out of you, and this can be very difficult. It can make you feel as if you should be put in a corner; it can make you want to run away and hide; and it can make you want to be someone that you are not. And if you are struggling with these painful feelings, you can sometimes take this out on friends, family members, or your own children. I had to learn to communicate my guilt and shame to others and not try and deal with them in isolation. I found the small groups during the Healing of Memories workshops so healing because they provided a nonjudgmental space where I could express my feelings of complicity in what happened under apartheid, acknowledge them, and communicate openly my apologies and remorse to my fellow South Africans who were harmed. I also realized that this is a continuous process of confessing, acknowledging, expressing real remorse and saying, "I'm sorry," and then contributing to reparation and restoration. I truly believe this is the only way.

At times I have found it hard to understand how my parents and their parents and the people they knew could have voted this monstrous system into existence. I was so disillusioned and angry with the white Afrikaner church I belonged to that I resisted being ordained for seven years. It has been difficult trying to relate to the older generations, particularly when they did not want to hear the terrible stories coming over the radio and television during the sessions of the Truth and Reconciliation Commission. But since these same people have contributed so much to my life, I now understand that I have an obligation to try and share the stories of victims with them and to try to talk about these things. I struggle with this. I sometimes feel alienated from my own people, and the Healing of Memories groups have offered me a sense of home. I try to stand alongside other white people who are willing to look at these issues, and I have a commitment to devote my life to this process. In order to do that, I must continually reach out to them, and as I do so, ask myself, "Have I done enough? Am I doing enough now?"

My commitment to redressing what we have done to our fellow South Africans in the name of God is to make sure that the students I teach attend a Healing of Memories workshop, and that I expose more and more people, especially my own children and members of my religious society to the stories of both victims and victimizers. In the past we were all so separated from one another, but now there are opportunities for friendships across cultures. I am called to be an advocate for reconciliation and to continue to build relationships across boundaries in my own life, in the lives of my children, my students, my religious society, and people that I meet from around the world. None of this would have been possible, however, had I not first started the journey of dealing with my own guilt and shame.

Casting my vote in 1994 for the first democratic election in South Africa.

◇ 11 ◇

Truth, Amnesty, and Restitution

◇◇◇◇◇◇◇

MONDAY, APRIL 15, 1996, was a momentous day in the history of South Africa. On that day in East London, a town in the Eastern Cape, the Truth and Reconciliation Commission met for the first time to begin dissecting the truth from the web of lies, obfuscation, and intimidation that had so characterized apartheid repression. So much of what had happened under cover of darkness was finally to be revealed in the light of day. A long and tortuous path had brought the nation to this juncture, six years since the unbanning of the ANC and two years after the first democratic election. The interim constitution under which Nelson Mandela's government had been elected provided the constitutional basis for amnesty. It had been hammered out in contentious negotiations, adopted as one of the last acts of the old apartheid parliament, and then implemented by the new democratically elected Government of National Unity. Its final section is worth quoting because it lays out an overarching moral vision for the democracy that we hoped to achieve:

This Constitution provides a historic bridge between the past of a deeply divided society characterized by strife, conflict, untold suffering and injustice, and a future founded on the recognition of human rights, democracy and peaceful co-existence and development opportunities for all South Africans, irrespective of color, race, class, belief or sex.

The pursuit of national unity, the well-being of all South African citizens and peace require reconciliation between the people of South Africa and the reconstruction of society.

The adoption of this Constitution lays the secure foundation for the people of South Africa to transcend the divisions and

135

strife of the past, which generated gross violations of human rights, the transgression of humanitarian principles in violent conflicts and a legacy of hatred, fear, guilt and revenge.

These can now be addressed on the basis that there is a need for understanding but not for vengeance, a need for reparation but not for retaliation, a need for ubuntu but not for victimization . . . .

In order to advance such reconciliation and reconstruction, amnesty shall be granted in respect of acts, omissions and offenses associated with political objectives and committed in the course of the conflicts of the past.[1]

These words are the most remarkable ones in the entire constitution. In its use of the African word *ubuntu* it invokes a generosity of spirit that looks toward the eventual reconciliation of the nation.

The new parliament set about creating a plan for what eventually became the Truth and Reconciliation Commission. Before being finalized it became the most debated legislation of the first democratic parliament, and many proposals were put forward. There had been truth and reconciliation commissions in a number of countries previously, particularly in Latin America, but in the end ours was unique in two important respects. First, its deliberations were open to the public and widely reported in the media. Many of us would argue that this was our media's finest hour. Initial drafts of the enabling legislation, supported by both the old apartheid National Party and the ANC, proposed that many of the proceedings would be held "in camera," that is, not open to the public. Fortunately South Africa has a robust civil society, including the Religious Response to the TRC of which I was a member. It successfully raised a hue and cry about the secrecy provisions, and they were largely dropped.

Second, South Africa's was the first commission ever to provide for amnesty as well as truth-telling. Amnesty was granted in exchange for full disclosure. The interim constitution mandated that amnesty must be offered to perpetrators, but it left the details up to the new government, so it was the government's choice to make amnesty part of the Truth and Reconciliation Commission process. This was its most controversial provision. Many people wanted perpetrators to be tried in the courts, but some form of amnesty was the price we paid for a negotiated settlement. In the end what resulted, I believe,

---

[1] The full text of the interim constitution is available online at http://www .servat.unibe.ch/icl/sf10000_.html.

was as favorable an arrangement as we could have gotten, given the political constraints. We managed to scuttle the proposal for a general amnesty in private that was initially favored by both the ANC and the apartheid regime in favor of individual amnesty in public. Though I sympathize with those who objected, I believe that had we rejected the amnesty provision altogether, the white government would have walked away from the negotiations, and sooner or later there would have been a blood bath, and we would have died by the thousands, if not the millions.

There were three separate committees of the TRC. The Human Rights Violations Committee led off first on April 15. It was charged with investigating "gross human rights violations" committed by all parties from 1960 to the date of President Mandela's election in April 1994. To its everlasting credit the ANC fully supported the investigation of abuses by the liberation movement. In fact, two commissions set up by the ANC prior to 1994 had uncovered human rights abuses in its training camps, and these investigations served as something of a model for the TRC. The Reparations and Rehabilitation Committee was intended to assist victims in their recovery and restore their dignity by recommending a reparations plan to the government. The Amnesty Committee was empowered to grant amnesty to perpetrators under three conditions: that they were politically motivated, that their actions were proportionate to the objective, and that they made a full disclosure. In its requirement for full disclosure the agreement traded amnesty for truth. Perpetrators who did not come forward or who, in the judgment of the Amnesty Committee, did not meet one or more of the criteria remained, and still remain, liable for prosecution. Quite a few applicants were rejected because, in the opinion of the committee, they did not make a full disclosure. Ironically, the vast majority of those who applied for amnesty were from the various liberation organizations, although there was a significant minority who were members of the apartheid security apparatus, especially the police. Many perpetrators, particularly of the apartheid government and the military, did not come forward, and so much of the truth remains untold. While they remain liable for prosecution, the new government has attempted to prosecute very few and has maneuvered to provide new forms of amnesty with considerable opposition from civil society.

I appeared before the commission on June 10, 1996, only two months after it began. The hearing was in Kimberley, a town located in the Northern Cape a little more than 180 miles from the village of Modderpoort where I had visited SSM's priory when I first came to South Africa in 1973. After being sworn in I was asked to tell something of my background and my work in the liberation movement. After that I recounted my recollection of the bombing and my convalescence. Though I had told the story many times before, I felt a special poignancy about relating it in a public forum set up by our first democratic parliament. My own story was now joined permanently with the giant mosaic of stories of what we as a nation had done to one another.

After that I turned to what for me was the central moral question—where does responsibility lie for what was done to me and to others? After my bombing I had often said, "I think people who send letter bombs should be locked up"—that's what I used to say. The old order brought out in me a desire for retributive justice. Increasingly I had begun to relate notions of restorative justice to my own situation. Now, the righting of the moral order that the hearings represented challenged me to be more generous and more forgiving. So I told the commission that I was not full of bitterness and I had no desire for revenge, but I did say that I hoped they would identify the person or persons responsible. Someone wrote my name on the envelope, and someone built the bomb. Whoever it was knew how to make a very sophisticated triggering device. The package was tossed about in the post from South Africa to Zimbabwe, and it lay unopened and unexploded in my living room for some time before I tore open the envelope and the bomb detonated. Although the government of Zimbabwe had created an attempted murder docket in my case, it had not found the perpetrators. I told the commission that the degree of technical sophistication suggested that it was a professional job undertaken by an arm of the state, probably the rather bizarrely named Civil Cooperation Bureau (CCB), a Special Forces unit of the South African military. In other hearings the TRC had established that this unit, which reported to Magnus Malan, the head of the South African Defense Force, was responsible for the killing or attempted killing of many people that the CCB identified as enemies of the state. Unfortunately, in my case, although several suspects were identified, the commission was never able to link anyone conclusively to the bombing, and this remains true to this day. Those who were involved in "dirty tricks" refused to answer any question that involved extraterritorial attacks, that is, those like mine that took place in countries outside South Africa. Their reasoning was that even if they were granted amnesty in South Africa, they would still be liable for prosecution in the other jurisdictions where the crimes had taken place.[2]

---

[2] The South African Broadcasting Corporation televised a weekly Special Report on the TRC hosted by journalist Max du Preez. Excerpts from my testimony,

During the investigation of my bombing I had been contacted by the commission to say it had some evidence that might lead to those responsible. I remember crying and becoming very emotional because what had happened to me was about to be given a human face. Now there were real people involved, as if faces came out of the mist. There were three specific names mentioned. They were white Afrikaans-speaking men. I didn't know any of them, but I began to wonder what each one told his children that night when he sat down to dinner with his family. "What did you do today, Daddy?" "Oh, I made a letter bomb to kill a priest." In the end, however, no one could unequivocally be identified.

While the person who made the bomb and the person who mailed it certainly have culpability for what they did—after all, they effectively pulled the trigger—the person with ultimate responsibility is well known; he is the state president, F. W. de Klerk. De Klerk has repeatedly said he knew nothing of death squads. On October 9, 1992, in a speech at Winburg in the Free State, de Klerk apologized for apartheid, but he said he would not allow any attempts in a new dispensation to break down history. He went on to say, "There are powers that are trying to manipulate our country's history by trying to portray it as dark, suppressive, and unfair." This would not be tolerated. "Yes, we have made mistakes. Yes, we have often sinned and we don't deny this. But that we were evil, malignant and mean, to that we say 'No.'" From this statement it is clear that F. W. de Klerk is not black. As some friends I met at a meeting in Latin America once said, "You cannot negotiate with the blood of the dead."

At a conference some time prior to my TRC hearing, I spoke with Frederik van Zyl Slabbert, a former leader of a white opposition party. Van Slabbert told me that he personally went to de Klerk and told him about the death squads. So I hold de Klerk politically and morally responsible for my bombing. He may not have personally ordered it. He may not even have known about it, though it's possible that he did. But he certainly knew about and did nothing to dismantle the machinery of state that carried it out. Despite this, I have yet to hear one word of remorse or acknowledgment of personal responsibility from F. W. de Klerk, a Nobel Peace Prize winner, about the evils perpetrated by the apartheid state that he headed. Instead, his attitude is, "I saw nothing, I knew nothing, and I did nothing." As a

---

photographs, and background information about my bombing, and an interview with du Preez are available at http://trc.law.yale.edu/view_all_requests.asp. Click on tape 6.

consequence, I asked the commission to make every effort to uncover the chain of command that led to the very top. When the final report of the commission was about to be released, de Klerk went to court and successfully sought an interdict preventing the sections from being published that found him to be an accessory after the fact in two notorious bombings, one that destroyed Khotso House, the headquarters of the South African Council of Churches, and the other that badly damaged the headquarters of the Congress of South African Trade Unions. The ANC also tried to have the court embargo the release of the final report because it held the ANC responsible for human rights violations. When the court refused, the ANC in the person of its head, Thabo Mbeki, boycotted the proceedings. Ironically, the commission's findings were based purely on what the ANC had itself admitted. It is probably also true that Nelson Mandela and Thabo Mbeki did not share the same perspective on this matter.

In May 1998 I had the opportunity to serve as visiting professor in democracy at the New School for Social Research in New York City. The New School was founded by Jewish refugees who fled the Nazi regime. One of its most famous professors was Hannah Arendt, a political philosopher whose writings grapple with totalitarianism, democracy, and the nature of evil. Inquiries like this were central to the mission of the university, so while the invitation was a personal honor, it was also one shared by the people of my country. The New School had made a connection with a South African university and the partnership was headed by Professor Mokubung Nkomo, a South African exile living in New York. So my visiting professorship was, in a sense, a recognition that what we were attempting in South Africa was of importance to the whole human family. I taught a weekly graduate seminar, and it was a bit scary for me because I hadn't been in a university environment for many years. I recall thinking, "What will happen when the students realize I'm not a real academic?" To my relief, my sense was that after a couple of weeks they did, and they were delighted! When I was interviewed for the post, someone asked me, "Can you tell us the ways in which you are a public intellectual?" I'd never heard the term, but I realized that the question acknowledged that someone like me, who had lived a life of activism in the service of human rights, had therefore made a contribution in the marketplace of ideas and could profitably be brought into the life of the university. Although the Truth and Reconciliation Commission had not yet filed its final report, its work was almost finished, and my professorship gave me a welcome opportunity to reflect on its successes and its limitations, especially in comparison to truth commissions in other countries. We made use of audio and video recordings of actual sessions of the commission, and the experience was very rich.

From the beginning South African opinion about the TRC was sharply divided, mainly because of the amnesty provision. Most people greeted it as a time of triumph and celebration that marked the beginning of a new era of respect for human rights. Some in the white community, on the other hand, viewed it with disdain, and the families of some victims vigorously opposed the amnesty provision with its bargain of trading justice for truth. They tried unsuccessfully to halt the proceedings by appealing to the newly formed Constitutional Court, which upheld the constitutional arrangement for amnesty that had been agreed upon. The Constitutional Court conceded that amnesty meant foregoing retributive justice. However, it asserted that the quid quo pro for amnesty would be restorative justice in the form of reparations.

Living in South Africa during the two years of the commission hearings was an extraordinary experience. The TRC held up a mirror to the country for anyone who cared to look. Day after day on radio, TV, and in the newspapers we witnessed the pain of what we had done to one another. The South African Broadcasting Corporation devoted a weekly television program to the proceedings that had extremely high ratings and was hosted by progressive Afrikaner journalist Max du Preez. In it he highlighted particularly significant testimony of the previous week, my own included. The stories were terrible, each in its own distinctive way, but some haunted the nation more than others, particularly examples of the security agents who killed people, set their bodies alight, and then held parties while the bodies burned. As a nation we saw paraded before our eyes a maelstrom of immense evil, a reflection of our ability as members of the human family to do terrible things to one another. Alex Boraine, the deputy chairperson of the TRC, has written:

> Torture was not something that took place in a handful of prisons, performed by perverted warders. Torture was endemic. There was no place we visited, no hearing we conducted, which did not contain stories of torture. Thousands were killed, not merely at roadblocks, in ambushes and raids, but also by abduction and design. Those who were seen as a threat to the apartheid regime were in many instances summarily executed.[3]

---

[3] Alex Boraine. *A Country Unmasked: Inside South Africa's Truth and Reconciliation Commission* (New York: Oxford University Press, 2001).

Those who were tortured were often told, "Scream all you like, there is nobody listening. Don't worry; we won't leave marks. No one will believe you." One of the great virtues of the TRC was that here at last was a forum where victims could be heard and be believed.

The apartheid state had been built on an inverted moral order going back to its foundation, even as far as slavery. It was a society in which the profession of torturer existed, and if a person was effective at it, he would be promoted, and at the end of his career he would be given a golden handshake for a job well done. In South Africa we had called good evil and evil good. By exposing these crimes and naming them for the evil that they were, the commission was laying the foundation for a new moral order. For the first time in our history both the tortured and the torturer stood before the country in the light of day.

One of the extraordinary things about the commission, and a sign that it was not simply victors' justice, was that whether one had been tortured by the apartheid state or by the liberation movement, every story was given equal dignity, and both were seen as wrongs. The TRC was uncompromising in asserting the moral unacceptability of gross violations of human rights regardless of who carried them out. As stories of torture in the ANC camps emerged in testimony, they had a painful impact on me, and I felt a deep sense of shame. I was, of course, conscious that we were at war and that infiltrators who were agents of the regime were a constant threat. During my time at the Trauma Centre it was humbling to hear the testimony of some people who had been wrongly detained by the ANC and maltreated but who were still loyal to it and who said that they did not want their stories to be used as a means to attack the liberation movement. The ANC insisted that there could be no moral equivalence between the just struggle to end apartheid and the injustice of defending it, and the commission agreed. Indeed, the commission was careful not to equate the violence of the state and that of the liberation movement, something that had been a tendency of some in the church. We do not equate fascism and liberation; one cause is seen as just, the other as evil. Nevertheless, torture is torture, and people were held to account for their acts.

The commission had limited resources at its disposal, but in some cases it went to extraordinary lengths to provide help for aggrieved witnesses, and a few of these incidents became iconic for the whole country. One story stands out especially for me because I had led a Healing of Memories workshop with the mothers involved. In the mid 1980s a black security policeman who pretended to be a freedom fighter abducted a group of teenage boys in Mamelodi, a township outside of

Pretoria. He promised to help them go and train to fight against apartheid, but in fact they were drugged and shot and their bodies disposed of. The mothers never found out what had happened to their sons and were tormented by the uncertainty. Though we all believed that it was unlikely that they could still be alive, as mothers do, they never gave up hope. Then one day ten years after their sons disappeared, they read in the newspaper an account by the security policeman who had kidnapped them and who was now applying for amnesty. These mothers simply couldn't rest until they knew where the bones of their children were buried. The TRC facilitated their being taken to the site, where they were able to perform the traditional ceremonies of farewell for the dead. These mothers will never forget their loss, but they can move on because the spirits of their sons can now rest. With the nation's sharing of their grief, the moral order has been restored.

The black community was transfixed by these revelations even if most were hardly surprised. It was highly regrettable that much of the white community either ignored the proceedings or found ways to minimize or rationalize the revelations. Whereas the hearings were always packed with black people, very few white South Africans attended. My own testimony is a case in point. Apart from the commissioners, myself, and Michael Worsnip, who accompanied me, there were almost no white faces in the hall. The white community's resistance to looking the truth squarely in the face was abetted by the terms under which the TRC was set up. Its mandate was to focus only on gross human rights violations, which were defined as murder, attempted murder, torture, and other forms of severe maltreatment. It therefore presented to the nation a steady stream of horrifying cases that rightly needed to be exposed. However, it had no mandate to examine the institutional violence that was the daily life of black South Africans—systematic discrimination and humiliation, inferior education, and such things as exploitative and forced labor, beatings by police with no recourse, and unremitting poverty. Under the state's racist social engineering, more than three million black people were forcibly removed from their homes as part of the nightmare that was apartheid. All of these indignities were forms of torture. None of them was considered sufficiently egregious to warrant an appearance before the TRC, but they laid a crushing burden of grief, anger, and spiritual damage on millions of black people. It was for them that we devised Healing of Memories workshops in parallel to the TRC hearings as a place where their sacrifices could be honored and recognized.

The focus of the TRC on dramatic violations of human rights had the unintended consequence that it enabled whites to say, "These things are appalling, but they represent the work of a few bad apples. Anyway, I knew nothing about them, and I had nothing to do with them." This was exactly de Klerk's argument. While the apartheid state deliberately tried to hide its worst atrocities from its white citizens lest it stir up opposition, white people surely knew about many of these abuses. After all, it was white people who carried out the abuses, and they had their own circle of relatives and friends. Even if some of us were against apartheid, it is still true that we benefited from it. Highlighting the institutional wrongs of the system would have confronted whites with the ways in which they enjoyed the fruits of an inhumane system and invited them to take some responsibility for it. This omission has had serious consequences in its failure to mobilize support in the white community for restitution in the form of reparations. In this respect de Klerk's own forms of denial have not helped the white community face its culpability for the past and its responsibility for creating a better future.

In the white community there was, and to some extent there still is, talk of wiping the slate clean, of forgiving and forgetting. But that is not the route to national healing. Healing cannot take place unless memories have been healed. The nation has to collectively face up to what has happened. In 1992 Professor Kader Asmal and I participated in a "phone in" on a program of the South African Broadcasting Corporation. The subject was the possibility of a general amnesty, then under discussion. We both made comparisons between apartheid and Nazism. Sheila Camerer of the apartheid National Party and another caller objected and said the remarks were "in bad taste." The lives and deaths of millions of people throughout Southern Africa were thus reduced to a matter of whether one uses bad language or forgets to use a table napkin. Even today I cannot help feeling that much of the white community still lives in cloud cuckoo land.

Apartheid's structural evils left no one untouched. Privilege gained through exploitation and suffering became an accepted "right" of white people and still blinds them to inequities and inequalities. Crime and corruption in the black community are partially the products of widespread contempt for laws that were actively hostile to all black people. Children, much too young to be soldiers, left school half educated and were drawn into the liberation struggle. White youths, not yet out of adolescence, were armed with assault rifles and perched atop armored vehicles, where they patrolled township streets like lords, while black youths their own age looked up at them with a mixture of fear and hatred. Lest anyone think otherwise, the evil took a dreadful toll on perpetrators. During the commission's hearings the wife of a former Special Forces agent sent a letter to the South African Broadcasting Corporation covering the TRC hearings. In it she shared some of her pain. Bishop Tutu quotes from her letter at length in his book *No Future without Forgiveness*.[4] It is worth recapitulating here because, while this woman was unusual in being willing to share her story with the nation, she would certainly not have been unique in her suffering. This is a little of what she said:

> [He was] a bubbling charming personality, humorous and grumpy, everything in its place and time. Then he says: he and three of his friends had been promoted, "We're moving to a special unit. Now, now, my darling. We are real policemen now."
>
> After about three years with the Special Forces, our hell began. He became very quiet. Withdrawn. Sometimes he would just press his face into his hands and shake uncontrollably. I realized he was drinking too much. Instead of resting at night, he would wander from window to window. He tried to hide his wild consuming fear, but I saw it. In the early hours of the morning between two and half past two, I'd jolt awake from his rushed breathing. Rolls this way, that side of the bed. He's pale. Ice cold in a sweltering night—sopping wet with sweat. . . . The terrible convulsions and blood curdling shrieks of fear and pain from the bottom of his soul. Sometimes he sits motionless, just staring in front of him. . . .
>
> I end with a few lines that my wasted vulture said to me one night: "They can give me amnesty a thousand times. Even if God and everyone else forgives me a thousand times—I have to live with this hell. The problem is in my head, my conscience. There's only one way to be free of it. Blow my own brains out. Because that's where my hell is."

In this corrosive moral environment there were people of courage and deep integrity who made submissions to the commission. One was a South African housewife named Lesley Morgan. A deeply religious woman, the simple eloquence of her statement has the quality of a confession not only before the nation but also before God.

> I grew up with all the advantages and opportunities afforded me because I was white. . . . Although I was fully aware of the

---

[4] Desmond Tutu, *No Future without Forgiveness* (New York: Doubleday, 1999), 52–53.

dreadful things that were happening all around my, fear paralyzed me. I was no activist. I was afraid of being arrested, afraid of being detained without trial, afraid of being tortured or killed. I do not even have the excuse of not knowing. I was well aware of what was happening, I read the Black Sash publications and knew the terrible consequences of the Group Areas Act, the Mixed Marriages Act, the Land Appropriation Act, the Separate Development Act, the Bantu Education Act. God forgive me, I did nothing to speak out against these obscene laws.

The TRC hearings on Gross Human Rights Violations have devastated me. I have watched them on television and read about them in the Press and in magazines and they have made me weep with anger and horror. There is a strong feeling of denial, not because I don't believe what has been said, but because I don't want to believe that such cruelty and systematic destruction has occurred so near me. There is a sense of complicity, a terrible feeling of failure. . . .

When I read of the reparations that people who have made submissions are requesting, it compounds the deep sense of shame I am feeling. A tombstone, a bursary for a child's education, a proper burial for a loved one, such simple requests, no vengeance, no desire to get even. It somehow makes it harder to face you. Given the same circumstances, I'm not sure that I would be so willing to forgive. . . .

The choices I made in the past to avoid what I perceived, in my fear and cowardice, as having consequences too dangerous to deal with have resulted in consequences worse than ever I feared. Poverty has moved into my street, crime has moved in next door, unemployment is knocking at my gate. The results of the Human Rights violations have left us all with a legacy of mistrust, suspicion and anger. I will not run away from what is happening. I acknowledge my part in the creation of our present. I pray that together we will secure our future. . . .

Finally, I need to say one last thing. While making (this) submission today has been painful for me, the hardest part is here at the end. It is so hopelessly inadequate to make right what has happened, so puny in the face of such suffering that I am overwhelmed at my temerity in even offering it, but it is all I have to give: I'm sorry.[5]

---

[5] Lesley Morgan's submission to the TRC is available online at http://web.uct.ac.za/depts/ricsa/commiss/trc/morgan.htm.

A surprising acknowledgment of complicity was articulated in their endearingly scholarly way by a group of black youths in their twenties who applied for amnesty for their "apathy." They said in a preamble,

> For millions of South Africans, the anti-apartheid struggle consisted of maneuvering around regulations designed to control their day-to-day activities [and] to stunt the actualization of their professional aspirations. Rather than change the system themselves they relied on others to force the changes they hoped would take place. For most ordinary people in South Africa and elsewhere in the world, apathy is a defense against oppression. It affords comfort zones where tyranny is tolerated for the sake of personal and professional survival, and the maintaining of the desired standard of living.

They continued,

> In applying for amnesty for apathy the persons here recognize the following:
> 1. That we as individuals can and should be held accountable by history for our lack of necessary action in times of crisis.
> 2. That none of us did all of what we could have done to make a difference in the anti-apartheid struggle.
> 3. That in exercising apathy rather than commitment, we allowed others to sacrifice their lives for the sake of our freedom and an increase in our standard of living.
> 4. That apathy is a real and powerful phenomenon and perhaps the most destructive one in society.
> 5. That society takes a leap forward when individuals hold themselves accountable for their lack of action commensurate with change that needs to be made.[6]

As my black friend in Durban had pointed out to me soon after I arrived in South Africa, I too was complicit. Though I preached against apartheid, I enjoyed the comfort and security of sleeping safely in my white suburb at night. He wasn't saying I shouldn't do it; he was saying that complicity was inevitable, and I should own it. The German existential philosopher Karl Jaspers, writing soon after World War II, spoke about criminal, political, and moral guilt, and the sin of indifference and passivity. He goes on to say that only by accepting

---

[6] The original text was given to me by one of the petitioners.

responsibility for the history of which we are a part can we make a new beginning as a nation.

Perhaps no event since the TRC has raised the issue of responsibility as much as the very public apology of Adriaan Vlok, the former minister of law and order under the apartheid regime and, as it turned out, I had the opportunity to speak with him directly. In January 2007 I was invited by Piet Meiring, a member of our board, to participate in a panel discussion about forgiveness and reconciliation organized by the Southern African Missiological Society. The meeting was held at the University of Pretoria where Piet was professor of theology. What was especially notable about the invitation was that I was to share the program with Vlok. He was a figure much feared and hated in South Africa because in his role as minister of law and order from 1986 to 1991 he was responsible, directly or indirectly, for organizing the abduction, torture, and killing of very many antiapartheid activists.

Vlok appeared before the Truth and Reconciliation Commission, a decision that he has said was prompted by the suicide of his wife in 1994. At the TRC he admitted to two notorious bombings, one of Khotso House, the headquarters of the South African Council of Churches, and the other at the headquarters of the Congress of South African Trade Unions, but he denied responsibility for other crimes. In 1999 the TRC gave him amnesty for the crimes he had confessed.

In 2006, after what he described as something of a religious epiphany, Vlok confessed to crimes that he had not previously disclosed, including the murder of ten youths in the Pretoria township of Mamelodi and the attempted killing of Frank Chikane, then the general secretary of the South African Churches, by putting contact poison in his clothing. In a famous incident he showed up in Chikane's office with a basin of water and a towel over his arm and announced he had come to wash Chikane's feet as an act of apology and humility. Taken aback at first, Chikane allowed him to do so and was ultimately gracious in accepting the gesture. The drama, however, provoked a contentious public debate about justice, forgiveness, and reconciliation, and this was the background for the Missiological Society meeting.

I was slightly uneasy about the encounter. When the foot-washing incident took place I was out of the country, though I had read about it. A number of my friends had joked about the incident in a disparaging way. I read and was moved by President Mbeki's passionate defense of Vlok's initiative. What did I think? I was not sure. I had felt uncomfortable that the person who was responsible for the suffering of so many had chosen to make his symbolic act with someone who is an official of the new order—was it just "old" power talking to "new" power?

The night before the encounter I did not think much about the next day, but I prayed for guidance and wisdom. Also I wanted to be open minded as to what would happen. I could not quite remember whether Vlok was still minister of law and order in 1990, at the time of my bombing. The night before the conference I had even checked on the Internet but only found out when he became minister, not when he stopped. I guess in the back of my mind was the question of whether and what Vlok knew about my bombing. Just before his presentation he told me that he had indeed been minister of law and order until about 1991. He said he was currently living in Centurion and caring for his elderly mother. He appeared to be an ordinary man, dressed in blue jeans and an open-necked shirt.

On the panel he told the story that led to his encounter with Chikane and the Mamelodi mothers. He said God had led him to the realization that at the heart of the apartheid issue was a lack of Christian love and his own sense of superiority and that people had to believe perpetrators because of their sincerity. At first I found myself growing in sympathy with the man, and then after a little while I began to feel a bit uneasy.

Then it was my turn to be the first respondent. I said it was a significant moment for me because I had been a victim of the apartheid state. I went on to reflect a little on the public response to his initiative as well as my own. I expressed respect for the step Vlok had taken. Many people were worried that he did not seem to be at all forthcoming about all that he knew about the past. I said that it was not easy for people to believe in an apology until people saw what perpetrators did with the rest of their lives, including their money, their time, and their energy. I also said that Vlok had done rather better than his leader, F. W. de Klerk. While I was speaking Vlok occupied himself with shuffling papers, putting them away, and then taking them out again.

The second respondent, Professor Nico Botha, said he could not question Adriaan Vlok's integrity and suggested that he might have a particular mission to carry out among his own people. From the audience the point was made that while perpetrators received amnesty, they were able to live in wealth while victims often still lived in abject poverty.

When it was time for Vlok to respond to the questions and comments, to my astonishment he ignored all that had been said and rather implored us all to love one another. He said he was sorry about all the hurt that had been caused but said they had been fighting a war against communism. I interjected to ask if he still believed that, and he said, "Yes," and that he had documentary evidence of the Soviet Union's plans. He also said that things like killings had never been discussed, referring to the State Security Council that he headed. I interjected to say, "But it was in the minutes," an assertion that he rejected.

After the meeting ended I pressed him again privately about what he must have known as a member of the cabinet and state security council. He admitted that he should have questioned more but that he didn't because he "didn't want to know." I wished him well as he waited for God to tell him what to do next. The scale of denial concerning what happened on his watch was disillusioning and difficult to swallow. The hour we spent together had been a roller coaster. I had been impressed, moved, and sympathetic during the first segment, and then confused and disillusioned by what followed. I have always been slightly incredulous that the whole world knew in significant measure exactly what was happening in South Africa during the apartheid years except for those who were at the top of the chain of command. The inquest into Steve Biko's death in police custody took place in 1978 and was comprehensively covered in the *Rand Daily Mail*. I remember saying to myself at the time, "Let no one ever say, 'We did not know.'"

I couldn't help reflecting on what Michael Worsnip had written in my biography, *Priest and Partisan,* about the use of the doctrine of deniability by the apartheid state—how the chain of command was deliberately broken in such a way to enable the political masters to seek to avoid political, moral, and criminal responsibility for heinous crimes such as death squads. But this was different—here was Vlok who was saying "sorry" and who had sought amnesty from the TRC, but claiming that such things were not discussed and that he knew very little. Telling me that he did not want to know was for me the giveaway, because knowing would bring with it moral responsibility, not to mention political and criminal liability. Not wanting to know suggests also, at the very least, that he had the suspicion that very bad things were happening.

What was also striking about Adriaan Vlok was his piety and religiosity. From his presentation he implied that he had always been quite religious. Until very recently his religiosity seemed not to have interfered with his own view of his conduct as minister of law and order. While in the context of his faith there has been a shift toward apology, when more information was requested his response was to preach rather than to confess. I was reminded of a Healing of Memories workshop some years ago that we did with members of the Riot Police. Some of them complained that there was not enough praying and singing at our workshop, which they preferred to telling others about their own woundedness and perhaps complicity, as well as touching and listening to the pain of the "other." Ironically, it struck me that religiosity can become an obstacle on the journey to healing.

As a nation, through the Truth and Reconciliation Commission we chose not to take the route of punishment. Instead we would give amnesty in exchange for truth. I wondered for a moment whether I should forgive Vlok for what happened to me, but how can one forgive what is claimed to be unknown to the person who is responsible? Then I remembered that I had once read that the words "I forgive you" can also be an accusation.

Taking responsibility is the first step in healing, but if we want full reconciliation we have to make material restitution in the instances where this is possible. This is true for individuals and for societies. In my case the bomb that almost killed me was not dropped from the sky in an impersonal act of war. My name, Fr. Michael Lapsley, was carefully inscribed on the envelope. It was a chilling act that links me forever with the unknown person who wrote it. Since I am not full of hatred and bitterness and my heart has softened, forgiveness is potentially on the table. For me, forgiveness is an I-Thou process, and since I don't know who bombed me, there is as yet no one to forgive. If someone were to come forward and say, "I am the person who sent you the bomb. Please forgive me," I would be willing to turn the key that frees that person from guilt. But first I would need to know if he still makes letter bombs. I live in Cape Town around the corner from the largest children's hospital in Africa, and if the person said, "Ah, I work at that hospital," I would know that he had had a change of heart. My response would be, "Yes, of course, I forgive you." How much better that my assailant should continue working in a hospital rather than being locked up in prison. This is the justice of restoration, not the justice of punishment. But there is more. In my imagination I might then sit down for a cup of tea with the bomber, now my friend, and during the course of the conversation I might say, "You know, even though I've forgiven you, I still have no hands; I still have only one eye; and I still hear very poorly. Of course there is nothing you can do to bring these things back, but because of what you did I will need assistance for the rest of my life. Of course you will help to pay for that." In this case my forgiveness is not conditional on restitution, but restitution is necessary to heal fully the relationship between the two of us. The same is true for the nation. The Reparations and

Rehabilitation Committee of the TRC was designed to embody the nation's acknowledgment of its complicity with the evils of apartheid and its commitment to restore the social fabric.

Many beneficiaries of apartheid expect those who were oppressed under the old order to just move on as if the past had not happened, and some Christian preachers too speak about forgiveness as if it is something glib, cheap, and easy. However, for most human beings forgiveness is costly, painful, and difficult. These preachers would have us act according to what I call bicycle theology. I steal your bicycle. Then six months later I come back to you and admit it, saying, "Yes, I'm very sorry I stole your bike. Please forgive me." Perhaps being a good person, you say, "Yes, I forgive you." Then I keep the bike! Forgiveness and healing relationships involve making restitution for what has been stolen. I have to return the bike.

Deon Snyman, a minister in the Dutch Reformed Church, is leading a wholly admirable effort to encourage white people to "return the bike," and in a statement that accompanies this chapter he describes his work. Deon was born and raised in a traditional Afrikaans family. In 1992 he was installed as pastor of an all-black Dutch Reformed parish in the heart of Zululand where he immediately set about learning to speak the language. For some years he worked to create dialogue between white and black congregations, and he now leads an organization called the Restitution Foundation that encourages white congregations to contribute tangible resources to the development of the black community. Even today his work is an act of courage within the white community.

Dr. Mapule Ramashala, while a member of the Truth and Reconciliation Commission, provided the nation with a living parable of restitution and restorative justice. Soon after the 1994 election she moved into a house in a predominantly white neighborhood of Boksburg, a town not far from Johannesburg. While she was away on a trip to Rwanda as part of a TRC delegation she received a telephone call telling her that a gang of sixty white youths had broken into her house, vandalized it, and burned it to the ground. The police had arrested twelve of them. When she returned Dr. Ramashala had a meeting with the young people and their parents. She told them she had no intention of pressing charges, to the fury of the police and several of her own family. Instead, she said to them, "Of course you're going to take responsibility for what you have done; my house will be rebuilt and you will be responsible for raising the money to rebuild it. Also, I want you to find people in the community, particularly old people and others who are vulnerable, and find out what you can do to help them. I want a report from each of you every six months telling me about your life, especially how you are doing at school." What would have happened to those youths in prison? What would a prison record have done to their lives after their release? And what effect did Dr. Ramashala's generosity of spirit have on that white community?

In the South Africa of the twenty-first century all of us, and I don't exempt myself from this, are overwhelmed and preoccupied with crime, its effects, and how to combat it. The response of a majority of the population is to call for the immediate reintroduction of the death penalty, which was a morally bankrupt feature of the apartheid regime. Meanwhile our prisons are bursting with people being incarcerated with longer and longer sentences. This is also the route taken by the United States. That country cuts back more and more on social welfare spending, and building prisons has become a growth industry. The death-row population is appalling, and a colossal number of young men, particularly African Americans, are abandoned to the prison system. Even though none of this solves the United States' crime problem, there is no sign that restorative justice is about to be taken seriously as an alternative.

Meanwhile in South Africa the sad truth is that torture continues in the criminal justice system, and television footage a year or so ago showed job seekers, some of them illegal immigrants, being set on by police dogs. Because of the scale of violent crime the public often lacks sympathy for the torture victims. Fortunately, there have been cases captured on camera that have received widespread local and international attention.

While there was a requirement for full disclosure before the TRC, there was no requirement for individual perpetrators to make restitution to those they had harmed, either as a condition for amnesty or as a form of reparation. Restitution did happen voluntarily in a few very public cases that the commission facilitated, but there was no formal provision for it. These cases were unfortunately the exception, though their symbolism to the nation was important. Of course it's also true that many perpetrators did not come forward. As an alternative to individual restitution, the Reparations and Rehabilitation Committee was charged with recommending a policy for reparations to the government. Amnesty International correctly asserts that torture victims have a right to reparation. From the beginning there was the irony that the new democratic government would find itself paying reparations to victims for crimes committed by the apartheid state. The Reparations and Rehabilitation Committee attempted to deal with this conundrum by proposing that the government finance reparations with a one-time wealth tax or a number of other mechanisms that would have tapped the resources of those who profited from apartheid. In response to these suggestions much of the white community and big business went ballistic. The government has inclined its ear to the business community, which remains overwhelmingly in white hands and has declined to do anything beyond requesting voluntary contributions from businesses. Not surprisingly, these have been minimal. As pressure built on the government from victim groups and civil society, it became increasingly hostile.

Faced with this situation, a victim organization, the Khulumani Support Group, tried another tack altogether. In 2002 it brought a suit for damages in a U.S. District Court against twenty-three multinational corporations for having aided and abetted the perpetration of gross human rights violations in South Africa by equipping and financing the apartheid government's military and security agencies. The suit was supported by an overwhelming majority of the TRC commissioners and much of civil society, but in an act of supreme callousness, the South African government intervened on behalf of the corporations, charging that the suit infringed on South Africa's sovereignty. Despite this, a U.S. appellate court allowed the suit to go forward. There was an attempted appeal by the multinational corporations to the U.S. Supreme Court, which failed because a number of the esteemed judges owned shares in the companies that were defendants. Perhaps having been shamed by the incredulous reaction of civil society in South Africa and around the world, in late 2009 the South African government withdrew its previous objection and now supports the suit, which stands before an appellate court that has as yet not rendered a judgment. However, in March 2012 General Motors made an out-of-court settlement with the plaintiffs.

Inasmuch as several thousand perpetrators were given amnesty, victims have felt cheated and believe, rightly under the circumstances, that the process was weighted in favor of perpetrators. Unquestionably it is true that those who qualified for amnesty received it immediately, whereas victims waited for many years—some are still waiting—for their quid pro quo. The "rehabilitation and the restoration of the human and civil dignity of victims" that was set out in the enabling law had become more of an epitaph than a promise, as the oldest of the victims are dying off without having received any payments whatsoever. Because many citizens do not understand that the TRC never had the legal authority to mandate reparations, only to recommend policy to the government, the TRC has been unfairly blamed, and the government has for the most part escaped opprobrium. This has unfortunately undermined what would have otherwise been the healing impact of the commission. For the rest of us it is hard to avoid the conclusion that the government has broken faith with its own people.

The quid pro quo of amnesty for perpetrators and reparations for victims is crucial for the moral legitimacy of the Truth and Reconciliation Commission. Moreover, the TRC identified more than eighteen thousand victims of gross human rights violations, and because many more were seriously harmed or unable to appear it recommended that the list of potential victims to be compensated remain open. The failure of the new government to hold up its end of the bargain and enact reparations in a timely and generous manner, to be seen as honestly grappling with the issue of financing them, and to insist without vengeance and rancor that the wealthy white community share in the cost of providing them, has undermined its moral authority. It is a tragedy that a process that was correctly heralded around the world is in danger of going down in popular perception as a perpetrator-friendly exercise. Sadly, many victims who gladly gave evidence to the commission are today disillusioned by its outcome. The worldwide community and a chorus of South African survivors and human rights organizations such as Amnesty International have been calling for the immediate full implementation of the recommendations and proposals of the Truth and Reconciliation Commission.

In May 2011 the government at long last approved a plan to pay compensation for educational and medical benefits to at least some victims and their relatives who meet the criteria of egregious human rights violations set out in the enabling law for the TRC. There is presently nearly US$145 million in a special fund set up to pay reparations. The devil, of course, is in the details, and it remains to be seen how much funding will actually be made available and how wisely it is administered. The guidelines promulgated by the government have been criticized by civil society as being unnecessarily restrictive. The delay in implementing the recommendations of the TRC has been unconscionable.

Opening to the Possibility of Making Restitution

by Deon Snyman

I am very thankful for the opportunity to minister to Zulu congregations in northern KwaZulu-Natal. I listened and learned from them how the history of our country shut down their dreams and aspirations for the future. Fathers had to leave their families because they had to go away to work in the cities. Inferior schools didn't prepare pupils so they gave up hope for a better future, and of course HIV/AIDS was rife. This experience made me aware of how apartheid destroyed lives. So, if we begin to think of restorative justice and restitution, we have a big job to do.

I also had the opportunity to minister to a city congregation in Durban where I led Healing of Memories workshops as a tool for reconciliation. When I talked to ministers about the workshops, they would say, "Ja, that is very nice. You come together; you hug each other; you give your email addresses to each other; and you shake hands and say you love each other, but the reality is that afterwards some of you go back to your comfortable living and others go back to living in desperate poverty. What are you going to do in your program about this?"

In the same vein, after a Healing of Memories workshop, a member of my congregation was riding in my car. We passed through a nice white neighborhood, and he said to me, "I don't know how to tell you this, but we must not drive a long time in this neighborhood. When I drive here, I feel very bitter, and that makes me uncomfortable because I have gotten to know some very good white people at the workshop. But I feel bitter because I know these white people are not more clever than I am, and yet their lives are so totally different from mine." Personal experiences like this helped me to realize that restitution forms a very important part of reconciliation. Restitution involves recognizing the harm that was done and then doing something concrete about it by sharing and giving back.

Promoting restitution, as I do, is not the easiest job in South Africa. My friends see that I have more and more grey hair. The difficulty with promoting restitution within the white community is that many of the people who benefited from this crime against humanity have thus far been unwilling to take responsibility for their actions. Religion has not helped; rather it has hindered. People hold a fundamentalist understanding of their faith that says "God has forgiven us. So now if blacks are good Christians, they must forgive us as well." They do not understand that forgiveness needs to be earned through some form of restitution. Most victims of apartheid are still not sure if white people feel real remorse about the past. This has serious consequences for our country. Black people deeply desire that whites acknowledge the evil that was perpetrated under apartheid and, lacking that, they are left with unhealed trauma that I think is one of the reasons why our country is so violent. The government has not helped by being so reconciliatory to the white community. This will haunt us in the future, as the majority of black people feel bitter that white people have not appreciated the generosity of spirit extended to them by the black community after the fall of apartheid. I believe the government should have implemented the reparations recommendations of the Truth and Reconciliation Commission with much more vigor and should have introduced a tax on those who benefited from apartheid to pay for it. If we in South Africa fail to deal with this issue, difficult as it might be, then we might have a country in the future that we will regret. The growing divide between rich and poor is not good news for a peaceful South Africa.

I feel a deep personal responsibility to advocate for the needs of the people who have shared their lives with me. It is quite difficult, but one must not give up. Fortunately, there are hopeful signs. For example, in the Paarl area near Cape Town there was a church building that once belonged to the Anglican Church. Because of the apartheid Group Areas Act, people of color were chased away and the church was given to the white community who moved in and it became a white Dutch Reformed Church. Naturally, people carried a lot of pain because their church was stolen from them. After the 1994 election when people had the opportunity to put in restitution claims, the Anglican Church put in a claim. The Dutch Reformed Church decided they didn't want to contest the claim and they gave the church back. There was a big celebration and the leadership of the two churches got together, and everybody hugged and kissed and shook hands. Nevertheless, I went to visit members of the church after it was returned and asked, "How do you feel today?" What I heard was that, even after receiving their church back, there was still pain and a lot of unfinished business. So restitution for me is not only about giving material things back, but by sharing yourself with another person, both materially and personally.

There are still very, very few close, cross-cultural relationships in this country. This is where Healing of Memories work is important because it lays the groundwork for restitution. Workshops provide an opportunity for those who benefited from apartheid to listen to the painful stories of others and to understand and appreciate the effect that it had on people. Then it becomes easier to consider restitution. The dignity that people lost because of the racist policies of the past was a huge price to pay. One way to begin restoring that dignity is by having the suffering acknowledged by those who benefited. Before that can happen, however, white people must open their ears and eyes to the truth of what was done in their name. Creating an opportunity for people from disadvantaged communities to tell their stories and feel understood can be deeply restorative, but alone it is not enough. Healing of Memories workshops help create the fertile soil in which I can then sow the seeds of tangible, material restitution as well.

*With Madoda Gcwadi at a Southern African conference
on healing of memories in Capetown.*

◇ 12 ◇

Deceptively Simple

◇◇◇◇◇◇

I RISE AFTER DINNER on the opening evening of a Healing of Memories workshop and smile encouragingly at a circle of hopeful, apprehensive faces, anxious in anticipation of what lies ahead. People come to workshops for many reasons, but the common denominator is almost always the feelings we share. "We're about to go on a journey together," I say. "As the weekend progresses, we're going to invite you to tell your story and share the pain of what brought you here. We hope you'll leave some of your burdens behind and be able to move on with the rest of your life feeling lighter. For many of us, this can be a challenging path to walk. We don't want you to feel pushed beyond your limit. This is not magic and we don't give you a certificate that says 'healed' when it's over. What we do offer you is the opportunity to take one step. But it can be a giant step, and in some cases, it may even be life-changing." With that we begin two and a half days of intense emotional work and reflective storytelling, during which people are often astonished at the strength of the bond they develop with others on the journey that transcends race, culture, and nationality.

When seeking healing, human beings naturally turn for guidance to whatever framework they have come to rely on. For me as a priest that framework includes my faith. Lying in my hospital room after the bombing, I experienced an outpouring of caring and concern from around the world. My reflection on my own journey became the starting point for imagining what a Healing of Memories workshop might be like. Above all, it is a deeply interpersonal experience wherein we listen to one another's pain as well as our own and acknowledge our suffering. At an international conference convened by the Institute for Healing Memories in 2004 on Robben Island, theologian Donald Shriver said,

Some say, "Laugh and the world laughs with you; cry, and you cry alone." I think it's precisely the opposite. Laughter can separate us; pain unites us. It's what in one way or another we all understand.

Again and again people bear witness that the common sharing of pain helps them feel less isolated and alone. There is another expression, "What you see is what you get," but that also is not true. We can look around the room and think we know what lies behind the individual faces, but in reality we have no idea. The trust that is generated among participants in a workshop as they tell their individual stories is healing and binds people together, and this in turn helps to restore a sense of belonging and mends the social fabric. That is surely one of the reasons that we have been invited to offer workshops in so many different countries rent by divisions and conflicts, such as Rwanda and Northern Ireland.

The workshop is a powerful psychological, emotional, and spiritual experience that I often say is deceptively simple. That is because it appears to flow with a seamless inevitability from start to finish. That sense of inevitability arises from a sequence of activities that has been painstakingly designed and is attentively watched over by a team of facilitators trained in the flexibility and perceptiveness needed to encourage participants gently along the way. Ideally the workshop is held in a residential setting where people are relieved of the cares and distractions of their ordinary and often difficult lives. There are usually about twenty-five participants, one facilitator for every small group of five or six people, and a lead facilitator who is responsible for setting the tone and presiding over the sessions of the whole group. The workshop begins with the evening meal on the first day and ends after lunch on the third day.

We try to create a sense of community as quickly as possible among people, many of whom have never met before, and so we begin with a shared meal. After dinner we gather in a circle and ask participants to adhere to a set of ground rules that includes a commitment to be present for the entire workshop, to observe strict confidentiality, and to listen respectfully to one another without criticism or giving advice. These guidelines are critical in creating a safe and sacred space in which each person feels respected and valued. A workshop is not an intellectual exercise; it is a journey of the heart. We begin immediately moving people into their feelings with what we call an emotional trigger, a sort of mirror that invites them to face their pain, particularly as it relates to their nation's past. In South Africa we use a small community theater group that enacts a brief but powerful dramatic sketch from the apartheid years. In the United States we have employed an improvisational theater group, and in other contexts we have used photographs, film clips, and newspaper articles to open up feelings. I am sometimes asked, "Don't you think it's a bit dangerous to plunge people into their feelings so abruptly?" Although I am tempted simply to say no, the fuller answer is that when people are greeted from the moment they walk in the door with warmth and compassion and are treated as persons of great value, this is very seldom a problem, especially when two more days remain to work through whatever has been triggered.

After giving people an opportunity to share their reaction to the trigger, we assure them that the next day in small groups they will have all the time they need to tell their story and share more feelings. Then we send them off to bed with a series of questions that we ask them to reflect on, and with a sly smile I often suggest that they sleep with them under their pillow.

> What were the most painful and wonderful experiences of your life?
> How did you survive? How did you find the resources to do so?
> What has been your faith journey?
> How has your nation's past affected you?
> How did the journey of your parents or your grandparents affect you?

And then, we ask three deliberately open-ended questions that are particularly important in relation to both the individual's life and the history of the nation:

> What have you done?
> What was done to you?
> What did you fail to do?

The next morning after a good breakfast and an opportunity to comment on anything left over from the previous evening, we gather in a room with large tables arranged with sheets of blank newsprint paper and an array of colored crayons. There I invite people to draw their life story in the light of the questions they have reflected on overnight and the feelings that are connected with those memories. The request to draw their life story is inevitably met by worried glances and sometimes groans of protest that this is an impossible task. However, after reassurance that this is not an art project and that they are free to draw anything that has meaning for them, along with some joking that representatives from the Museum of Modern Art have agreed to defer their arrival until they've had time to polish their work, people settle into what most find a surprisingly satisfying experience. Some of the drawings are figurative, others abstract; it makes no difference. The drawing is simply an entry point into the person's story, especially his or her feelings about it. It's another way of getting out what is inside of us.

After the drawing the mood shifts. People are still a bit apprehensive, but drawing has energized them. We break into small groups, each with a facilitator. People who know each other are put into separate groups that are constituted to be as diverse as possible with respect to race, religion, ethnicity, gender, and sexual orientation. This is the heart of the work for the second day. Here people begin to tell their stories with a focus not so much on what they think about what happened to them but on what they feel about it. The drawings provide a starting place. A little girl from Fiji once described her drawing as an opportunity to vomit onto the page what she felt. I told this story in Namibia, which prompted another participant to describe the experience as "positive vomiting." Though it sounds crude, even vulgar, it captures an element of what we are doing—acknowledging the pain of the past and letting go of that which is poisonous. It is a powerful image, because in our small groups one can sometimes feel as if someone is, almost literally, vomiting something toxic, and the group often shares the feeling of relief when the poison is out. People must be encouraged to feel to the fullest, no matter how uncomfortable, because we cannot let go of feelings that we don't own. People need space to be weak and vulnerable for a time before they can become strong. Healing can be painful, a bit like the surgeon's knife.

Groups continue for about four or five hours with a lunch break and shorter breaks during the day. Some groups need almost no facilitation, whereas others do. A skillful facilitator can unobtrusively guide a group without getting in the way, yet still be prepared to step in if a difficult situation arises. Facilitators in our model are on the same plane as group members, so they too share their stories. What follows can seem quite magical. People take turns speaking, leading off from their drawing. We welcome group interaction after a person has shared, but at any given moment the focus remains on one person's story. As the day moves on great pain is expressed and an equal measure of compassion. No feelings are discouraged or declared illegitimate. Some people say at the beginning of the workshop, "I totally hate such and such a person or category of persons and I will never, ever forgive them for what they did to me." But in the context of the workshop they begin to confront what this poison is doing to them, and they begin to realize that for the sake of their own freedom, they need to let go of it. Intimacy is generated by the authenticity of the sharing. Pumla Gobodo-Madikizela, a psychologist and a member of our board, who was part of one of our small groups, described the experience in this way:

> There were tears in the room. People cried about the pain that was being shared, but they were also crying about their own pain. And that is the beauty of what I experienced. It's what psychologists have observed so often—that when you begin to articulate what the pain is about, that is when you begin to heal. Many people shared things that they have never shared before, things they had only thought and felt, but never actually put into words. The healing and the cleansing begins with the tears, and the words, and finding the language to talk about your pain. Experiencing other people's pain connected us, and that was the beauty of the moment. . . . The way to healing what has happened in our countries is not within private rooms with our private therapists. Instead it involves ways that our stories can become linked together as they have today.

The depth of pain touched in some workshops is almost more than the human spirit can bear. I think of a workshop we held in Port au Prince, Haiti, that was arranged by our Haitian American friend Georgette Delinois. There, one Haitian mother said simply, "I have been humiliated all my life." The words seared my flesh and entered my soul. I prayed that the workshop would give this woman an experience of being valued and respected for once in her life. In some groups the intimacy can feel transcendent and holds those present in a loving warm embrace, even when great pain, anger, and grief have been the dominant emotions. Often the depth reached can be measured by the silence that follows, and that can be the sign of a powerful healing force at work and a manifestation of God's grace.

After the small groups we reconvene for about an hour before the evening meal to talk about our experiences and provide a little conceptual framework for understanding what has transpired. The change in mood is dramatic. Faces are bright and filled with energy. A gentle liveliness permeates the room mixed with emotional exhaustion. We invite people to share feelings and reflect on the overall experience. One hears comments like,

> I was so nervous before we began, and I thought, "I can't do this." And the truth is I've never in my life shared some of the things I did with the people in my group. It was wonderful. I feel lighter.

Recurrent themes emerge such as loss, grief, anger, and abandonment, but also joy and hope. Articulating them unites the whole group and underscores the commonality of the human experience across boundaries. A sense of relief and camaraderie is palpable. Confidentiality mandates that what is said in the small group stays there, so people do not share specifics of anyone else's story, but they can share their own if they choose and some do. One South African woman said,

> I haven't spoken to my mother for years because she left us. Now I realize she was probably afraid the police would kill us after she got involved in the antiapartheid struggle. It's changed my whole feeling about her. (This woman subsequently reconciled with her mother.)

In some instances there is an opportunity to help people begin to make sense out of their past in ways they may not have previously thought possible. For example, an inmate in a prison workshop said during this discussion,

> I never thought much about myself before, but now I can see that the anger I felt at my father when he came home drunk and beat us was connected to why I got so angry and killed that policeman.

This is also the session in which people begin to make sense of what their Healing of Memories process is really all about. They begin to "get it." People also often raise conceptual issues, asking, "But how do we forgive?" "Is it possible to forget the past?" Participants gain wisdom and insight from one another. This is empowering, and the discussion can enable people to fashion a new, more hopeful meaning to their life experience. After everyone who wishes has spoken, there is a sense of quiet satisfaction. People are tired, but they feel happy and victorious.

After this we adjourn for dinner, and that evening we have a party. Its character varies greatly from group to group, but it is a chance for people to relax and enjoy one another after what has been a deep and intense experience during the day. Sometimes it is lively with impromptu performances, singing and dancing and much laughter, or it can be an opportunity for informal conversation with music playing quietly in the background. Either way, it is a time for enjoying refreshments and nurturing new friendships. Facilitators relax as well but are also available for quiet conversation with participants who may need to follow up loose ends from the small groups.

Liturgies point us in a direction, which is why they are important elements in rites of passage. I am writing this during Easter week with its message that crucifixion is not the end of the story—there is Easter morning in all its glory. Life arises from suffering and death, promise triumphs over despair, and victims become victors. So, on the third and final day of the workshop, we begin to move away from a focus on the past and create a liturgy of celebration that looks to the future. The form it takes can be, and often is, completely secular. However, if everyone present is from a particular faith community, it may be clothed in religious imagery and can even include the Eucharist. It is up to the group. The morning is spent in preparation.

When we are victims, we are passive. As we heal we become active and take back agency. In the Christian tradition Paul speaks of us as coworkers with Christ in building God's kingdom. In that spirit participants create a peace symbol out of clay into which they later incorporate a lighted candle. They may add flowers and greenery or any other elements they wish to give the symbol a special vitality. When all the peace symbols have been prepared, the whole group chooses a theme and devises an overall plan for the celebration, after which each small group meets for a short time and creates an offering for the ceremony such as a song or dance, a skit, or a reading that reflects its members experience of the workshop. By now the mood is upbeat and forward looking, reflecting the creative energy that has gone into the planning. We break for a final lunch together.

After lunch we invite participants to choose something from the past that they wish to leave behind, whether a burden or a destructive feeling. Everyone is given a small sheet of paper and writes on it whatever he or she has chosen. What the participants write is private and known only to them. Then the liturgy begins with a solemn procession, either silent or accompanied by singing, from the meeting room to a spot outdoors where a fire has been prepared. When I lead the workshop I always wear a beautifully embroidered stole that was given to me by Albie Sachs, a former judge of South Africa's Constitutional Court, who like me was injured, in his case by a car bomb. The stole, made by mothers whose children disappeared in Chile during the Pinochet dictatorship, symbolizes their loss and their struggle to know what happened to their children. After briefly describing the significance of the stole, I invoke the spirit of solidarity with people around the world like these mothers and acknowledge the important work that people have done at the workshop. Then each person, in turn, places his or her paper in the fire. When all have been burned and a few moments of silence have been observed, the procession returns to the meeting room for the remainder of the ceremony.

The skits and presentations that follow are a wondrous mixture of sadness and joy, solemnity and laughter. A recent ceremony at a workshop we did in White Plains, New York, stands out in my mind. A group of African Americans presented verses from Ecclesiastes 3 as a rap that was jaw-droppingly creative, joyous, and moving:

> To every thing there is a season, a time to every pur-
> pose under heaven:
> A time to be born, and a time to die; a time to plant,
> and a time to pluck up what is planted,
> A time to kill, and a time to heal; a time to break
> down, and a time to build up,
> A time to weep, and a time to laugh; a time to mourn,
> and a time to dance.

The presentation of the peace symbols concludes the liturgy and the workshop. Healing is leaving behind the poison of the past and reclaiming the ability once again to build and shape the world. That is an idea that resonates with human beings whether they are religious or secular, and the ceremony we are about to perform embodies this. We gather in a circle. Candles are lit by passing the flame from one person to another, and then each in turn steps forward, relates the meaning of his or her symbol, and places it in the center of the circle. Some honor a person dear to them, living or dead; others recognize someone who has hurt them or express the willingness to reconcile with someone from whom they have been estranged. When all have spoken, we stand in a moment of reverence before this flickering mandala of light and hope that symbolizes the wisdom and healing power we have generated for one another and the world.

All humans, whether religious or not, are spiritual beings. In a Healing of Memories workshop we use the physical enactment of liturgy to access the world of the spirit. For some people the workshop provides an extremely deep experience that can be the turning point in a long journey. It can be the point where people leave victimhood behind and see new possibilities. People have embraced the Healing of Memories methodology in cultural contexts as different as post-apartheid South Africa, Rwanda, and Berkeley, California. It's something we ourselves have marveled at ever since our first offering outside South Africa at the Riverside Church in New York. At the same time, when we work across the globe in varied situations of culture and conflict, facilitators must necessarily attend to the particularities of the local context.

On reflection, I have come to believe that, while there are indeed cultural differences among people, human beings are human beings the world over. People know when they are being treated with the love and respect accorded a child of God, whether it is articulated in those words or not. The workshop is a sort of open container into which people are free to place their unique and valued personal and cultural contributions. I am fond of a lovely photograph on the wall of our office in Cape Town that was taken at a Healing of Memories workshop that I did some years ago in Alice Springs in the heart of Australia's Aboriginal territory. It was a very hot day in this arid country and we had moved outdoors. There is a lot of motion in the photograph depicting drummers and dancers decorated with body paint in colorful patterns joining in our celebration at the end of a workshop. Nothing could be more different in appearance and tone from a workshop in New York or Hamburg, but underneath there is a common spiritual language of pain as well as joy and peace that speaks to everyone.

We can think of the entire Healing of Memories workshop as an extended liturgy. Religious liturgies have a transcendent quality that opens our hearts to relationships—with those with whom we share a common faith and with God. In a Healing of Memories workshop those relationships may include others on the workshop journey and significant persons living or dead who are not physically present. The safe and sacred space we create not only allows participants to feel connected with one another but also to be in touch with whatever each person understands as the ultimate ground of being, whether or not that is personalized as God. From the beginning I was clear that all faith traditions have gold to mine in relation to journeys of healing and wholeness. While the majority of people in South Africa are Christian there are also many Muslims, Jews, and Hindus, and we seek to provide a home for people of different faiths and those who have none. Sometimes in interfaith work people look for the lowest common denominator rather than being willing to share the riches of their faith tradition with one another.

Another thing about liturgy is that it is used to mark a rite of passage. All cultures have celebrations that signify important life transitions. So, for example, two individuals come as single people and leave as a married couple; or a child comes for circumcision and leaves as an adult. The role of liturgy as a celebration of these rites of passage fascinated me. It seemed to me that we could create a liturgy that would allow us to let go of poisonous feelings from the past and claim victory. In a Healing of Memories workshop we hope that while people may come with heavy burdens, they leave feeling freer than when they arrived and move from being an object of history to becoming an agent of history once again. Of course this rite of passage may be only the beginning of a journey, just as circumcision is only the beginning of becoming a man, but liturgies nonetheless have great power.

For some, whether or not they think of themselves as religious, the experience can be transcendent. A man wrote me recently about his reflection on a workshop he had attended a month previously:

> I have found it difficult to relate the experience to others because every description falls so far short of the power of the moment. It's a bit like trying to convey a dream to someone else. I guess it's a matter of grasping how something so simple can be so profound.

While a Healing of Memories workshop does not depend on Christian imagery, there are echoes of the gospel that are implicit in its design. The heart of the gospel story is that Jesus triumphs over crucifixion and death, and Thomas, overcoming disbelief, thrusts his hand into the still-visible wound of the resurrected Jesus. So like Jesus, our wounds may remain visible but they can be healed, and then we are no longer their prisoner. The signs of the crucifixion had not disappeared, but Jesus' wounds were no longer bleeding. I think that tells us something about God's will for the human family—that we are called to recognize and acknowledge the terrible things that we have done to one another, but then we are called to stop being crucifiers. We are called not to be a Good Friday people but to be an Easter people. The idea of the wounded healer is thus deep within Christian theology. The victim triumphs not by becoming a victimizer of others but rather by becoming fully himself or herself. It was St. Irenaeus of Lyons who asserted that the glory of God is a human being fully alive.

◇ 13 ◇

Founding the Institute
for Healing of Memories

◇◇◇◇◇◇◇

OUR FIRST OFFICE WAS IN A COTTAGE next to Braehead House, a home for retired priests. It was September 1998 when Shanti, Barry, and I said our goodbyes to the Trauma Centre and moved to the Kenilworth neighborhood of Cape Town in what are called the southern suburbs, really just a residential area at some distance from the city center. I was pleased that Shanti and Barry had decided to accompany me. After all, they could have said, "Thank you, but no thank you. We're going on to other things," but instead they signed on to an enterprise that none of us was entirely sure of. Still, this was only four years after the election, and there was a sense of possibility everywhere in the air. We felt we were embarking on an exciting adventure that would contribute to the healing of our country. Without the continuity that Shanti and Barry provided, the Institute would have had a far more difficult start. Shanti had been my personal assistant at the chaplaincy project, and she knew our work inside out. At the Trauma Centre we had a support staff that kept track of finances, ordered supplies, provided maintenance, and managed the thousand small things necessary to keep a organization running. Now Shanti took over every aspect of running our little office, a role she filled quite capably; later, when our staff increased, she was able to relinquish her other duties and concentrate on managing our finances. Barry had already shouldered great responsibility in helping organize the first Healing of Memories workshops as part of the chaplaincy project, and for the past four years we had offered workshops together in every province save KwaZulu-Natal. He was a skilled facilitator and when I was traveling outside the country, as I was increasingly, I had full confidence in him. Barry, a trained social worker, stayed with the new Institute for Healing of Memories for two more years, after which he returned to his home in Upington to become chief social worker at an agency there.

Our quarters at Braehead House were a bit cramped. Shanti complained that they were quite chilly in winter and that many of the sweet, elderly, retired priests assumed that we were there to provide fax services for them; they tottered up our stairs to request assistance whenever the occasion arose. Eventually, we relocated to a larger office suite in the building occupied by the Western Cape Provincial Council of Churches, and that remained our home for several years. We shared office equipment and some services with the Council of Churches, and we offered Healing of Memories workshops jointly with the Centre for Ubuntu, which occupied an office next to us.

I was keen from the start that we should have a board of directors that was diverse and harmonious. Coming from my experience of conflict at the Trauma Centre, I thought, "Let's carefully choose people who believe in Healing of Memories work, people who will have their own opinions and not be afraid to express them and will bring a range of gifts, but also people who will work together smoothly." I think we achieved that very well. We were very fortunate that Glenda Wildschut agreed to be our first board chairperson. During her tenure as a board member at the Trauma Centre she had been a staunch supporter of Healing of Memories work, and President Mandela later appointed her to the Truth and Reconciliation Commission. Glenda provided our board with leadership and stature for more than a decade. These were historic times, and the board members had a sense that together we were helping to create the future. I remember one of our first meetings when we worked on developing a mission statement. As I looked around the table I thought to myself that it was quite a marvelous thing we were doing, for our decisions were shaping the organization for years to come—an organization we all hoped would make a significant contribution to healing our damaged nation.

Not long after our successful workshop at the Riverside Church in early 1998, I received an invitation to offer a Healing of Memories workshop in Rwanda. It would be only the second workshop we had offered outside South Africa. At the very moment in April 1994 when we South Africans were celebrating our first democratic election, Rwanda was in the midst of the terrible genocide. The truth is that most of us South Africans were so busy enjoying our hard-won victory that we hardly registered the terrible atrocities engulfing our neighbor to the north. It was a painful irony, and ever after our countries' destinies have seemed joined by some incomprehensible twist of fate. The invitation to come to Rwanda was not completely unexpected. Earlier that year I had been visited at the Trauma Centre by a delegation from World Vision in Rwanda. World Vision, an international Christian organization, was struggling to help Rwandans cope with the aftermath of the genocide. Its staff had learned of the chaplaincy program at the Trauma Centre, and some had come to see for themselves what we were doing. While with us they joined one of our workshops. The result was the invitation to conduct a workshop in Rwanda. In some ways I dreaded the visit. I worried about whether I had anything to offer a nation still coming to terms with the enormity of the genocide.

I was accompanied to Rwanda by Brenda Rhode, one of our most experienced facilitators. It was an emotionally grueling experience for both of us. The Rwandese had made a decision to keep a number of the genocide sites exactly as they were. I remember being deeply concerned about how I would cope with the gruesome sight of thousands of bodies in varying stages of decay. When I shared my misgivings with a Rwandan friend, he looked at me and said quietly, "Well, Father, if you can't cope, how do you imagine we can?" I knew in that moment what would be required of me, and I prayed fervently that I would not be found wanting. Of course part of our humanness is that we should be deeply, deeply moved. What would be wrong with us if we could see such things and not be profoundly affected?

We were taken to sites where, four years after the genocide, we witnessed sickening piles of skeletal human remains often surrounded by a tangle of clothing that had been worn by the victims. What seemed particularly horrific was that large numbers of people were killed on the altars of churches. We human beings did this. Our fellow Christians did this. What does it mean to be part of a human family that is capable of such monstrous atrocities? As a Christian the reality that the genocide happened in churches totally confronted my own faith. How could this possibly have happened? What does it say about people's understanding of the Christian gospel? It threatened to completely overwhelm me.

Our Healing of Memories workshop, organized by World Vision, was attended almost entirely by survivors of the genocide and relatives of those who had been killed. We were told beforehand that Rwandese men don't cry, but we discovered that given permission and a safe and caring space, they do cry, and they did. This is something we've seen time and again in cultures where it is said that men don't cry; yet we find they welcome the opportunity when the setting is right. It is not that we in the Institute have a need for people to cry, but crying is part of the human response to terrible things. For many of those present the workshop provided an opportunity to confront their deepest feelings about the genocide and the magnitude of their loss. In the case of Rwanda, it will take a long time for most people to recover fully, if they ever do, but I think we succeeded in providing a healing presence for those who trusted us enough to share their terrible stories.

The resilience of the human spirit is impossible to overstate. I think of a workshop I did with people in Northern Uganda who had been victims of the Lord's Resistance Army. Some of the pain we listened to was almost unbearable. Layer upon layer of the most horrendous things had been done to people. The word I like to use about some stories is that they *imprint* on us. We are marked by them. It's almost as if they are etched into us physically. In that workshop there was a woman who had lost limbs, and she said to a group of other people who had also lost limbs, "You know, I was a peasant farmer before I lost my legs, and I am still a peasant farmer." What she meant was, "It's OK. I'm living a life," and she was saying that to other people, some of whom had given up hope. So she became a role model of possibilities. I think we are called to be signs of hope, but to do that we must be able to deal with our own woundedness. Time after time in our work around the world I am humbled by people who have been victims of terrible violence and yet have been able reach deep into their hearts and touch a place that enables them to move into the future with a measure of peace and hope and to become a light to others.

The Riverside Church workshop and the one in Rwanda taken together marked a turning point in my vision of our future work. No two contexts could have been more different, and yet in both instances people claimed the process for their own. The pain of the human family knows no boundaries of geography, culture, or class, and it became evident that with God's help we had devised a method that spoke to people in their great diversity. Going forward, I began to foresee our work unfolding on a larger stage than I had dared to imagine previously. At the same time we never move into a situation unasked; rather, we always seek to respond to invitations that come from partners who request our help. I needn't have worried; requests from overseas soon rolled in.

At the same time we continued offering workshops throughout the length and breadth of South Africa through our partnership with the South African Council of Churches. The workshops in South Africa focus on the apartheid experience, which, directly or indirectly, underlies almost every other trauma. Still, people bring to the workshops what they bring, and so we have found ourselves dealing with a range of issues including abandonment and abuse of children, marital abuse, criminal and political violence, and the violence of poverty itself.

The problems in KwaZulu-Natal (KZN) were particularly fraught. Many years of violence between communities that were historically loyal to the ANC and others loyal to a rival political party called the IFP had left deep rifts in the social fabric. While much of the violence was originally fomented by the apartheid state, once set in motion it escalated out of control and internecine warfare wracked the province for many years up to and beyond the 1994 election. Unhealed wounds lay just beneath the surface, and by the early 2000s the conflict had settled down sufficiently that, working with local partner organizations, we could begin offering Healing of Memories workshops in areas that had been the sites of conflict. Because of the social disruption caused by the political conflict, criminal and domestic violence were rife in families and communities, and, in a not unrelated way, KZN also became the epicenter of the HIV/AIDS epidemic in South Africa. The pain associated with these traumas, including the stigmatization of people living with HIV, surfaced in nearly every workshop.

We continued to work with the aftermath of the political violence, and in 2005 we began partnering with the Pietermaritzberg Agency for Christian Social Awareness (PACSA) to offer workshops specifically designed to serve the needs of people infected and affected by HIV/AIDS. In 2007 we appointed a full-time coordinator for KZN, Mpendulo Nyembe, and in 2009 we opened a satellite office in the Durban area. Our HIV/AIDS workshops are offered in conjunction with already existing HIV/AIDS support groups, so people have ongoing support. Intolerance often based on fear was and still is rife in South Africa, and people infected with the virus often suffer in silence, fearing discrimination, abandonment by their families, and even violence. For example, a member of the staff of a partner organization who is herself living with HIV said, "Long before this virus kills me, the loneliness will." We began to think of people as suffering from "multiple woundedness." For example, an elderly grandmother who attended one of our workshops carries pain typical of others in her community. She is supporting several of her grandchildren on a wholly inadequate state pension. Her adult son, the grandchildren's father, and his wife have both died of AIDS, and this same woman is living with unworked-through grief from the death of several of her children who were casualties of the struggle against apartheid and the later political violence.

South Africa is not alone. HIV/AIDS is rife throughout the subcontinent. In 2007 and 2008 we were asked by Norwegian Church Aid and the Norwegian government to train facilitators working with people living with HIV/AIDS in Zambia and Malawi. The idea was that, step by step, we would enable caregivers working with those affected to offer Healing of Memories workshops.

South Africa is the most developed economy on the continent, and it has become the destination of many thousands of refugees fleeing instability, war, famine, and persecution in countries as nearby as Zimbabwe and the Democratic Republic of the Congo and as far away as Rwanda and Burundi. In South Africa these refugees find welcome and kindness as well as antagonism and violence. Some of our own people fear competition for scarce jobs and government services, do not understand their languages, and resent what they often see as their strange ways. As an Institute we have organized community forums to combat xenophobia, and we have spoken out sharply against the violence directed at refugees, many of whom are already traumatized by war and the death or disappearance of family members in their home countries. For some years we have cooperated with refugee organizations in offering Healing of Memories workshops for the individuals they serve, overwhelmingly women. There are many challenges with these workshops, not least that several languages may be spoken in a single workshop. Some refugees have experienced unspeakable violence that has left them disturbed, distrustful, and quite fragile emotionally, so these workshops require especially sensitive and delicate facilitation. On the other hand, responses we receive from participants afterward indicate that they came away with more confidence to deal with their difficult life situations and a feeling that there are South Africans who care. A welcome benefit that we did not anticipate is that a sense of solidarity develops at the workshop among women from different countries who are residents in the same shelter. As one woman put it,

> I live in the refugee center with stress and depression that I carried from my country. The women there do not get time to talk to one another because everybody is busy with their problems and there is lack of trust among us. Also, we do not have a safe place that allows us to meditate and share our experiences in privacy.

This same woman went on to say that the bond she made with the women from other countries will make her life in the center easier, and it will be possible for the women to come together and better advocate for themselves. Following serious xenophobic violence in 2009, we changed tactics and, in order to further mutual understanding, we began to place South Africans and foreign nationals in the same workshop.

It had been my dream for some time to be able to offer Healing of Memories workshops to prison inmates, and in 2005 we began an ongoing series of workshops in prisons. Despite having done terrible things to others, most inmates have themselves been victims of serious abuse. The public sees only the perpetrator, but deep inside these men early wounds have festered and emerged years later in the criminal behavior that brought them to prison. Healing of Memories workshops seek to break the chain whereby the victim becomes the perpetrator by acknowledging the pain of the past and helping inmates to see the connection between their own mistreatment and their victimization of others. When inmates are able to tell their stories in small groups, protected by the promise of confidentiality and treated with respect for their humanity, pent-up emotions of anger, hurt, rejection, guilt, and shame come tumbling out, and they often spontaneously make the link between the abuse visited on them and their abuse of others. I believe this is a precondition for perpetrators to experience genuine regret and to take responsibility for what they have done. In our experience it is not uncommon for inmates to report in follow-up interviews that they have contacted those they have harmed to make apology or amends. On the occasions when our Healing of Memories workshop has been offered as a part of a course on restorative justice, this outcome has been even more evident.

I am often asked what evidence we have that Healing of Memories workshops make a difference in people's lives. From earliest days we have given questionnaires to participants at the end of a workshop, asking them to tell us how the experience was for them, and the responses have been overwhelmingly positive. Most of our facilitators also tell us that they volunteered because their first Healing of Memories workshop changed their lives. So we have a great deal of anecdotal information. Still, we understood the need for a more systematic look at the evidence.

As a preliminary to embarking on a formal research study we conducted in-depth interviews with key figures in several partner organizations. In one interview, a case worker from an agency that serves abused children related that sending teenage girls who had been abducted into sexual slavery to a Healing of Memories workshop had sufficiently unlocked their feelings that for the first time it had become possible to work with them in their day-treatment program. A professor of social development at a university said she sent students to Healing of Memories workshops because they learned essential listening skills that made them more effective community workers. Recently, cooperating with the University of the Western Cape, we have put in place a program wherein our workshop facilitators can obtain university certification.

In 2006, with the help of a research grant from the Rehabilitation and Research Centre for Torture Victims (RCT) in Copenhagen, we undertook a more formal evaluation of our workshops. The subjects were facilitators and former participants, and we were particularly interested in whether the workshops had a long-term impact on people's lives. To that end we interviewed and sent questionnaires to participants several months after they had attended a workshop. The results were quite positive. For example, one person said,

> I was carrying anger and hatred toward my mother for so many years. This stopped me from forgiving and reconciling. During the workshop I realized that I am the one who is carrying the burden and this burden is destroying me. Soon after the workshop, I decided to go and talk to my mother. I reconciled with her and I forgave her. We have started a new relationship since then.

People were realistic; they understood that this was only one step. For example,

> I managed to let go of anger and guilt caused by apartheid while I was growing up. It is not to say that all my pain has gone, but when I look at the picture of how I was before the workshop, I realize that at least my pain is not the same now.

The workshops also had an impact on racial understanding,

> I was a white person in a predominantly black group. Nevertheless, through the small-group sharing, I felt accepted as I am and encouraged to be myself. It is important for me to be accepted by black people because of the history of our country.

Facilitators who were interviewed spoke about their motivation for volunteering, one saying,

I continue to be motivated by seeing participants dropping the burdens of the past . . . listening to a participant saying, "I do not need to carry that anymore. I do not need to hold it that much. I want to go back home after the workshop with a sense of rightness."

Positive results have come from other research, including three doctoral dissertations, one in South Africa and two in the United States.

A second important strand of our work in South Africa has been with youth who are too young to have experienced apartheid directly. Some of them who attended Healing of Memories workshops said to us, "Actually, we didn't come for healing so much as to learn what happened to our parents under apartheid, because they don't like to talk about it." Reflecting on this, I realized that as a country if we were going to avoid the mistakes of the past, we had to involve these young people who were the first generation who grew up after apartheid but who were nevertheless living with its effects. It happened that on my travels to the United States I had encountered an organization called Facing History and Ourselves. It partners with organizations in other countries to aid them in preparing school materials that teach history and a culture of human rights. We were able to establish a relationship and, working with it, we designed an innovative school curriculum that used specially created audiovisual materials and experiential exercises to teach the history of apartheid and encouraged students to open a dialogue with their parents. It challenges them to think about what they can do in their daily lives to develop a culture of human rights among their fellow students in post-apartheid South Africa. Themba Lonzi, our youth coordinator at the time, put it very aptly when he said, "Education needs to have a moral component if it seeks to develop more humane people."

We recently redesigned our youth program to nurture young people with the potential to become leaders whom we hope will in turn affect the lives of others. We decided to focus on developing the knowledge and leadership skills of a core group of thirty young people through a year-long program in three Cape Town communities. The young people attend training workshops and have established Restoring Humanity youth groups in their communities. They visit important historical sites related to the history of apartheid as part of their investigation of how the wounds of the past shape the present, and they practice leadership skills by being mentored in organizing youth events in their own communities. They are encouraged to develop their own solutions for building a more humane and nonviolent society, and at the end of the year they will have produced a case study based on their observations and analysis and a self-critique of their interventions. The program is now beginning in KwaZulu-Natal as well.

A third strand of our work concerned ex-combatants. In 2002 we opened a comprehensive social development program for them. During the apartheid years many school-age youth joined the liberation struggle, some left the country and went into exile, and most missed out on their schooling. Now in adulthood, they are an uneducated group often living in abject poverty with resentment that their sacrifices have gone unrecognized and susceptible to being recruited for criminal behavior. They are sometimes referred to as the lost generation. Our program was a combination of career guidance, skills training, personal counseling, and Healing of Memories workshops. The name of the program, Ndabikum, means "Now it is my turn," a phrase that underscores the program's dual emphasis on recognizing the contribution they have made and insisting that they take personal responsibility to use the help that is available. Unfortunately, the government funds that supported the program dried up, and it never reached full maturity. We are hopeful that in the future we may once again secure adequate long-term funding for the project. The need has not gone away.

14

◇◇◇◇◇◇

Cuba

◇◇◇◇◇◇◇

I FIRST LEARNED ABOUT CUBA from Bishop Colin Winter soon after I arrived in South Africa. He described Cuba in gospel terms as providing good news for poor people, and I dreamed of one day seeing for myself what a socialist society looks like close up. I admired Bishop Winter because he was a fearless Anglican bishop who criticized the unjust, racist exploitation of Namibian migrant workers by the South African colonial government, and he acted on his convictions by mobilizing the resources of the church in their defense. As a result the apartheid regime expelled him from Namibia, just as it would soon banish me from South Africa. His outspoken witness made a deep impression on me, a young priest still reeling from the impact of my first encounter with apartheid. From him I drew support for my own conviction that a commitment to justice and the gospel are and should be intertwined, and this too reinforced my interest in the Cuban experience. However, it was not until 1985, when I was working for the Lutheran World Federation in Zimbabwe, that I had an opportunity to go to Cuba. What I saw affected me greatly, not only because it offered an example of a country striving to create a more egalitarian society, but because in its military and medical aid to other struggling countries it exemplified the meaning of international solidarity in the cause of human liberation.

I feel a great debt to Cuba both for what it has given me personally and for the contribution it made to the freedom of the countries of Southern Africa. Its efforts to create a society organized in the interests of the poor majority make it a role model. Beyond that, although poor itself, it provided generous technical assistance to other developing countries, including South Africa. While I was living in Zimbabwe I knew Cubans working there, and the ambassador was a friend of mine. In fact, I had been in Cuba only the week before my bombing, and so it was in that context that I was offered free medical care in Cuba. I promised the ambassador when he came to see me in the hospital that when I returned to South Africa I would repay Cuba's generosity. That I did by founding the Friends of Cuba Society with a group of likeminded South Africans. I became its first national president and remained its chairperson in Cape Town until recently.

Over the years I have made many visits to Cuba, and Cubans have come to know me well. For them, as for me, there are echoes of Che Guevara's story in my own. He was a foreigner who came to Cuba from another country and fought alongside Fidel, and although people in Cuba may not have been conscious of this, I feel a powerful personal identification with him, in that when he was killed in 1967 in Bolivia his hands were chopped off. So even though I'm a tiny figure by comparison, our lives were in some ways parallel. Che's body was returned to Cuba after his death, and his remains are interred in a mausoleum in Santa Clara where he fought in the final victorious battle of the Cuban revolution. I made a pilgrimage there, and the opportunity to lay flowers at his grave was a deeply poignant moment for me.

In 1996 I was honored by the Cuban Council of State, which awarded me the Cuban Friendship Medal in Havana, and Cuban television made a prize-winning documentary in South Africa about me. Not long after it was shown in Cuba, I was shopping in a Havana street market and a souvenir vendor stopped me and recounted to me my life story that he had just seen on television. Then he said I could choose whatever I liked from his wares as a way of thanking me for the contribution I'd made to the liberation of South Africa and my support for his country.

I was used to traveling to poor, developing countries that built showy stadiums, splendid first-class hotels, and prestigious public buildings. Cuba demonstrated a different set of priorities altogether. Here was a place where the government allowed its capital city, Havana, to remain relatively shabby so that it could put its resources toward the development of its human capital and address people's social needs. In Cuba a child could go from crèche to university at government expense. There was no sign of hunger, and unlike other poor countries, no one was begging in the streets. The health-care system provided doctors in every locality, including rural areas, and they lived in the communities they served instead of in expensive homes in upmarket suburbs. Everyone had a job and a place to live, however modest. Of course much of this was possible because of the support of the Soviet Union. The socialist countries provided Cuba an economic lifeline in exchange for sugar and other agricultural commodities. With the fall of the Berlin Wall in 1989, only four years after my first visit, much of this support evaporated. The implacable hostility of the United States created very hard times for Cuba, and some of these achievements began to unravel. Nevertheless, to this day I stand in awe of the extraordinary accomplishments of this very poor society in providing health care and reducing infant mortality, in offering quality education, and in excelling in culture and sports. As a visiting South African who was fervently looking toward the eventual liberation of my own country, I found these achievements deeply encouraging.

Some other countries make the assumption from a distance that Cuba is a "Godless society." While it is true that its programs are not motivated by Christian faith, I have been welcomed in my role as a priest. I met the dean of the Episcopal Cathedral in Havana, Fr. Juan Ramon de la Paz, on a trip to Guantanamo and the two of us became friends. I was invited to preach there and concelebrate at mass several times. In 2000 while I was visiting Cuba the South African ambassador, Mosia Makhaya, was taken sick and died. I was blessed to be able to minister to the ambassador, who was also my friend, while he was dying, and I conducted the memorial service at the cathedral in Havana, which was packed with mourners. On another trip I visited a tiny church on Holy Thursday where the parishioners were mainly from the Caribbean and had immigrated to Cuba years earlier. They were practicing their faith at Easter freely. I have also spoken at the Martin Luther King Center in Havana, an ecumenical organization that actively promotes Christian social responsibility and nonviolent progressive change. The view that Cuba is hostile to religion is also challenged in a thoughtful book published in 2006, *Fidel and Religion: Conversations with Frei Betto on Marxism and Liberation Theology,* in which Fidel speaks about the compatibility of liberation theology and socialism. So, while in reality Cuba is not a particularly religious society, in its view of the world it has a strong spirituality. It is true that there are those who complain that things are very tough for the church, but others are appreciative of the gains and benefits that the revolution had created. Over the years I have made good friends with Cuban Christians, and while they may have their own criticisms, many nevertheless see the government's policies as a living out of gospel values.

As much as I admire the immense achievements of the revolution, I disagree with certain of its policies. Of course, that is equally true of my attitude toward South Africa. Still, even on my first trip in 1985, there were hints of authoritarian strands in the fabric of the society.

Although I detected nothing overt, I was aware that the space for dissent was contested, and of course Cuba is a one-party state. Nevertheless, the country was dedicated to meeting the basic needs of its people, and that captured my imagination as a Christian. At that stage it was probably the only country in Latin America where no child went to bed hungry. So while I was conscious that there were elements I might not agree with, there were immense achievements. Ironically, the only part of Cuba where there is torture and unlimited detention without trial is in the area under the jurisdiction of the United States.

One issue that has troubled me over the years in many countries is the status of gay and lesbian people. Most socialist countries have been quite homophobic, and Cuba has been no exception. It has, however, moved a long way, step by step. The prize-winning film "Strawberry and Chocolate," now more than ten years old, was a breakthrough. It is about a friendship in Cuba between a gay man and a member of the Cuban Communist Party, and I think it enabled the country to take another look at the issue of the rights of LGBT people. The second issue that has deeply concerned me is the death penalty, which I have always opposed. I campaigned against it in South Africa, and it was a major triumph when we constitutionally abolished it. In Cuba, by contrast, in 2003 a ferry boat was hijacked and within one week the hijackers were tried, convicted, and three of them were executed by firing squad. When I was invited to Cuba the following year to speak about the achievements of ten years of democracy in South Africa, I took the opportunity to call for an end to the death penalty, and I personally raised this matter with the Cuban foreign minister. The media ignored my comments, but privately a number of government people expressed their own opposition to the death penalty.

Cuba taught us the meaning of international solidarity, for it gave generous support to the ANC and the South West People's Organization (SWAPO), not just militarily, but by providing education and training in many fields to a great number of exiles. There are today in South Africa Spanish-speaking members of government who received their education in Cuba. It is also true that Cuba supported the liberation struggle militarily. In 1987–88 their troops saved the day by joining with Angolans to corner the South African army during the Battle of Cuito Cuanavale in Southern Angola. It was a decisive battle in which the South Africans received their comeuppance. The Cubans could have taken a large number of South African lives, but they chose not to. The victory of the liberation forces was a turning point that led to negotiations for the independence of Namibia and foreshadowed the freedom of South Africa itself. In 1998 Fidel Castro came to South

Africa to address parliament. During his visit I had the unforgettable privilege of meeting him face to face and chairing a fascinating three-hour meeting where he laid out in detail the strategy and maneuvers the Cubans had used to win their victory at the Battle of Cuito Cuanavale. I think people in the West saw Cuba simply as a tool of the Soviet Union, but Cuba was always its own master. Cubans rightly say, "We went into Africa and the only thing we took out was our dead." They didn't come for gold or diamonds or oil as the colonial powers had done, and we in the liberation movement owe them a great deal.

Less controversial, but equally exemplary, has been the example of Cuban doctors and other health personnel and professionals who have gone to the ends of the earth to aid the development of other poor countries. And it isn't only poor Africans who have received the benefit of Cuban medical education. Despite the embargo and hostility of the United States, Cuba welcomed young African Americans and provided them with a free medical education. Once South Africa became a democratic state, Cuba began sending us medical doctors and provided medical training to our own students. Cuban doctors were prepared to go to remote parts of South Africa where young South African doctors would not go. To this day they have a number of personnel in our country, in a range that includes physicians, housing specialists, and even architects. So practical solidarity continues and not just with South Africa. An article in the November 8, 2011, issue of the *New York Times* highlights Cuba's role in fighting the cholera epidemic in Haiti after international NGOs and other governments had abandoned the country. The Cuban commitment has staying power. The article reports that the Cubans have asked the United States to join them and help finance a major hospital that would be part of the remaking of the Haitian health care system, but "no deal has emerged."

The illegal blockade of Cuba by the United States seems to me to be a case of David and Goliath that has tragically curtailed Cuba's economic development. Cubans, for their part, sometimes seem to be characterized by a war psychosis that comes out of the objective conditions that have been imposed on them. Cuba has been on a war footing for decades, and that has meant that the kind of socialism that has developed and the security restrictions the government has put in place can justly be criticized. On the other hand, one might ask why the United States hasn't normalized its relations with Cuba when it has done so, for example, with Vietnam, a country where there was enormous loss of life on both sides. There is something rather pathological about the United States' aversion to socialism in its backyard.

When the United States questioned the friendship between Cuba and the new democratic South Africa, President Nelson Mandela remarked that he was glad the United States was our friend but said that there were others who were our friends when the United States was not and who remained consistent. So, he said, we would not abandon the friends we had during the dark days of struggle when others were not with us.

There is a long history of acts of terror being planned on U.S. soil by anti-Castro extremists, so the Cuban government decided to send Cuban agents to infiltrate these terrorist groups in order to get information necessary to head off these attacks. In a case of blaming the messenger, the U.S. government hunted down these men and arrested them. Known as the Cuban Five, they were tried in Miami in 2001, convicted, and are now scattered throughout maximum-security prisons in the United States. One was recently released on parole, but he is still not free to return to his country, and the other four remain incarcerated. One of the small ways that I have tried to repay my country's debt to Cuba is by visiting one of them, Gerardo Hernandez, who has been sentenced to two life terms, to be served consecutively. Gerardo, a decorated hero of the war in Angola, has not seen his wife, Adriana, in more than eight years because the U.S. government has denied her entry, contrary to international humanitarian law. A particular sadness for Gerardo and Adriana is that they have no children and that her biological clock continues to tick while Gerardo is imprisoned. There have been various attempts to challenge the convictions of the Cuban Five. All have been opposed by the U.S. government and have been ultimately unsuccessful. As a South African these visits with Gerardo have a particular poignancy because they remind me of how our finest leaders were imprisoned, not because they were criminals, but because they sought freedom and justice for us all.

Cuba has taught me many lessons, but perhaps two especially stand out. First, its commitment to international solidarity in support of human liberation is an example that I have tried to follow in my own modest way. The Institute for Healing of Memories attempts to respond to need wherever it is manifest and resources permit, and our scope includes the whole of the human family. Second, although Cuba offered military support when necessary, its primary goal through its medical and educational missions was aiding the healing and development of the full potential of human beings. This is precisely the value that animates Healing of Memories work the world over. So while Cuba, like all countries, is not a perfect society, its example commands my appreciation and respect.

PART IV

A WORLDWIDE MISSION

15

Rwanda and the Genocide

SOON AFTER OUR SUCCESSFUL WORKSHOPS at the Riverside Church and in Rwanda in 1998 requests for Healing of Memories workshops began to flow in. The result is that by now I have spoken or offered workshops on every continent save Antarctica, and much of my life is spent on airplanes. Besides South Africa, in Africa alone we have worked in Namibia, Zimbabwe, Lesotho, Malawi, Zambia, Uganda, Rwanda, Burundi, and Eritrea. Some of the invitations have matured over the years into long-term relationships. Seeds sown in any one visit germinate and grow in unpredictable ways that in some cases I may never know about. That is not important. What matters is that people are touched and lives transformed, and they in turn touch others in life-giving ways that are perhaps known only to God.

People sometimes express surprise that Healing of Memories work is embraced so readily in such a wide range of cultures, religious traditions, and political contexts. I think one reason is that while workshops provide a clear structure, people bring to them whatever personal or collective offerings have deep meaning for them. It is also true that, in my own case, my visible brokenness gives me a point of entry. When people see that I have no hands, no one says, "Why are you here? You don't know suffering." Even though most people's brokenness is less visible than my own, pain unites us at the deepest level of our humanity. In places like Northern Uganda, where the Lord's Resistance Army has cut off limbs and horribly mutilated people, there was of course a special bond, but everywhere my disability offers a point of connection across boundaries.

Each context in which we work provides its own challenges. In Northern Ireland, for example, I found that people on different sides of the conflict may compete for victimhood. Members of each side see themselves as the "real" victims, and they are not sure about the authenticity of the suffering of others. In his essay at the end of this chapter Alistair Little, a skillful and sensitive Healing of Memories facilitator in Northern Ireland, describes the difficult emotional terrain that must be negotiated in this situation. Alistair is himself an ex-combatant, and his essay illustrates the flexibility and perceptiveness required of facilitators who work in situations where conflict has engendered strong feelings.

Working in many different countries has taught me that while history and geography are unique, at the most profound level there is a range of human emotions, destructive or life giving, that we have in common. That is why our simple, powerful methodology, carefully executed, heals people across the world. Human beings bring pain from great depths to the workshops. Facilitating them can be emotionally draining and sometimes daunting, but it's also immensely rewarding. Over and over we are touched by human beings' extraordinary beauty and resilience, particularly where the experience has been life changing for them.

This and the subsequent two chapters tell something of our worldwide work. Each illustrates how the need for healing often arises from historical events such as colonialism or political or inter-ethnic conflict. In this chapter I relate our experiences in Rwanda, where we have worked with survivors of the genocide. The next chapter, on Australia, highlights our work with indigenous people, particularly with respect to children, now adults, who were forcibly removed by the state, in many cases never to see their families again. They are referred to as the Stolen Generation. Chapter 17 describes the seemingly never-ending conflict in Zimbabwe and the terrible toll it is taking on that country's people. In each of these countries we have had the opportunity to return again and again, allowing us to build long-lasting relationships and foster a sense of continuity and experience across time.

After our first workshop in 1998, I returned to Rwanda in 2004, as before at the invitation of World Vision. This was the tenth anniversary of the genocide, and Rwandan friends alerted us to some of the complexities, challenges, and pain we could expect to encounter. As a South African I sometimes felt impatient when visitors from other countries seem surprised that in ten years of democracy we had not finished dealing with the legacy of apartheid. We have traveled so far, and yet we have just begun. So it was with Rwanda ten years on. The presence of the international community at the tenth anniversary ceremonies and the apologies by the United Nations and others poured a welcome balm on the wounds of the people, yet the pain remains palpable. There is no denying that the world abandoned Rwanda and did nothing while hundreds of thousands were mercilessly hacked to death.

The first three days of our visit were occupied with a Healing of Memories workshop that was attended mainly by leaders of Pentecostal and evangelical churches. It was apparent on the first day that, while the pastors faithfully preached to their deeply wounded people, they themselves struggled with their own unfinished business. Indeed, some expressed worry about the impact that listening to so many painful stories has had on them. Some of the pastors, coming from a strong evangelical persuasion, were of the view that their Christian identity meant that they no longer harbored feelings of hatred and bitterness toward other ethnic groups because these had been overcome through prayer. During the course of the workshop they began to see that although they were Christian they still had to struggle with these feelings and that their Christianity was not the end of the journey. For some, this realization was a breakthrough. While the participants were overwhelmingly positive about the experience, several commented that there was a disappointing imbalance between the two ethnic groups, Hutus having been mostly absent. Nevertheless, in small groups where both ethnic groups were present, there was a depth of sharing that may well be life changing for particular individuals.

The day after the workshop I was invited to address the commissioners and staff of the National Unity and Reconciliation Commission. An official government body, it is quite different in scope and powers from South Africa's Truth and Reconciliation Commission. The Rwandan commission was not designed as an investigative body in any except the broadest possible sense. It was intended to identify and promote education and public discussion of human rights violations, discrimination, and other abuses that are seen as having led up to the genocide. I shared some of my own life journey with the commissioners and explained the context in which we developed our Healing of Memories process. Some people had difficulty with the notion that I as a white person had been part of the liberation struggle in South Africa.

The judicial process in Rwanda is moving forward, and that brings its own problems and anxieties. For example, the executive secretary of the commission said that she did not sleep for a week when many prisoners were scheduled for release, fearing violence either from the community or from the prisoners. Fortunately, neither happened. There can be a mistaken belief that an outsider can provide solutions to complex national challenges, and some people looked to me for answers to the difficult problems that they face. In reality, all I could do was share what I had learned from my experience in South Africa and express my feelings of solidarity with the intention of fanning the embers of hope. The present generation of leaders in Rwanda face many unenviable challenges, and it would be wrong to make judgments from an armchair.

One sign that unattended trauma is rife was the eagerness of people to talk about what had happened. I was invited to address the weekly devotions of the World Vision staff in Kigali, and I led a reflection on issues of remembering, forgetting, and forgiveness. Although it was scheduled for one hour, there was enthusiastic participation, and two-and-a-half hours later we had to cut short the discussion, as I was late for another engagement. We met with staff members of a national association of widows of the genocide, numbering some twenty-five thousand. Hundreds of women are known to be HIV positive as a consequence of gang rape, and children were born from these rapes. It was there that I met a woman named Estha, who used the image of a journey from being dead-alive to becoming alive-alive. She said, "We have physically survived the genocide, but many of us are dead inside. Even though we wake up in the morning, make breakfast, and go through our daily lives, actually inside we're dead." So for her, healing was becoming alive-alive once again. In a similar way, one of the men who came to our workshop told us that this was the first time since the genocide that anyone had seen him laugh and dance. So for him, coming alive meant being able to experience humor once again and enjoy the simple pleasure of dancing to music.

On the final day of our week in Kigali we went to the Memorial Centre, a burial site for more than 250,000 people killed in Kigali Province alone. It also houses a permanent exhibition of events pertaining to the genocide. Particularly heart wrenching are the stories of child victims and survivors. An exhibition about other genocides reminded us that genocide challenges the whole human family, not only Rwandans. The role of churches in the killings brings shame and guilt to all of us in the faith community. Although less than 1 percent of the population, the stories of how Muslim Rwandese protected one another across ethnic lines is an important lesson for Christians. It is clear that for many Hutus who were not themselves driven by ethnic hatred, the choice was either to kill or be killed. Those who refused to cooperate were murdered along with their Tutsi neighbors. Vast numbers of people have blood on their hands, and for survivors of the genocide, who are often left with no or very few living relatives, every normal family occasion or anniversary has within it deep sadness.

The journey of healing will surely take more than one generation. New and innovative methods as well as tried and tested ones will need to be employed as Rwandese and their friends travel down this road together.

I returned to Rwanda again the following year, accompanied by my dear friend Ndukenhle Mtshali, a very compassionate and keen facilitator whose heartfelt observations of our visit accompany this chapter. Ndukenhle has since died, one of the tragic casualties of the AIDS epidemic in our country. For myself, I wondered how it would be this time. Before leaving I felt a need to ask people to pray for me and for the success of our work and I began to ask myself, 'How would I have acted if I had been a Tutsi? How would I have acted if I had been a Hutu?'

Rwanda has adopted a traditional form of justice called *gacaca* as a practical way to deal with the thousands upon thousands of people who had been detained on suspicion of having contributed to the genocide. Gacaca takes place in a community gathering, the focus of which is reconciliation and reintegration. In South Africa, even though our TRC process asserted that apartheid was a crime against humanity, it nevertheless provided a platform to people on all sides of the conflict whose rights had been violated. Some have charged that gacaca, on the other hand, provided an opportunity for Tutsi pain to be acknowledged, but not the pain of the Hutus. I tried to put myself in the position of those who have to make difficult decisions. How would I deal with the aftermath of genocide? At a Healing of Memories workshop later on we asked participants what memories had been stirred up for them by the gacaca process. There was a lot of ambivalence. Even those who defend it concede that there is space for the system to be abused. The danger is that the process can be used to settle old scores that have nothing to do with the genocide. People worry that many of those in prison actually should be free while others who are free deserve to be incarcerated. Nevertheless, without gacaca vast numbers of people would remain awaiting trial for the indefinite future—and it is already more than ten years on.

I met with a group of several hundred adults in a reintegration center who were among those about to be released after years of imprisonment. One older man said he had confessed his involvement and had asked to be forgiven. What advice could I give him? he wanted to know. I suggested to him that he was returning to a society that was still hurting, and that would affect greatly how people responded. Some would welcome him and accept his words of remorse, some would not, and some would take a "wait and see" attitude, reserving judgment until they saw if his words of contrition were sincere. I reminded him that the only person he could depend on is himself, and I pointed out to those in the group that they had an important role to play in creating peace or war in the future.

At our next visit we met a group of thirteen hundred young adults on the eve of their release back into the community. Most were contrite, and as we arrived they sang songs about returning home and not knowing whom they would find. All of them were minors at the time they participated in the genocide, and some were shockingly young. They had simply been swept up in the maelstrom, and many of them are still profoundly haunted by the very terrible things they had done. They feel a great sense of sorrow, and they don't want to rot in prison; they want to find a way to be part of creating a different kind of society. As we left, these young people were singing their hearts out about their commitment to rebuild Rwanda with their own hands. I prayed that they would find the space to make that contribution. Their future remains uncertain, because it is asking a great deal of people in their communities to accept back the very individuals who may have killed their mother, father, brother, or sister, and then to continue as if life is normal.

Interestingly, in our workshops the pain was deepest in people from mixed marriages, where one parent was on one side of the ethnic conflict and one was on the other side. How does one choose between mother and father? It is a problem in a number of places where people straddle the divide between the sides of a conflict through intermarriage and are not fully accepted by either side. It is present among some of the colored population of the Western Cape in South Africa and among people of dual parentage in the indigenous community in Australia. People literally embody the two sides of the conflict within themselves. How does one separate sinew from sinew?

Leaving these young people with hope and prayers, that same afternoon I spoke to several hundred inmates at a Kigali prison. Many of them bear heavy responsibility because they are the ones who helped organize the genocide, and they now face the possibility of life in prison. In a brief discussion afterward that made reference to my life story, one prisoner asserted that what had happened to me was God's will. I replied that I did not believe God sends letter bombs or, for that matter, that God commits genocide. What is of God, I said, is the choice of how we respond to evil. I was asked to return to the prison the next day. Suddenly, after meeting with the head of the prison, I found myself facing an open microphone where I was expected to give an extemporaneous address over the public address system to all six thousand inmates. For a brief moment I hoped the floor would open up and provide me with a quick exit, but I guess I rose to the occasion. I have to confess that I have no memory of what I said.

As I had the previous year, I met with the commissioners of the National Unity and Reconciliation Commission with whom I shared some of our learning over ten years of Healing of Memories work. For me, the question that I posed many times in Rwanda was, "How do we prevent the genocides of tomorrow if people don't deal with the poison they have inside them?" Of course a lot depends upon the political maturity of those who hold power. If it is not exercised wisely, Rwanda could reap a harvest of such deep bitterness that it would guarantee another genocide. In particular, I emphasized to the commissioners that memories can be recalled in a way that is either destructive or life giving. This is especially important in the public sphere. During April every year Rwanda remembers the genocide, and I pointed out that these memories can be presented in a way that encourages healing and reconciliation or that retraumatizes people or stirs up ethnic hatred. I suggested that horrible memories might be paired with stories of people who acted with generosity, compassion, and self-sacrifice to protect others. There were many people who risked their lives and even died for their neighbors by hiding people and helping them escape, and these need to be lifted up. So the leaders themselves need to be on a journey of healing so that they are willing to exercise that sort of leadership.

The central question in Rwanda, then, is how to prevent the genocide of tomorrow. In our own humble and modest way I have no doubt that the Institute made a contribution in this regard. There are no easy answers. As I thought about it, I recalled the words of Bertolt Brecht: "Woe is the land that has no heroes. Nay, woe is the land that needs heroes." In situations of great injustice, heroism is required simply to be a decent human being, but most of us are not heroes. While it is easy to be overwhelmed and feel despair, there are many Rwandese who are themselves signs of hope through their courageous and compassionate lives. I met a young woman named Juliette, and she is one such person. A genocide survivor, she promised God that if she lived she would care for orphans, both Hutu and Tutsi. She has indeed cared for three hundred orphans. Eventually the government began to give some assistance, so the number under her care has finally lessened. Juliette and others like her are the hope for Rwanda and indeed for all of us.

Journey to Rwanda

by Ndukenhle Mtshali

This is the testimony of what I experienced during our visit to a camp in Rwanda that housed about 722 prisoners. They had been in jail for ten years and were being released because they had confessed and told the truth about their part in the genocide. During the month they stayed in this transitional camp, they were taught about human rights, reconciliation, and a traditional form of justice called gacaca in order to prepare them for fitting into their communities once again. About ninety of them were women.

It was a very painful experience to see that even very old people had been imprisoned. These elderly people should have been telling stories to their grandchildren, but instead they have been isolated from the community for the crimes they have committed. As I listened to them speak about what they had done during the genocide, I asked myself how human beings could possibly have done such cruel acts to others? When one realizes that these were Christians killing other Christians, it makes one to go into a state of shock, and I concluded that there must really be forces of darkness and evil that hovered over all human life in Rwanda and propelled such beastly acts.

Another day we visited a camp that is a halfway house for youth who are also about to be released. There were about two thousand of them, ranging in age from fourteen to early twenties. It was excruciating to listen to what they had done, but when they told their stories, it became very clear that they were both victims and victimizers during the genocide. Most of them were very young at that time and there was no way they could have committed such atrocities unless they were forced to do so. Indeed, they shared that they had no choice and they either had to kill or be killed, and so they ended up committing those crimes. I was very much touched by a young man who stood up and shared with us that at age fourteen he murdered about twenty-eight people, using guns and pangas to kill them painfully. While this young man was indeed a victimizer, on the other hand, he is also a victim. He spoke of being filled with shame and guilt for a long time and said he was ready to go to Gacaca Court to give testimony of what he did and ask forgiveness from the relatives of the people he had wronged. This was very painful to witness because these young people have been robbed of their youthfulness and burdened with these unpleasant and horrible experiences. In addition to that, they have to struggle with the uncertainty of whether or not the community will accept them back.

Nevertheless, they were singing and were filled with hope, looking forward to going back and reconciling with their communities.

The diabolic acts of the genocide have left Rwanda with deep scars that still lie on the surface. This was evident when we visited the center called Avega where the widows of the genocide meet. They are facing big challenges of having to come to terms with the loss of their husbands and other dearly loved ones, and they are raising their children alone. Now they have to meet face to face with people who have been released from prison, who come and tell the stories of how they killed their relatives including their husbands. This opens up the wounds that were beginning to heal and it is a very big challenge for both the victims and victimizers to be so directly confronted once again with the pain of the genocide.

Within this deeply disturbing context the Healing of Memories workshop experience was very powerful and taught me a great deal. The sharing of stories very much assisted the participants. Some of them are involved in the gacaca process, while others are counselors and pastors, and they are used to dealing with the painful experiences of others. Now they were given the safe space to share their own stories, some of which were told for the first time. They themselves got a chance to be listened to and to be in the position to bring some of the poisonous memories they hold up to the light of day. Last, for me, I was so much encouraged by the people of Rwanda, the way they hope for the future. They gave me hope as well, to go on and on, and to strive for a peaceful and safe future for us all.

Healing Memories in Northern Ireland

by Alistair Little

I am a former combatant in the Northern Ireland conflict. I became involved in the conflict when I was only fourteen years old. When I was seventeen, I became a political prisoner, and I was released when I was thirty. So I was imprisoned for sixteen years. My prison journey was about coming to terms with the violence in the Northern Ireland conflict and becoming convinced that violence is not the way forward. A big part of that was rediscovering my own humanity and that of those I had seen as my enemy. After I was released from prison more than twenty years ago I began working with people who had been traumatized by violent conflict. My counseling work has taken me to many different parts of the world.

In 1999 Fr. Michael Lapsley came to Northern Ireland and held a workshop to train Healing of Memories facilitators. At that workshop a number of the participants said that ex-combatants like me shouldn't been there and certainly shouldn't be facilitators. Michael's response was to point out that that attitude reflected the sort of discrimination against the "other" that Healing of Memories workshops were intended to overcome, and so I became a facilitator. Over the years my background has become an asset because former prisoners and combatants attend the workshops and they identify with me.

Making peace is not about talking to your friends but about talking to your enemies. The workshops in Northern Ireland are for the most part made up of people who have lost loved ones, as well as former paramilitaries of either Loyalists or Republicans and members of the state forces. So we have all the enemies in the room. Therefore my experience has been beneficial in understanding the sensitivities of the different kinds of people. At the same time, I felt the need of additional skills to help me understand these complexities, so I took some additional training as a counselor. The best facilitators internalize a certain way of life and way of being. It's a question of values and sensitivities and how we treat other human beings. This then is reflected in how we conduct a workshop—for example, in our effectiveness in not allowing some people to dominate and making sure everyone has a place, a voice, and feels valued. All of this really is about how we want people to treat us in everyday life. The skills we learn can be helpful, but if we don't fundamentally internalize and believe in the process itself and what it's attempting to achieve, then we could be the most highly trained facilitator in the world but it will not make any difference.

Despite my commitment to nonviolence and my training, I wasn't prepared for how I felt when I walked into the same room with people who were willing to kill me and whom I had once been willing to kill. That wasn't something that I had expected to be so difficult. I think this is where Fr. Michael is right when he says that some things about facilitating cannot be learned from books but are rather about our personality and who we are as human beings. We either have them or we don't. At the same time there are people who were not combatants and haven't had my particular history who nevertheless bring an important strength of character to the work. In fact, much of my own learning has come from people who haven't had my experience, and they bring different insights. Facilitators who are noncombatants are able to ask questions that I might not even think of asking. So it's important that facilitators come from many different backgrounds. What makes good facilitators is the ability to reflect and learn from our experiences, whatever they were.

Facilitating in Northern Ireland brings its own particular challenges. The politics around conflict are very difficult, especially in situations where there is no clear line between victim and perpetrator. Many participants were perpetrators and yet suffered themselves. That is quite difficult.

There is also a hierarchy of victims. In Northern Ireland some people call themselves innocent victims and say that others directly involved in the conflict, such as combatants, are not innocent. So they refuse to legitimize combatants' experiences. All of this becomes problematic and difficult to work with. It requires a facilitator to adapt quickly to what is going on as it happens in the room. That requires flexibility and understanding that these attitudes arise out of people's trauma, pain, and loss, even though they are expressed as prejudices and judgments. Another serious difficulty is that a lot of people who have lost loved ones struggle with a sense of betrayal by virtue of simply entering the workshop with people who represent or come from organizations that were responsible for their loved one's suffering.

Preparation for these workshops is vital. The workshop organizer must know the background of each person who is coming to the workshop. Participants must be informed in advance that there is a possibility that they may end up in a small group with someone from the other side. They need time to think about that and discuss it with their family. Often, relatives totally oppose a family member going to the workshop with people whom they see as perpetrators. Even though active hostilities are over, the wounds are still very raw.

At the same time the possibilities for creating mutual understanding among people on different sides of the conflict are enormous. At one workshop recently a former prisoner who had been involved in quite serious violence came with his daughter. She told about what it had been like for her during those years. It was very, very challenging for the father to hear how his daughter had been affected by the choices he made, and how it had affected her relationship with the wider community when it became known what her father had done. Some of those present who had lost loved ones said they had never considered what the consequences were for the children of the men involved in the violence. They had assumed that the family and the children were all supporters of the violence, whereas in reality it had destroyed their lives. The father and daughter created a new relationship that hadn't existed before. This was a powerful experience that created a deep understanding of the complexity of the conflict for all who were involved.

Then too some people come with unrealistic expectations despite being briefed in advance. They are told one thing and they hear something else. It is not that they don't listen; it is where they are as human beings in their suffering and fear. So some people expect answers that they have been seeking for years, some aspect of truth. It can be difficult if people want to ask perpetrators specific questions about what happened to their loved ones. Of course, that is not what a Healing of Memories workshop is about, and facilitators need to go over those guidelines every day.

I have been working with the same facilitators for five or six years, and we have developed a deep trust among us. We all understand that we are not there for ourselves; we are there for the needs of the group. We give the participants ownership of the process. That means that while the workshop has a clear structure, we try to be flexible and work with the needs of the group. If someone needs a time out, for example, we take a break. Once people understand that they are not going to be interrogated, judged, or threatened, that makes a huge difference. As facilitators we must let go of our own need to control the process and respond flexibly to what participants need.

We also have to be clear that we are not doing this work for our own ego gratification, but rather to help create the kind of society we want to bring into being. Sometimes people will say, even at the end of a workshop, that they still don't fully trust me because I was a combatant and that they still wonder if I would be capable of using violence again because I used it in the past. Or can they really trust me with their innermost thoughts? Will I go off and talk to their former colleagues? Although that can be worrisome, it is also a joy because they trust that expressing those thoughts is not going to change our relationship, that the process embraces that, and that they are not expected just to say "nice" things. It is a joy that people feel so liberated. It is rare that I don't learn something about myself from other people's experiences. Sometimes I feel a little guilty that people who have such traumatic stories are giving so much to me. Then there are the stories that are so inspirational that they go beyond normal expectations of what human beings are capable of. For example, a participant who has lost a loved one puts his arms around another person who belonged to the organization responsible for the loved one's death and says, "Never, never in my life would I ever have thought that I would be able to do this."

It is also a nice surprise when people phone, send a card, or buy a little present. All that says how they are feeling. This is not to say that everything is going to be wonderful, but people can experience for that moment the possibility that they don't have to be crushed and paralyzed by their pain and suffering. Sometimes people who may have been quiet through the process ask to come back a second time. I have learned that silence is not to be understood as a person not being involved. Silence for some people is part of the process. So there are many satisfactions.

◇ 16 ◇

Australia's Stolen Generation

◇◇◇◇◇◇◇

AUSTRALIA IS DEAR TO MY HEART. I left New Zealand at the age of seventeen to go there to seminary. There I joined my religious community and was ordained a priest. It was Australian surgeons who repaired the damage to my body after I was bombed; Australian nurses nurtured my recovery; and Australian physical therapists helped me adjust to my disability. In the years since then I have offered Healing of Memories workshops for Australians of European descent, as well as a large refugee community from Burma and Sudan, but here I highlight our work with indigenous Australians.

In 2002, at the invitation of Anglican Bishop Philip Freier, we began working in Alice Springs, a small town in the central part of Australia that is the heart of Aboriginal country. A member of my own community, Fr. Colin Griffiths, was the parish priest there at the time. Australia has a regrettable history of mistreatment of Aboriginal people beginning in 1788 with the first European settlement. The early settlers referred to the country as *terra nullius*, "an empty land," a legal fiction that was used to justify the exploitation of the continent with disregard for indigenous interests. The reality is that indigenous people inhabited Australia for at least forty thousand years before the settlers arrived. It is a classic example of European colonialism that championed its own superiority and trampled the rights of indigenous people with impunity across Asia, Africa, and North and South America. Beginning in 1869 and continuing for at least a century thereafter, thousands of Aboriginal children, especially those of mixed race, were forcibly removed from their families by government agencies and in some cases by church missions. They came to be called the Stolen Generation. The motives for this were varied, but the removals were typically rationalized as being for the children's own protection.

An official government investigation into this practice was presented to parliament in 1977. Titled *Bringing Them Home,* the report documents the findings of hundreds of interviews held with survivors and their descendants, including dramatic stories of terrified children who were snatched from their parents' arms, never to see them again. In extreme cases even newborn babies were taken from hospitals. Totally unqualified people, such as policemen and ordinary town officials, were authorized to remove children forcibly. Some ended up in orphanages and boarding schools, and others were adopted by white families where they often became domestic servants as soon as they were old enough to work. Because they were regarded as wards of the state, there was no obligation to maintain family records, and many children permanently lost contact with their families. As adults, they lacked ethnic and family identity and were usually undereducated and without employment skills, so predictably they fell prey to a variety of social ills. Some survivors of those experiences are still bitter, angry, and frustrated, while others say, "Actually, I was cared for and people were kind, so I don't see myself as having been terribly mistreated." So there is a kaleidoscope of opinion among people who were victims of these policies, although more are inclined to see their experience as horrible rather than viewing it as relatively benign. Even those who feel they were treated kindly paid an enormous cost in losing connection with their birth parents.

In response to a national movement, in 2008 Australian Prime Minister Kevin Rudd made a formal apology to the Aboriginal people on behalf of the nation that was ratified by both houses of parliament. However, there has been no effort to pay restitution or compensation. The traumatic aftereffects of this terrible policy will linger for generations in the form of alcoholism, drug abuse, and domestic violence, all of which are endemic in traumatized Aboriginal communities, rather as they are in Native American communities in North America for many of the same reasons. In all the key social indicators, members of the indigenous community lag very far behind the rest of the population.

I had a personal encounter with the toll that these social problems take on their communities. I was invited to spend the weekend at an Aboriginal community, called rather ironically Utopia, as the guest of an Aboriginal friend. Tragically, the day before I arrived, a family murder took place, said to be alcohol and drug related. The community immediately became involved in a grief process, and my visit was canceled. Only a few days previously the mainstream nonindigenous media had headlined an assertion by a national Aboriginal leader that domestic, family, and sexual violence had reached epidemic proportions in the Aboriginal community and that it required urgent national intervention. This situation dramatically illustrates the complexity of the social environment in which the Healing of Memories process seeks to make a small and modest contribution. How do we break the cycle whereby victims become victimizers of others? It is easy either to have a highly romanticized view of the situation of Aboriginal people or to be overcome by hopelessness and despair in the face of the enormity and seriousness of the challenges facing these communities. The situation is not without hope, but undoing the damage will surely take several generations and considerable resources, together with a deep willingness to heed the desires and aspirations of indigenous people themselves.

That willingness seems still to be very much in question, and resentment continues to run very high. A recent indication occurred on Australia Day just this year when Aboriginal protestors mobbed the prime minister, Julia Gillard, as she was leaving a public presentation with the opposition leader, Tony Abbott. Australia Day commemorates the arrival of the British fleet in 1788 and marks the beginning of the British settlement of the land. For the majority of Australians it is a day of celebration, but Aboriginal activists refer to it as Invasion Day. In his remarks Abbott said that since the government had already offered an apology and that in his view the lot of Aborigines had improved so much, it is now "time to move on." According to the January 26, 2012, issue of the *Australian,* one protestor responded, "What Tony Abbott said was disgraceful. Our people are living in awful third world conditions, they're dying, and this government just continues to turn a blind eye to it." Aboriginal activists want the government to sign a treaty with indigenous people that would recognize their sovereignty and give them ownership of their historic land.

The Anglican Diocese of the Northern Territory under Bishop Freier's leadership has sought to respond creatively to the pain and anguish of the Aboriginal community in Alice Springs. The church may feel a special responsibility to do so because beginning in 1948, a number of children who had been removed from their families were placed under the care of the Anglican Church at St. Mary's Hostel and School in Alice Springs. At a reunion at St. Mary's in June 2010, one of those children, now grown up, described her experience to an Australian Broadcasting System newscaster in these words:

Our parents made a sacrifice and I really feel quite emotional about it, as we just don't know how they felt. I was living out on the homelands but every now and then we would come into town. I was getting to an age where they decided that it was time for me to have a good education and this is where I was brought. I didn't really know what was happening to me and I didn't realise that I wasn't going to see my parents again, I think for about a week I just cried my eyes out, not realising what was happening.[1]

What is evident from this report is that the situation was complicated because some parents willingly gave up their children, although it is questionable whether they understood that they might never see them again.

In some ways Alice Springs was the most challenging assignment I've ever had. I've been interacting with Australia since I first went there in 1967 to go to the seminary, and I have relatives and dear friends who live there, so in one way I know the country quite well. Nevertheless, indigenous and nonindigenous cultures are dramatically different, and in some respects Australia is an apartheid society. There are two worlds that don't often meet. I therefore took up this challenge with a high degree of humility.

I recall one particular workshop with a small group of seven or eight indigenous women who were all artists. At the end of the first afternoon of what was to have been a two-and-a-half day workshop, they said I wouldn't be seeing them again because they were going to go out hunting the next day. That seemed like the end of that, but I turned up the next day just in case any of them had changed their mind, and to my astonishment the number had trebled. Clearly, the women had gone away and talked among themselves and decided this was something worthwhile. In the end we had an extraordinary workshop, and I was proud that the women felt safe enough to share the stories of their struggles. When the workshop was over, as a way of saying thank you, they allowed me to choose one of their paintings, which I still have in my house in Cape Town. It is called "Women Talking Stories," and it is done in the Aboriginal dot painting style that has been acclaimed around the world. The wonderful thing about it is that the design formed the inspiration for the logo of the Institute that we use to this day.

Having met with a degree of success, we embarked on a three-year partnership with the diocese and I returned to Alice Springs each year.

---

[1] Full text and a video are available at http://www.abc.net.au/local/stories/2010/06/22/2933376.htm.

Each workshop was a challenge in its own way. I remember another in which the women present sat silently and impassively as I spoke. I described the Healing of Memories workshop and said, as I often do, that we would concentrate not on thoughts but rather on feelings. Still the women seemed unresponsive. Then I recalled an expression that a friend had quoted to me from the Arrernte language, the Aboriginal language spoken in Alice Springs. The saying was that "we see through our stomachs." So I said to the women that one way of translating the statement that Jesus was "moved by compassion" would be to say that "Jesus was moved by his stomach." Suddenly the women became engaged and began to talk, and the workshop fell into place. Although these women all spoke English, my small acknowledgment of their native language made all the difference in their willingness to join with me.

In addition to our program in Alice Springs, we also worked in Perth, a large city in the southwest of Australia. Though more than a thousand miles from Alice Springs, Perth has an urbanized Aboriginal population, and this provided us with the opportunity to bring together people of Aboriginal and European descent. Our workshop was sponsored by the Christian Brothers Edmund Rice Centre and thus took place in a Christian context. For an opening drama we used an excerpt from the film "Rabbit-Proof Fence," a true story of three Aboriginal girls who were part of the Stolen Generation and who ran away from the settlement where they had been placed. The film traces their epic journey to return to their families. It gave the workshop a good start by opening up memories and strong feelings on the part of both the indigenous and nonindigenous Australians present. On the Sunday following the workshop there was an ecumenical service for healing and reconciliation at St. George's Cathedral. During the service those who had participated in the workshop presented as an offering the clay peace symbols they had created at the end of the workshop.

Our work in Perth was organized by Marlene Jackamarra. An Aboriginal woman herself, Marlene coordinated an indigenous ministry at the Edmund Rice Centre. Healing of Memories work captured her imagination, and our workshops were the fruition of her commitment. In the short essay that accompanies this chapter Marlene shares a small part of her personal journey from pain to hope.

In incidents noteworthy for what they say about the lack of openness on the part of some in the Christian community, one of our newly trained facilitators and her husband paid us a visit prior to the workshop to express reservations about our methodology because it was not couched in evangelical language and was respectful of different faith traditions. Regretfully, both decided not to attend the workshop, even though the wife, who had been trained as a facilitator, had hitherto been very positive and had contributed to the process. The withdrawal of this wife and husband reminded me of a similar experience in Alice Springs, where on another occasion we had organized a workshop that included both indigenous and nonindigenous Australians. Sadly, two of the non-Aboriginal participants pulled out after the first night, unhappy with the evident respect shown for Aboriginal spirituality coexisting with Christian commitment. The other participants gelled quickly and bonded throughout the course of the workshop, and for a number of them it was the first time in their lives they had the opportunity to tell their own story in a trusting and safe atmosphere and to listen to the story of someone from another racial background.

I believe that God has a dream for Australia. Indigenous people have lived there for thousands of years, and I have been a visitor for just a moment in time. Even so, I have heard painful stories of broken hearts, of separation, and of racism and violence. Alice Springs lies at the heart of Australia, geographically and spiritually. Are we willing to seek out and cooperate in God's dream for this country? Are we willing to do the "heavy lifting" that would provide an opportunity for people to heal from the past and furnish the resources to create a better future? I hope that in our work we have made a modest contribution in providing a place where people could be heard, acknowledged, accepted, and received with love and compassion. That is God's dream for Australia. It is also God's dream for the human family.

A Long Way

by Marlene Jackamarra

I would like to acknowledge my people and the land from which I come. I am a Yamuji woman of the Inguda people. I want to acknowledge my mother, my father, and my grandmother whose stories I was very fortunate to learn since so many others of the Stolen Generation know nothing of their ancestry. My story is also one of struggle. I was born in an Aboriginal settlement, the same place my mother was born. In fact, we had an entire family in this mission home, but very many members of different generations were taken away from their mothers and fathers. Priests and nuns brought me up from when I was seven years old until I was sixteen. The orphanage was a strict and cold place and I am sure this is linked to the reason that I didn't feel I belonged anywhere as I was growing up. I still feel very alone sometimes.

For most of my life I have been an abused person. It took me some time to find the words to describe my experiences, to tell the truth about what happened to me, and what happened to others in our communities. I have lived in violent relationships. I was "black and blue" from the violence, as they say in Australia. Alcohol was a comfort for a time. I became a heavy drinker and most of my days were taken up looking for booze. I have been a member of Alcoholics Anonymous for twenty years. The day I stopped drinking was a turning point in my life in dealing with the effects of sexual abuse. I have had to deal with my share of shame and guilt and sometimes also a sense of hatred toward some of my own people. The violence I experienced was at the hands of my own people and this takes time to deal with.

We are a marginalized community in Australia. Much of this is due to government and legislation. I know that our communities have been terribly affected by colonization, but I also know that we must now take our own action and responsibility for ensuring that violence in our communities stops. Our spirituality has sustained us, the Indigenous Peoples of Australia, for many thousands of years and enabled us to defy great odds. Healing comes from honoring our collective courage to survive the violence of Australia's colonial history. Now we need that courage to look within our own souls in order to define and live by what it means to be truly human. Healing comes through the gift of forgiveness and our ability to listen to and share in the stories that people find sacred, including the pain of being a child of the Stolen Generation. I believe that the Indigenous community is mature enough to turn the mirror inward, to find a common ground where there are no scapegoats and no victims, and to construct a new Dreaming that combines the old and the new, the past and the present.

When I started on this healing journey there was just me—me and God. And for a very long time that was all there was. Now I am mother of five children. I have six grandchildren and one great-grandchild. I think I have twenty-three stepbrothers and sisters. It is a big family and I am the eldest and I therefore have the greatest responsibility. I've had to do a lot of healing of memories. Sometimes I have found it hard to forgive myself and love myself again. I take it one day at a time. It's a long road, and walking it requires courage and faith. I've already come a long way.

In Northern Uganda with victims of the Lord's Resistance Army.

17

Zimbabwe—The Agony Continues

◇◇◇◇◇◇◇

I HAVE VISITED ZIMBABWE nearly every year since I left there to return to South Africa in 1992, and for me, having made it my home for so many years, the turmoil is especially painful. I include here accounts of two visits, one in 2002 and the other the following year. Who could have imagined when I wrote them that this dreadful situation, now nearly ten years later, continues to roll on? I decided to leave much of the narrative as it was written then, because it conveys the immediacy of the suffering that continues to this day.

In July 2002 Themba Lonzi, our youth coordinator, and I traveled to Zimbabwe to conduct two Healing of Memories workshops. It was Themba's first visit to another African country. We were invited by Women's Net, a group of Christian women seeking to live out their Christian faith in a practical way and to contribute to national reconciliation. One of their members, Brenda Adamson, had experienced Healing of Memories as life changing at a workshop in Cape Town.

Having decided that it would not be appropriate to visit until after the presidential election in March, the visit had already been postponed once because of the deteriorating political and economic situation. I asked myself whether it would be possible to deal with issues of the past while the difficulties of coping with the present were so overwhelming. However, our hosts encouraged us to come, and so we agreed. Indeed, a recurring theme everywhere we went was how to keep hope alive. The continuously rocketing inflation, widespread shortages, looming famine, and mass starvation—without even speaking of the politics of fear and repression—mean that for most people their standard of living goes down every week.

Our first workshop was in Mutare, about four or five hours drive from Harare. We had twenty-five participants, including five facilitators.

The group was intergenerational with first language speakers of Shona, Ndebele, and English, mainly black and a few white. There were also a number of people living with physical disabilities. We began as we usually do on Friday evening. Despite their present problems people were able to speak about how events in the country's past had damaged them as well as bringing up more personal hurts.

On Sunday morning I had the opportunity to share with the congregation of St. John's Anglican Cathedral and I sought to bring a message of hope and encouragement. After the service, I met with an old friend I had not seen for many years. She told me about two members of her immediate family who had died of AIDS, and she spoke of the number of young people who had gone to Britain in order to survive. AIDS and people leaving the country were to be among the recurrent themes of our visit.

Sunday evening, now back in Harare, Women's Net held a small reception to welcome us. We had the opportunity to meet a couple who had just been told that they would have to leave their land as a consequence of the government's latest plans to acquire more farms. This particular couple had only owned the property for four years and had not believed that they would become a target of forced land acquisition. As traumatic as it is for the farm owners, the much more painful issue is what happens to the farm workers, many of whom have lived on these farms for many years and have nowhere else to go. The next day I was interviewed for a radio program called "Faith in Action." To my astonishment, in the briefing beforehand the interviewer asked me not to even mention the situation in Zimbabwe in my remarks.

We began our second Healing of Memories workshop at the Christian Counseling Centre in Harare. There were twenty-one of us altogether, including five facilitators, with a good racial mix. Since there were only about three people in addition to the facilitator in each individual group, there was ample time for people to share at great depth. As in the first workshop, the challenge was to focus on how the past of the country had affected us and not dwell on the overwhelming realities of the present. As someone said, "We talk about the present and about what is happening in the country every day." A number of people at the workshop talked of never feeling that they belonged or felt they were of less value because of race, tribe, gender, or unfortunate things that had happened in their families. During the liturgy of celebration three women, each with different racial backgrounds, read out letters to their mothers that they had written in the light of what they had shared of their own journeys. Another poignant moment came during the thank-you speeches, when a white Zimbabwean man spoke of his indifference to my bombing in Harare in 1990 and his opinion that I had gotten what I deserved. He characterized what he was feeling then by saying, "If you play with fire, you will get fire." He asked my forgiveness for his attitude. I had a sense that people left the workshop with a renewed sense of self-worth and a willingness to contribute to the healing of others.

The day after the Harare workshop ended I was invited to address a meeting of pastors coming from many different church backgrounds. In the discussion that followed they attempted to discern God's will in the here and now under these very trying circumstances. One inquired whether I had forgiven those who had bombed me, and another asked if I thought things would continue to get worse in Zimbabwe. Underlying both questions were unresolved issues of hope and despair, how to endure, and whether forgiveness is possible.

Roman Catholics and Anglicans in particular are deeply divided along political lines at the leadership level. Many, many Christians feel abandoned by God and agonize about what they can and should do. My last couple of days were spent in Bulawayo, a city in Matabeleland that was the scene of huge loss of life due to conflict between rival political groups soon after the fall of the white Ian Smith government. For many people there the killings of the 1980s in Matebeleland are still very fresh wounds compounded by recent events. Once more I met with clergy and others working with victims of violence. I was also grateful to meet Archbishop Pius Ncube of the Catholic Church, who has been under attack because of the way he has championed those who have been deeply hurt during the present conflict. I also had the opportunity to meet with Judith Todd and her father, former Prime Minister Sir Garfield Todd. Like me, originally from New Zealand, Sir Garfield became a Zimbabwean. A man of liberal political leanings he nevertheless remained a controversial figure in some circles until the end of his life, because although he opposed racial discrimination and acted to improve the lives of the black majority, he was nevertheless a member of the United Party that protected white privilege under the colonial government. Out of office, over the years he became increasingly outspoken in his opposition to white minority rule, and at ninety-four years of age he remained up to the minute with current events. He and his daughter both had a lifetime commitment to social justice, and both were rendered stateless by the Zimbabwe government.

I had a sense that those in power in Zimbabwe are committed to retaining political and economic power no matter what the cost. With

frequent shortages of basic commodities and mass starvation looming, one wonders how long it will be before there are food riots or
desperate responses coming out of anger and a sense of hopelessness.
It is frightening to contemplate how the state may respond. There
seems to be a lack of clarity from the opposition about a clear way
forward. Numerous Zimbabweans expressed great frustration about
the failure of South Africa to take a stronger stance, particularly in
regard to the recent presidential election. In my own tiny way I tried
as a South African to come with a loving embrace to show people that
they are not forgotten and abandoned. The narrative accompanying
this chapter, written by Immanuel Hlabangana, who was a participant
in the Mutare workshop, vividly portrays the personal dimension of
what it is like to live through these troubled times in Zimbabwe.

It is easy to become discouraged in the face of what seem like in-
surmountable forces that operate to crush out hope and sometimes life
itself. Yet when given even a little nourishment, human beings show
remarkable resilience. A month after the Mutare workshop the participants held a reunion, and I received the following account from Shirley
De Wolf who had organized the workshop and attended the reunion:

> We started our reunion by sharing what has emerged so far as
> the most lasting effect of the HOM workshop. It was remarkable
> how many changes have taken place in people's lives as a direct
> result of that event.
>
> The workshop helped some people to identify the need to take
> a major directional decision in terms of future career—as though
> somehow they had been walking backwards all this time unable
> to look at what lay ahead and map out their forward direction.
> One man has accepted a calling to the ministry as a result of
> what he cleared away in the workshop.
>
> For other participants the workshop helped them to open
> up to receive insight and nurturing from others. One man said
> this experience helped to save his marriage; another that it had
> changed his whole concept of pastoral style. He used to stand in
> the pulpit as a tower of exemplary strength and morality—now
> he can see "his natural smallness and his needs as a human being
> alongside his parishioners."
>
> The workshop gave people the courage to come out of their
> shells and to seek and find belonging in the community. For
> some, the workshop taught new listening skills, and they have
> begun to make use of some of the exercises and rituals in their
> churches, classes, and other groups.

Rarely have I known such a short event to make such a strong impact on people!

In February 2003, upon our return to the country, I heard someone say, "We are witnessing the death of Zimbabwe." Yet despite this I remembered the words of the old hymn,

> Yet saints their watch are keeping,
> Their cry goes up, "How long?"
> And soon the night of weeping
> Shall be the morn of song.

Together with my colleague, Mongezi Mngese, I visited Zimbabwe for twelve days in mid February. I had expected a phone call asking us not to come because of the deteriorating political and economic climate. I was doubtful that people who were struggling with survival would have the emotional and spiritual resilience to focus on how the past of the country had affected them when the present was so crushing. I am happy that I was proved wrong. People seemed eager to leave the worries of the present for a little time and focus on some of the poisonous residue from the nation's past. When Zimbabweans tell their stories, it is apparent that there are many layers to their pain. During the struggle for independence up to 1980, many had bitter and painful experiences of torture, death, discrimination, and exclusion at the hands of the white regime. Then, during the conflict in Matabeleland in the mid 1980s following liberation, several thousand people lost their lives at the hands of the Zimbabwean army in a conflict with a rival liberation group—a conflict that the apartheid regime sought to fuel. Now, since the government lost a referendum on constitutional changes in 1999, Zimbabwe has been characterized once more by increasingly violent political conflict culminating in the still bitterly contested outcome of the presidential election in 2002. I have long felt that one of the negative influences that fuels the present situation is the memory of past conflicts that Zimbabweans tended to bury rather than acknowledge and work through.

From the moment of our arrival we were confronted by the crisis facing the country. Everybody speaks incessantly about "the situation." Visually, the first impact is the sight of endless lines of cars waiting for gas, often with no signs of their drivers. Much more disturbing were the long queues of people hoping to buy basic foodstuffs like bread, mealie meal, cooking oil, and sugar. Recently the government has fixed the prices of certain basic commodities at the point of sale, but because the prices are not fixed throughout the chain of production it is not economically viable for companies to produce at the official price. Virtually anything can be obtained at a price on the black market. Vast numbers of people on basic wages or without formal employment do not earn enough to buy sufficient food to eat. Survival is often dependent on relatives who live in South Africa or the United Kingdom. I asked a friend if he still cycled for pleasure, as I knew him to be a keen cyclist. "No," he said. "I no longer have the energy. I am too hungry."

Our visit began in Zimbabwe's second city, Bulawayo. We had been invited to lead a residential Healing of Memories workshop and train new facilitators. All the participants were from churches or community organizations, and most were involved in caring professions. We arrived on Valentine's Day, and an organization of women of all races and tribes had seized the day to demonstrate and distribute flowers in the streets calling for peace and love. To the delight and amazement of our participants we ate well during the workshop but only because a number of items on the menu had been specially imported from South Africa and Botswana. However, in case we needed to be awakened to the reality of life in Zimbabwe, one of the women who was to prepare food for our workshop spent the night in a police cell and was released without charge the next day.

Several Ugandans presently living in Zimbabwe, together with our own presence from South Africa, helped to bring a continental perspective that was most welcome. On the second evening we focused on the ways in which we are all called to be signs of hope. As is so often the case, crisis brings out not only the worst in human beings but also the best. People spoke of the long queues as places where new friendships have been created and common bonds forged in adversity. People are listening and responding to one another's pain and need, and they share what little they have. This generosity exists alongside great tension and frustration.

I spent the last five days in Harare at the outlying centers of Marondera and Ruwa. Friends pointed out to me the place where food is distributed weekly but only to those who can produce a party card; it is too late to join for those who don't have one. In order to survive the majority if not all Zimbabweans are involved in illegal or immoral activities on greatly varying scales. For example, nobody changes foreign currency in the bank with an official exchange rate of US$1 to Z$55, as opposed to the black market exchange rate of US$1 to Z$1300. Many people spoke of the police as partisan instruments of coercion, intimidation, and repression, not defenders of law and order.

Crisis, economic meltdown, and the breakdown of law and order also have their beneficiaries, some through good fortune and others through criminality. Over and above the legal process of land reform, individual greed has emboldened some to illegally commandeer land belonging to others purely on the grounds of race.

On my last morning in Zimbabwe I went to meet with a senior office bearer of ZANU-PF, the government party, who had been a cabinet minister for more than twenty years. I asked him specifically about the politicization of food distribution. He said that he himself had been responsible for food distribution in 1994 and that food was distributed to everyone regardless of political affiliation. He seemed to think that if that was true in 1994, it was evidence that it was still true in 2003. He suggested that partisanship on the part of ZANU-PF was a response to actions by the opposition party, the MDC. I asked about torture. He conceded that two journalists had been tortured a year or two previously but asserted a lack of knowledge of any other cases. He blamed the opposition, the white farmers, the NGOs, and the British for all that is wrong in Zimbabwe. He agreed that the issue of Mugabe's successor had to be addressed but said Mugabe had to be provided with a dignified exit. He then went into a bit of a tirade, saying, "Who are these young people who know nothing? Who are they to tell us how to run the country and deal with the economy?" He conceded that there had to be reconciliation and negotiations between the government and the opposition, but only if the opposition MDC dropped its legal objection to the outcome of the presidential election. I wondered if the government in return would be willing to drop its high treason charges against the leader of the MDC. I guess many of us, especially politicians, are generally better at blame than responsibility. How many leaders carry within them poison from the past that still infects the present? As I was taking my leave, this gentleman said that he welcomed my role in contributing to healing Zimbabwean's memories.

The truth is that the older generation of Zimbabwean freedom fighters cannot accept that they no longer govern with the consent of their people. One person said to me, "We Zimbabweans are socialized to internalize pain. South Africans would not put up with what we are enduring." Almost all the Zimbabweans I spoke with expressed a mixture of incomprehension, anger, frustration, and disillusionment at what they perceived as South Africa's apparent disregard for their plight and failure to speak out in defense of basic human rights. I wondered, as have so many others, if the generational dimension given voice by the ZANU-PF official that I spoke with, along with the historical solidarity of liberation movements in Southern Africa, were factors in the dogged support of President Mugabe by our own President Mbeki. The assertion by President Mbeki and President Obasanjo of Nigeria that the situation in Zimbabwe has improved was met by widespread disbelief. Many people I encountered were long-time supporters of ZANU-PF, and some only now have begun to support the MDC out of disillusionment with the ruling party. In looking to South Africa I had the impression that most Zimbabweans were expecting neither the megaphone diplomacy of Tony Blair denouncing the Mugabe government nor the South African army to appear on their doorsteps to liberate them. However, they did expect that we would publicly distance ourselves from the violations of a range of basic rights that are enshrined in our own constitution. They expected from us the kind of solidarity that they have received from Botswana, Kenya, Senegal, and Mozambique, and that the world gave us during our struggle.

The situation in the country is quite dire, and again and again people said with a great sense of foreboding that this year the crisis in the country will climax and something will have to give way. Almost everyone I met of all races spoke in support of land redistribution. The objections are to the method that has helped turn a country that was once the breadbasket of the region into a begging nation. The economic meltdown together with famine and AIDS means that nearly eight million people now face death by starvation and disease. With thousands of farm workers mainly of Malawian and Mozambican descent driven off the land there is a rapid increase in criminality often accompanied by the violence of hungry and desperate people.

Tragically the Christian community in Zimbabwe is deeply divided over what is happening in the country, and this too echoes the divisions within the church in South Africa over apartheid. In spite of this we are beginning to see an increasing number of voices from a wide spectrum of denominations acting collectively in a prophetic way. After a service at which torture survivors spoke of their experiences, Archbishop Pius Ncube of Bulawayo was warned by the police that the service should be of a purely religious nature and that he was not to mention aspects critical of the government. He said he had told the police that it was impossible to separate issues of hunger, economic hardship, and violence from religion. "If people are suffering the church cannot excuse itself." Paulo Freire once said that the oppressed's idea of being human is to be like the oppressor, which is unfortunately what has happened to the rulers of Zimbabwe. Will its next government break the cycle that turns victims into victimizers?

Under varying auspices together with different colleagues I have visited Zimbabwe virtually every year since those two visits in 2002 and 2003. In recent years we have partnered with the Zimbabwean Christian Alliance, an ecumenical formation that arose as a faith response to Operation Murambatsvina, which means "Operation Drive Out Trash." This was a government undertaking that was designed to forcibly clear out poor, informal residential settlements and the informal trading sector from Harare and elsewhere because they had dared to support the opposition MDC. It was widely condemned by civil society, religious organization, and even the United Nations. Nevertheless, the Mugabe regime continued violating human rights and has ruthlessly clung to power. For example, on May 30, 2011, the *New York Times* reported that truncheon-wielding riot police broke up a meeting at a Nazarene Church in which people were praying for peace.

Most recently our own partnership has been with the Anglican Diocese of Harare, which is made up of seventy thousand congregants and seventy-two parishes. Unfortunately the diocese itself has become the site of conflict with the government. The bishop of Harare, Nolbert Kunonga, who was elected in 2002, began replacing priests who criticized the government. In 2007 he attempted to withdraw the Diocese of Harare from its parent body, the Church of the Province of Central Africa (CPCA) on the pretext that the church was sympathetic to homosexuality. The province rejected this move, a caretaker bishop was appointed in Kunonga's stead, and Kunonga was excommunicated. Subsequently Bishop Chad Gandiya was elected bishop of Harare. The conflict has proceeded in the courts, and people are prevented by the police from attending church in their own parishes; priests are even prevented from burying the dead in Anglican cemeteries. Those who oppose the moves by Kunonga are arrested, and the *New York Times* reported on October 7, 2011, that bishops who have remained loyal to the CPCA are being followed and have received death threats. The Harare Anglican Cathedral stands virtually empty on Sunday mornings and its parishioners worship in a tent set up in the garden of the dean of the cathedral. The police have chosen to support Kunonga and his allies violently despite court orders. When questioned they said they were acting on orders "from above." Beyond the facts of the matter, ordinary faithful Anglicans have suffered greatly. At the time of this writing Bishop Gandiya and the congregation of the parish in Mbare where I had been the priest were all arrested for holding a service in the priest's house, not a crime in anyone's book. In one particularly shocking incident, on the morning of February 7, 2011, an eighty-nine year old grandmother and Anglican lay leader, Mrs. Jessica Mandeya, was murdered, supposedly because of her consistent refusal to join Kunonga's church. She had received numerous death threats in the weeks before her murder.

In the midst of this deeply unsettling situation, the Institute for Healing of Memories has been asked to begin leading workshops for parishioners and priests of the CPCA in Harare. These people carry an extra layer of woundedness beyond what vast numbers of Zimbabeans have experience for a long time. In the midst of widespread political repression they are even prevented from practicing their faith freely.

Clearly it is true that Healing of Memories is not yet the most important agenda item for most Zimbabweans; their priority is surviving and enduring. However the day will come when healing and reconciliation will become the order of the day. If all goes well we will visit Zimbabwe again to train facilitators and offer further Healing of Memories workshops. It is important that when the present problems are finally resolved and a measure of stability returns, some people are farther down the road of healing and are not caught up in fantasies of revenge so that they can point the way forward to others. In its own modest way the Institute for Healing of Memories will continue to offer our workshops as one way in which people can acknowledge the poison from the past and begin to let it go. In so doing we can help to heal the wounds and begin to lay the groundwork for a new order in Zimbabwe.

Reflections from Zimbabwe

by Immanuel Hlabangana

The history of our nation is filled with violence and the survival of the fittest. First there were tribal wars. Then came colonization by the British for almost one hundred years, and by the time we got our independence in 1980, we had gone through a bitter struggle leaving almost fifty thousand civilians dead in a period of twenty years. In 1980 we had to integrate four armies into one—the Rhodesian army of Ian Smith's white supremacist regime and three different liberation forces. The prime minister then, now president, Robert Mugabe, declared "reconciliation" as the way forward to building the nation, although the process was never spelled out.

The year 1980 also saw the start of my primary education, but because of the war it was delayed by two years. The running images of white soldiers beating up people in my village were still vivid in my mind as I started school. Thus I grew up as an angry child. The seven years of my primary education were marked by two major incidents that affected me mentally and emotionally. First, after three years of bliss after independence, our nation was once again at war, this time black-on-black violence, which after the so-called Unity Accord in 1987 between the two main liberation groups left twenty thousand people from my tribe dead in mass graves. Among them was a seventy-five-year old lady who was affectionately known as Gogo (Granny) MaMlosthwa and who was my paternal grandmother. She died two weeks after being beaten up for "hiding dissidents" by soldiers of the new black government in what President Mugabe has termed "a moment of madness." Another layer of hatred and bitterness was added. The second emotional challenge I had to deal with was when we had to move from the township to a suburb that was once dubbed "whites only," and I had to go to a multiracial, multilingual school. From an early age I saw the need for a process that dealt with issues of justice, truth, peace, and mercy, for a process that dealt with our past yet had a forward-looking aspect as well.

In 2002 I attended a Healing of Memories workshop with facilitators from South Africa. By the time I attended the workshop I had layers and layers of scars. Since the year 2000 a group of about twenty or thirty pastors, priests, and church lay leaders from different denominations had been meeting to talk about how to respond to the sociopolitical environment. Among these ministers I had developed a special relationship with the Rev. Shirley De Wolf, a fully Zimbabwean white United Methodist minister. She had gone through a Healing of Memories workshop, and she highly recommended that our group and the whole nation needed to go through a healing process. When the Healing of Memories facilitators came from the Institute in South Africa, an added challenge for me was that the core facilitator, Father Michael Lapsley, was white, and part of my journey to healing was dealing with the "white" factor of my history. I had many questions about this healing process. Should I be honestly committed to the full weekend? Or should I just please my friend Shirley and go through the motions? Why not let sleeping dogs lie? Why bring up issues that I have put to rest?

The friendliness of the facilitators helped to settle me in. Hearing the personal stories of both facilitators, Fr. Michael and Themba, allowed me to let go and become involved and find a measure of healing. The workshop had twenty-five people altogether; fifteen females and ten males; five whites, two coloreds, and eighteen blacks; three Ndebele speaking, and the rest Shona and English speaking. I mention this to show the diversity of our country, its culture, history, and the different perceptions of our journey and hurts as a people. The icebreaker, which came in the form of dance and song by Themba, set the mood for the whole weekend: "If we are to progress as a people the past has to be dealt with." The storytelling aspect of the Healing of Memories workshop allowed me to dig deep, and having people listen was the most important part of the healing process. I really appreciated the methods and techniques used in teaching us, and I benefited a lot.

Our country is still going through a difficult time, yet my attitude toward nation building has changed. Our nation has to look at its past and go through a process of healing, and I am glad that among the twelve million people at least one of us, me, has been convinced to be a participant. Yet because of the difficulties we face, we continue to hurt one another. Through the Healing of Memories program I am able to look at my arrest in 2003 under section 24 of the dreaded Public Order and Security Act as part of the challenges that face us as a people to coexist in our differences. I am able to reach out to perpetrators in a reconciliatory manner. The things that are meant to destroy us can become the doorway to being better people if we allow a healing process to work and to play a positive role in our communities. I now run on a full-time basis a department within a Christian NGO that deals with conflict transformation and healing of memories. Without the support system that we created by being involved in this healing process, I would be developing more and more layers of scars and hurts. Yet like the apostle Paul, I can say, "With the same comfort that we have been comforted, we now comfort many."

18

Torture

◇◇◇◇◇◇◇

IN 1975 WHEN I WAS A STUDENT in Durban, Raymond Suttner, a law lecturer who was the brother of a friend, was detained and physically tortured, including electric shocks to his genitals. A woman with him was also detained. In her case her parents were brought to see her in detention. The parents told me what considerate, kind people the security police were. What they didn't know was that as soon as they left, the police told their daughter that if she did not tell everything she knew, she would not see her parents again. In this case she did tell all, and they did not lay a finger on her. In many other cases the outcome was quite different.

The South African government certainly did not invent torture, but it became a principal weapon in the government's arsenal of repression. Never particularly sensitive to irony, the apartheid regime justified its very existence as a struggle ordained by the Creator against godless communism, yet it employed a variety of dehumanizing instruments including torture against fellow human beings whom scripture tells us were created in God's image. Of cardinal importance for those of us who are Christians is that we are followers of the tortured one.

Apartheid was based on a lie about the human person, namely, the false claim that our value as human beings comes from the color of our skin rather than from our very humanness. It is this lie and this dehumanization that provides the milieu in which all forms of torture flourish.

Sad to say, torture became a normative part of the South African way of life, especially during the 1980s when repression and resistance were strongest. People were tortured in order to extract information, though of course the information provided was often deliberately inaccurate if not downright fictitious. It was also a form of punishment and used to intimidate others and prevent them from following the same course. So torture became part of the arsenal of state terrorism. It was an instrument whose primary purpose was breaking the will of the people to resist and to be free. The regime tried to crush their spirit by crushing their bodies. Despite the horrific toll that torture took, for the most part the South African spirit was unbroken. Those of us who were in exile were less subject to the threat of torture by the South African government; instead we faced "dirty tricks" engineered by agents of the apartheid regime that included assassinations by letter bombs and other explosions, such as the one that almost killed me, as well as poisonings and mysterious disappearances. On top of all that there were the direct attacks, such as the Maseru massacre. Meanwhile the torturers and assassins were respected members of their own communities, and their families may never have known how they passed their days. They were rewarded, promoted, and given golden handshakes when they retired.

In 1963 the government instituted detention without trial for up to ninety days, which was soon extended to 180 days, and in 1967 "indefinite detention" was legislated. After the Soweto uprising in 1976 preventive detention swelled the ranks of those detained even more. In the late 1980s estimates of the numbers in detention reached more than eighty thousand, and of those more than ten thousand were under the age of eighteen. Evidence suggested that more than 90 percent had been tortured. Detention without trial, unlike imprisonment, exposed the detainee to horrendous uncertainties: For how long will I be detained? Will I be tortured? How long will it last? Will I be able to endure it? Will I betray my comrades? Will I die? Wouldn't if be better to die than to survive? In the 1980s a group of mental-health workers who were themselves part of the struggle against apartheid sought to provide services to people who were in and out of detention, to people on the run, and to people coming out of prison. Some, for example, taught techniques to people likely to be arrested that helped them cope with torture. Among them were the founders of the Trauma Centre for Victims of Violence and Torture where I was chaplain.

Although many have written and spoken about their experience of torture, I am not sure that anyone who has not had the experience can know the full horror and terror experienced by the torture survivor. Survivors of torture were portrayed by the state as lying criminals who deserved to be disbelieved and punished. Because of their degrading and humiliating experiences, torture victims often speak of their own sense of shame at what they have endured. Survivors sometimes wait for many years, even decades, before they speak of what has been done to them. "Will I be believed? What will people think of me if they know what has happened to me?" This is particularly true of sexual torture and the rape of both women and men. In the recesses of the human heart the victim sometimes blames himself or herself for being the victim. These feelings are very powerful, and they can arise in people who understand that in a logical sense they were in no way responsible for what happened. For example, not long after I survived the attempt to kill me, I apologized to my friend Phyllis Naidoo for having survived when her own son had been killed.

Although the apartheid government attempted to hide its egregious violations of human rights, they nevertheless came to public attention through the medium of political trials. One of the terrifying features of torture is that it takes place in isolation. No one hears the victims scream, and the torturers are careful not to leave marks. Ironically, the courtroom was one of the few places where victims were able to speak about the torture they had experienced, often giving names, dates, and detailed descriptions of what was done to them. Nevertheless, very many of the judges refused to take the allegations of torture into account and accepted evidence given under torture. The English-speaking press recorded these details, and although the government made attempts to suppress the information it often became public. In 2000 I made a brief visit to New Zealand, and while I was there a friend, Fr. Michael Blain, told me about a conversation he had with a visiting South African woman. My friend mentioned to her that I worked with victims of violence and torture in South Africa. The response of this woman, six years after the democratic election and two years after the Truth and Reconciliation Commission had completed its human rights hearings, was to state unequivocally that there had been no torture in South Africa, though she conceded that some people had been killed. My friend, with a certain degree of irony, promised her that he would deliver her message that I was wasting my time since no one had been tortured. I could not help wondering how many ostriches New Zealand had imported from South Africa.

An environment of torture and human rights abuse corrodes the moral fabric of society. I am sometimes asked about the horrific form of killing known as "necklacing," which means placing over the head of a victim a tire doused in gasoline and setting it alight. This was particularly used in black townships against those who were believed to be collaborators with the apartheid regime. "How could this happen?" people ask. "How could a group of human beings do this to another human being?" Often it was young people who were in the lead in necklacing. My answer is in the form of another question: "What had been done to these young people to so warp their sense of a common humanity that they would relish this option?" So, without excusing them for their responsibility, the finger nevertheless points to apartheid's widespread use of torture and brutality against young people, who unfortunately learned from this experience that human life is cheap.

In November 1980 in Geneva, President Oliver Tambo made a solemn deposition that the ANC and its military wing, Umkhonto we Sizwe, would be bound by the Geneva Convention and its more recent protocols relating to armed conflict. It was the first liberation movement ever to do so. Nevertheless, after its unbanning in 1990, accusations began to surface of abuses that had taken place, especially in its detention camps in Angola. The ANC set up several commissions of inquiry that were antecedent to the TRC while at the same time it insisted that there could be no moral equivalence between the just struggle to end apartheid and the injustice of defending it. Nevertheless, it took responsibility for those acts and admitted that they were contrary to the ANC's own values. Later it made detailed submissions to the Truth and Reconciliation Commission. During my time as chaplain of the Trauma Centre I listened to the stories of those who had been tortured by the ANC, to which I belonged. To put it mildly, this was very troubling to me, even though I understood the context of war. Strikingly, many of those who spoke to me wanted to make a clear distinction between the acts of certain individuals and the liberation movement as a whole, which they continued to support.

In the eyes of the TRC all people who appeared were treated with the same dignity and respect regardless of whether the perpetrator of their abuse was the apartheid state or the liberation movement. However, with great importance both for the individuals concerned and for the establishment of a moral order in the democratic South Africa, the TRC asserted the moral unacceptability of gross violations of human rights regardless of who carried them out. In the eyes of the commission, the ends did not justify the means. Torture was torture was torture.

As so often happens, it is the victim who liberates the victimizer. This is true of Johnny Issel, an antiapartheid activist whom I knew well. His story is one of attempting to rehumanize his torturer and their rediscovery of their common humanity. In pursuit of his own healing the torture victim discovered that the torturer was the one more in need of healing. With Johnny's permission, Glenda Wildschut recounted the story of the meeting between Johnny and his torturer at our international conference in 2007. Her account of Johnny's story accompanies this chapter.

Unfortunately, with the demise of the apartheid state torture has not disappeared in South Africa. While there are challenges around definitions, it is clear that torture is implemented by both state and nonstate actors. We would be naive to deny that torture also happens within intimate relationships. In some ways those tortured under apartheid at least for a time were "popular" victims. Today's victims are often very unpopular and have few advocates. Allegations come most frequently from criminal suspects. Because of the scale of violent crime the public often lacks sympathy with the torture victims in criminal cases, but there have been exceptional cases that have been captured on camera and have received widespread local and international attention. Torture in the criminal justice system remains a serious problem. Xenophobia has also become a feature of the South African landscape in the face of growing unemployment and widespread poverty. There have been instances, documented by television footage, in which illegal job seekers have been set upon by police dogs, and these stirred an outcry. While technically not instances of torture, since they were the result of mob action, xenophobic riots in 2008 engulfed the country, and sixty-two people were reported killed, hundreds injured, and much property destroyed. Riots of this sort occurred in 2009 as well.

One of the many reasons that South Africa's constitution is hailed and celebrated is because of the provisions outlawing discrimination on the basis of sexual orientation. Tragically, that has not prevented the torturing and killing especially of African lesbians. Our government has responded with very mixed signals. On the one hand, it appointed an ambassador to Uganda who was notorious for his homophobic utterances, for which he has had legal sanctions. The appointment was particularly problematic since Uganda is known for its horrific treatment of the gay and lesbian community. On the other hand, the government has led the way in raising the treatment of people based on their sexual orientation in the UN Human Rights Council despite widespread opposition from other African governments, and it is considering new domestic legislation to protect people from discrimination.

Torture is a world problem, and the United States, which I visit frequently, is no exception. The United States has always maintained that it does not torture. Capital punishment is its own form of state torture. Fortunately our new constitution in South Africa has abolished it. According to the U.S. Death Penalty Information Center, in 2010 there were 3,242 inmates on death row in the United States, of whom 41 percent were black and 12 percent were Latino. They included Mumia Abu-Jamal, who spent three decades on death row before his death sentence was finally vacated in December 2011, thanks to growing pressure from around the world. How many times does a death-row inmate die before the actual moment of execution? Moreover, Abu-Jamal still remains incarcerated for life without the option of parole.

Some years ago I received an email from Sr. Dianna Ortiz, a Catholic sister who had been tortured in Guatemala. She was then working for Torture Abolition and Survivors Support Coalition International (TASSC), an organization opposing torture. To my astonishment she suggested that from within the legal community, including Alberto Gonzalez, then the attorney general of the United States, new defenses of torture had emerged. I was so shocked that I phoned her and asked if it was really true. She told me that it was, and increasingly I read such material in the public domain. It is worth underlining that these legal defenses were antecedent to the horrific abuses that scandalized the world emanating particularly from the U.S. military prison in Baghdad, Abu Ghraib, as well as from Guantanamo. Equally disturbing was the suggestion by the Bush administration that there were human beings called "unlawful combatants" who stood outside the jurisdiction of the Geneva Convention. As the president of the International Committee of the Red Cross told me personally, every human being on the planet is covered by the convention, as either a combatant or a civilian. Several times I have pointed out to U.S. audiences that even for the most selfish reasons abandoning the Geneva Convention for some has endangered the life of every member of the U.S. armed services. Subsequently, I became good friends with a retired U.S. general, General James Cullen, who had led the fight against torture within the military and had lobbied Obama hard on the issue before he became president. Tragically, the Obama administration remains morally compromised by the continued existence of Guantanamo and its refusal to investigate and hold accountable those responsible for authorizing torture. In the wake of the assassination of Osama Bin Laden, voices in defenses of torture have been raised once more. Torture is always wrong, and the failure of moral leadership by the strongest military power in the world is most disturbing.

The Story of Johnny Issel

recounted by Glenda Wildschut with Johnny's permission

Johnny Issel was a very widely known political activist. During the years of struggle he was probably one of the individuals most hunted by the police in the Western Cape. He was often detained and arrested and was severely tortured. One of the police who tortured him is also well known, a policeman called Frans Mostert. Hearing that name, many people here in the Western Cape would tremble. Those interrogated by Mostert were in for a very hard time, and Johnny was interrogated by him many times. After apartheid ended Johnny tried in many ways to heal his woundedness. He spent some time in Europe and Australia, and I think in Canada as well, where he went to various treatment centers and saw many therapists. At one of the treatment centers he realized that unless he released himself from this person who had tortured him so severely, he would forever be linked to him. Ironically, they would be prisoners of each other.

I think Mostert himself went through his own journey, though I am not familiar with the details of that. I became involved when Johnny asked me if I would walk alongside him and assist him in a victim/offender mediation session that he wanted to have with Mostert. It was logistically compli- cated because Mostert lives in Pretoria and Johnny in the Western Cape. Nevertheless, Johnny managed to set up the sessions, and we had a series of meetings together to prepare Johnny for the encounter with Mostert. Those meetings were often quite difficult because even the preparations for meeting Mostert evoked strong feelings in Johnny, but he went through with them. Eventually they met in a little chapel on the University of Stel- lenbosch campus.

For me, the amazing part of the encounter was Johnny's interest in the well-being of Frans Mostert. The first part of the encounter was a "where have you been since I last saw you?" and so on type of conversation. Then Johnny began to share his pain, the dread, and the horror this man had caused him. It was not said in a pathetic way, but rather in a way of set- ting the record straight, of simply stating the impact that the torturer had had on his life. Throughout the sharing Mostert sometimes returned to simple human questions, such as, "So, how is your ex-wife?" "How are the children?" "Do you remember (a particular thing that happened)?" And together they remembered a particular encounter that they had had. For those of us who were observing, we were witnessing the rehumanization of the relationship. These two persons who had previously been in such a totally unequal power relationship of torturer and tortured were now beginning to engage with each other on a human level, initiated by the one who had been tortured. To me, that was extraordinarily powerful. Issel had become the liberator of Mostert, and he became the liberator on behalf of others as well.

At one point Johnny said to Mostert, "In my community I am very well respected. People look up to me as a leader." He then recounted a little bit of what he had achieved in his life. Then he turned to Mostert and asked, "What have you achieved with your life?" At first the policeman didn't know what to say. Then he sighed very heavily and said, "I think I was a very good policeman." You could hear a pin drop in that little chapel. There was absolute silence. At that moment the power passed from the perpetrator to the victim. Those who perpetrate human rights violations against others have nothing now. They must travel their own journey alone. It reminds me of how often Fr. Michael reiterates that the system damaged us all. None of us can say that we were left unmarked or undamaged by it.

Immediately after the meeting Johnny said to me, "I am instructing you to make sure that you do something for Frans Mostert and the other people in his circumstances. Make sure that in your work you ensure that these people are healed." So I am looking to the clergy and others in our community to take up the task. Johnny called me not long after the encounter and we had a short conversation. What moved me also was that Johnny felt compassion for his torturer. I must admit that I was blown away by that. He felt sadness for this man and the emptiness of his life. But despite his healing path, Johnny's health is still quite fragile. I think it's a beautiful story, but it is not that everything is fine now. There are still struggles and the fragility is there. So, yes, there is hope, but there is still pain and still a journey to be traveled. Yet there was a breakthrough of gigantic proportions.

On January 23, 2011, Johnny Issel died at the age of sixty-five. Before his death he was accorded many honors, including the Order of Luthuli, which was presented by President Thabo Mbeki. The premier of the Western Cape, Ebrahim Rasool, cited him as one of the great architects of our freedom. His leaving us is a great loss.

◇ 19 ◇

Healing Memories
in the United States

◇◇◇◇◇◇

THE UNITED STATES OCCUPIES a special place in the history of the Institute. In 1998 we offered the first Healing of Memories workshop outside South Africa at the Riverside Church in New York, and its success convinced me that our methodology speaks to people across boundaries of geography and culture. In a sense the Riverside workshop launched Healing of Memories work on a global stage. At that time I was a visiting professor in democracy at the New School in New York, and as I talked with my seminar students I began to realize how many progressive people in the United States had been inspired by the South African victory over apartheid. It was as if they were saying, "If it could happen in South Africa, it could happen anywhere, even here in the United States." One of the people who attended the Riverside workshop was Steve Karakashian, who subsequently volunteered at our office in Cape Town during each of three years writing grant proposals, devising a strategy for evaluating our work, and facilitating workshops. Now he has undertaken to assist me in preparing this memoir. So, although I had made a number of visits to the United States during the struggle years, the connections I made on that first visit were exceptionally fruitful. I returned again and again, not always offering workshops, but always doing some work on behalf of Healing of Memories. Over the years our work has grown incrementally, and in 2009 the United States became the only country other than South Africa where we are legally incorporated as a nonprofit organization.

In my experience traveling the world, opportunities to offer workshops often arise out of personal relationships, some of which later mature into ongoing institutional connections. That has certainly

227

proved to be the case in the United States where our work now is focused in New York, Minnesota, California, and Hawaii. In each of these locations it has been a key individual who has organized our work. For example, in 1998 Connie Hogarth, a long-time social justice activist, and her husband, the late Art Kamell, attended the seminar I taught at the New School, and they became lifelong friends and supporters of the Institute. Connie determined that I should have more exposure in New York City, and so she organized another visit in April 2002, the cornerstone of which was a series of six weekly seminars at Manhattanville College under the auspices of the Connie Hogarth Center for Social Action. During that visit I also spoke to a number of activist church congregations and a Jewish community center. This latter engagement was arranged by an old friend, Donna Katzin, a long-time antiapartheid activist and now the executive director of Shared Interest, an organization that uses loan guarantees to promote social and economic change in South Africa. I was interviewed on radio and television and visited women at the Bedford Hills Correctional Facility and a youth prison in the Bronx. By the end of my six-week stay I had developed relationships with a number of progressive communities in the New York region that I have continued to nurture over the years.

The events of September 11, 2001, are etched in the memories of many, particularly those who lost loved ones. Everyone can tell you where they were when they heard that the twin towers had been attacked. My visit to New York in 2002 was only a little more than six months after the attack, and I preached at St. Paul's Chapel at Ground Zero where I saw for myself the moving tributes to those who had died. I also was invited to an event at the Episcopal Cathedral of St. John the Divine where I met Colleen Kelly, who belongs to an organization called September 11th Families for Peaceful Tomorrows, all of whose members had lost family on that terrible day. The organization took the position that the United States should not go to war in the name of those who died. I felt strongly supportive of these courageous people whose viewpoint has not always been popular in the United States, especially among some other families who also lost loved ones. A further blessing came when, at a Fellowship of Reconciliation meeting, I met Phyllis and Orlando Rodriguez, also members of September 11th Families for Peaceful Tomorrows, whose son was killed in the twin towers. Phyllis has become the volunteer coordinator for our work in the New York region and is a member of our board. It is a demanding job. She organizes my itinerary and makes arrangements for speaking engagements, Healing of Memories workshops, and has sought opportunities for us to work in prisons, as we also do in South Africa.

On September 11, 2006, the five-year anniversary of the attacks, September 11th Families for Peaceful Tomorrows organized an international conference called Civilian Casualties, Civilian Solutions. The conference took place in New York, and I was one of the invited speakers. The conference gave rise to the International Network for Peace, an organization comprised of survivors of political violence from seventeen different countries; it promotes peaceful responses to violence. Among the affiliates of the International Network is an Iraqi organization called La'Onf, which means "no violence." In 2009 La'Onf was awarded the International Pfeffer Peace Prize by the Fellowship of Reconciliation at a ceremony in New York where I was the guest speaker. The award was accepted on behalf of La'Onf by an Iraqi, Abdulsattar Younus. Not long thereafter, Sattar attended a Healing of Memories workshop in White Plains, New York, and his presence proved to be a poignant experience for everyone concerned. Participants from the United States had the opportunity to express to him their grief and regret about the terrible things the United States had done to his country. Sattar, for his part, was visibly moved and told the group that until his trip to the United States, his only experience of U.S. citizens was soldiers at the end of a gun. Now, he said, he had made the discovery that there were peace-loving people in the United States who not only opposed the war but cared deeply about the Iraqi people and who carried their own pain as well. He said with considerable feeling that he would take that message home to Iraq. It was one of those special moments when a prolonged stillness fell over the group that marked the depth of what had just taken place.

At the same workshop were two survivors of the November 3, 1979, Greensboro, North Carolina massacre, Paul and Sally Bermanzohn. On that day they were part of an interracial group of unarmed activists who were demonstrating against the Ku Klux Klan. In the midst of their demonstration and without warning the Klan suddenly opened fire while the police stood by. Five demonstrators died as a result of the shooting and two, including Paul Bermanzohn, were shot in the head and received permanently debilitating injuries. Though Paul and Sally had recounted their story many times, they nevertheless felt that the deep sharing of pain in the workshop opened a new dimension of healing for them, and I include an excerpt from an interview with them that took place at the conclusion of the workshop.

On one of my later visits to New York I spoke at Holy Trinity Episcopal Church. In the audience was Paul Feuerstein, like me an

Episcopal priest, but in this case with very many years of experience in the field of domestic violence. Paul is the CEO of Barrier Free Living, a nonprofit organization that offers nonresidential services for abused, disabled women and also operates a large, well-equipped residential shelter for women who are survivors of domestic violence and who either live with a disability themselves or have children with disabilities. Although most of us don't think about it, women with disabilities are particularly vulnerable to domestic abuse. As Paul observed my disability and listened to me speak about Healing of Memories, he was able to relate it to his own work. Our discussions afterward resulted in a partnership between the Institute for Healing of Memories and Barrier Free Living. We have trained Paul and a number of his staff in facilitating Healing of Memories workshops that, in turn, have become a part of the services that his organization offers to its clients. One of the challenges and exciting opportunities of the partnership has been the need to adapt the three-day Healing of Memories workshop format to accommodate a nonresidential population. When we were ready to incorporate in the United States, Paul became the first chairperson of the board of the new Institute for Healing of Memories—North America.

In Minneapolis our work has been made possible by the Rev. Margaret Fell, an Episcopal priest whom I first met when she visited South Africa. Margaret was attending an Anglican Communion conference on prophetic witness at which I was a keynote speaker. Healing of Memories resonated for her in relation to her own life journey and her passion for the welfare of returned war veterans. Margaret has now succeeded Paul Feurstein as chairperson of our board and has organized our work in Minneapolis. I have, through a number of visits there, developed a relationship with a program for returned war veterans called the Warrior to Citizen Campaign, a grassroots effort organized in 2007 by the Humphrey Institute's Center for Democracy and Citizenship and now affiliated with Augsburg College. As one Vietnam veteran put it, "Reentry into civilian society from military life is an ordeal, whether or not the skids are greased for you. Facing a life of uncertainty at such a young age can be a nightmare," and he pointed to the proliferation of suicides within the ranks, both before and after discharge. The Warrior to Citizen Campaign seeks to develop the leadership potential of these men and women by working to address issues of veteran reintegration into the community. As one part of that effort, in 2008 a working group was formed within the Warrior to Citizen Campaign to plan Healing of Memories workshops for veterans and those who care for them. Since October 2009 we have held two workshops each year, and we have now trained a core group of facilitators. Many of the participants have been homeless veterans living in transitional housing.

Many people wish to deal with the past but are fearful of confronting it, and some may even have developed an identity that makes the prospect of becoming free quite daunting. From my experience in South Africa I know that this can be especially true of ex-combatants, who often have special sensitivities, so I was a little anxious at the prospect of working with the Minneapolis veterans. I thought, "Will this be the time the model fails us?" But the response was very positive. For many people there's a road to a Healing of Memories workshop wherein trust has to be developed gradually. People carry pain that they may be reluctant to face themselves and even more reluctant to share with strangers. That has proved to be the case in Minneapolis as well. Consequently, our first two workshops were for veterans only, though as trust has been communicated through the veterans' informal channels, the subsequent two workshops have included others who care for them. Although I am not technically an ex-combatant myself, I bear the visible marks of the South African struggle, and that created a special bond with the vets. One of our first workshops was held at a Benedictine monastery, and there was quite a lovely welcome from the sisters. I wondered at the time if the veterans would feel comfortable in this, in some ways, very religious environment, but the naturalness and openness from the sisters seemed to be part of creating the safe space in which we worked. Many of these veterans have layers and layers of pain, not all of which have to do with military service. A few of them have attended more than one workshop, and one person described the process as "peeling the onion of my pain."

The other thing that's important to say in relations to war veterans is that nations send their young people to war, but when they come back, if it is an unpopular war, nobody wants to hear their stories. That was especially true in the United States for the Vietnam War. However, if it's a popular war, we are happy to mystify it by having marches and parades and medals, but again we really do not want to hear about the nightmares and enduring pain that those who have survived come back with. So I think Healing of Memories has an important contribution to make in this regard.

For some vets military service was the defining event of their lives, for good or ill, while for others that was not true at all. Some joined the military out of patriotism and love of country, whereas others joined because they came from poor families and saw it as a way to obtain an education or training. For some, drug and alcohol abuse has become a major problem, for others not. I think one of the beauties of Healing of Memories workshops is that we see each person as unique, and we enable people to place even the most traumatic memories within the wider context of a life journey. Focusing on just one aspect of life, however horrendous it may have been, can be reductionist and dehumanizing. We may be a veteran, we may be disabled, but we are not only that. We are all many things, and there are multiple dimensions to who we are. Framing the workshop in a wider way enables people to integrate the terrible things that have happened into their overall life journey. So in reality there has been a kaleidoscope of issues and stories in the workshops, and each is acknowledged and reverenced.

Turning to quite another dimension of our work, in California we have developed a relationship with Professor Jerry Diller of the Wright Institute, a professional graduate school of clinical psychology in Berkeley. Jerry turned up in our office in Cape Town while on holiday several years ago, met with several of our staff, and developed a lively interest in our work and we in his. He is now a member of our board in the United States and has spent two extended periods working with us in Cape Town. We, in turn, have offered Healing of Memories workshops for graduate students and members of the surrounding community at the Wright Institute. Jerry has enabled us to develop our capacity in regard to research, and two of his doctoral students have completed dissertations that focused on Healing of Memories.

Jerry is training a core group of facilitators that is poised to take this work beyond the Wright Institute into the San Francisco Bay area. He has also offered a course on Healing of Memories for graduate students at the Wright Institute that involves participating in a workshop, classroom discussions of the experience, and facilitator training for those who are interested in learning more about the methodology. Jerry wrote the following comments about the effect of a workshop on these future clinicians:

I was nothing short of blown away by how powerfully the students were affected. They will be far better clinicians for having gone through the experience. I was a bit concerned initially that our students were a bit too jaded and professionalized to truly appreciate what they had been offered, but they really surprised me. They really "got it" and were able to verbalize the significance of the safe space we create, the power of telling stories and of witnessing those of others. Even more, they said that that kind of intimacy and witnessing of another's pain should be the bread and butter of psychotherapy and what we should be teaching our students. I was so proud of how much they had learned and grown as individual and professionals.

Similarly, referring to what we call the power of multiple witnessing in a Healing of Memories group, Margaret Fell commented on its cultural dimension in the United States when she said:

We are imprisoned in this country by our dogged individualism. We don't see ourselves as benefiting from group support, yet the comments I hear from war veterans are, "For the first time in my life someone wanted to listen. Somebody cared." As Americans we are starved for acknowledgment of what has happened to us. We are a lonely people.

When I first told friends that I was working in Hawaii they looked at me in disbelief. While it is true that Hawaii has the appearance of heaven on earth, there is a great deal of pain below the surface. This relates to poverty, drugs, and unresolved issues about Hawaiian sovereignty and the history of the U.S. takeover of the Polynesian kingdom with its marginalization of indigenous inhabitants. I was there because in 2007 our then board chairperson in South Africa, Glenda Wildschut, was invited to give the Watada Lecture at the Church of the Crossroads in Honolulu. Crossroads was founded in 1923 by a racially diverse group of high school students who believed they should be able to worship together at a time when Hawaii's churches were segregated by ethnicity. The church has lived out this inclusive legacy through the decades, declaring itself an open and affirming church and providing a progressive Christian witness for peace, justice, and care of the environment. The Watada Lectures are one expression of that witness. Glenda's title was "The Pain of Injustice and the Promise of Reconciliation," and during her talk she spoke of our Healing of Memories work. This was the seed that has now flowered into an ongoing Healing of Memories presence in Hawaii.

Our work there has been spearheaded by Linda Rich and Liz Nelson, who have obtained grants to support it and on one occasion traveled all the way to New York in order to participate in a facilitator-training workshop. On my first visit to Honolulu I led a Healing of Memories workshop open to the general public and made a presentation in a women's prison. Hawaii is literally half a world away from Cape Town, and Linda and I wondered if our message would translate meaningfully to those in these islands. There was no need to worry. The women at the prison confirmed immediately the notion that those who become victimizers have often been victims themselves. They were predominantly women of color, and their willingness to share and examine their own behavior was inspiring. Their beauty and hope shone through in the graceful hula they offered and in the lei and bouquets they gave us, made from flowers from their own garden. They shared aloha, that Hawaiian spirit of love, generosity, and hospitality, despite their circumstances. At another presentation a Native Hawaiian woman spoke of how the indigenous people of these islands still live with injustice and the loss of their culture. She expressed surprise and gratitude when I responded with respect and expressed solidarity with the aspirations of indigenous peoples. Perhaps future workshops will bring together Hawaiians and non-Hawaiians to help heal the painful history of these islands and foster the mutual understanding that will allow them to move toward being a more just and peaceful community. The foundation has been laid and we will continue to develop our work in Hawaii.

I am sometimes asked why we are interested in working in the United States. The question perhaps reflects a perception that because the United States is such a wealthy country it is not in need of healing. But the United States is, of course, many different things, among them pockets of deep poverty with a super rich elite at the top, racial and ethnic discrimination, substandard health care and public education, one of the highest incarceration rates in the world, and a growing ethos of "every person for himself" that has led to a dangerously atomized and unfeeling society. Many people carry a burden of deep pain and alienation. We provide a place where they can unburden themselves in the context of a safe and caring community, and this is very much a part of the healing process.

The United States also has quite a troubled past. I recall a workshop in Hamburg, Germany, that was framed by the participants as "Dealing with the Burden of History," and I have spoken a number of times of the parallels between the denial of history on the part of some Germans and some white people in South Africa. But Germany and South Africa are not alone, and this pattern has echoes too in the United States where there is a purposeful national forgetting about slavery and the treatment of Native Americans. Right now the United States is the world's only superpower, and although with the emergence of countries such as China and India the preeminence of the United States is already beginning to fade, it is likely to remain a country of disproportionate importance in the world. For this reason alone it is important that it face up to when it has fallen short and its own brokenness so that it can become a model of morality and compassion, instead of being renowned for having the most weapons of mass destruction or executing more of its citizens than most countries in the world. Helping it acknowledge its past and its troubled present is one way that we in the Institute can contribute in our own modest way to the realization of a different kind of United States of America, one that the rest of the world can aspire to emulate.

Our New Old Friends

by Paul and Sally Bermanzohn

Paul: I'm a street psychiatrist in Poughkeepsie, New York. I came to the workshop because I'm interested in issues of trauma since a lot of my patients are poor, bitterly depressed people who have been through unspeakable trauma themselves. I myself was a victim of the Greensboro massacre almost thirty years ago. I was shot in the head and arm and I have a very serious limp to this day. The workshop experience was quite intense for me. There was a wonderful sense of connectedness, especially among the people in my small group. What we get from listening to people's stories is how much alike we all are. It's really true. Yes, it can be a cliché, but it's a fact, and it's a fact we all need to be reminded of often. What connects us is more fundamental than what divides us.

I'd also like to comment on Fr. Michael's leadership style. He is such a charismatic person and has such a powerful magnetism. He sets a marvelous tone for everybody. He makes people feel welcome and that they are a very important part of what is going to happen. Nothing starts until everybody is present. He is also a very funny and self-deprecating guy. I asked him how his prostheses work—you know his two hooks—and he said "faith and hope." And then we talked about how one hook was called "faith" and the other "hope," his two "hands" *(laughs)*. He really does work that way, with a lot of faith in people and a lot of hope for the future. He radiates that and it permeates the whole proceedings. He's a very positive kind of guy. At the same time, he is a gentle soul. If one weren't careful one might think he is passive, but watching closely what he actually does shows he is a powerful but unassuming leader.

Sally: I want to pick up on what Paul said about Fr. Michael's style. His leadership of the group was subtle in a delicate sort of way, but it was unmistakable. It was a rather large group and we had only one weekend, so we had a lot to do, and he didn't want to waste precious time. He was gentle, but he would let us know that we were all expected to be there right now. I was also impressed with how engaged he was. He leads these groups very often, so you might have expected his attitude to be, "Oh, I've done this a lot before, so you all talk among yourselves," but instead he listened intently and pointed out how our group was unique compared to other groups. He is a good teacher and shared his wisdom about the meaning of ideas like forgiveness and compassion.

I also want to speak about what the workshop meant for me personally. I came to the weekend anticipating the anniversary of the Greensboro massacre. I was feeling very sad and somewhat depressed and I wanted to tell my story and get it off my shoulders so I would feel better and happier. I tend to wall off those feelings and not deal with them, and the workshop gave me a really great opportunity to engage with my sorrow and think deeply about what it means for my life. It was a gift. During the course of the weekend I was able to identify things that I need to work on more. I want to engage with this sadness because I cherished being empathized with by others who were also going through things that are painful. I want to be able to respond to them in the same way they responded to me, and the experience helped me do that. Of course I felt sadness, but I also felt relief and a powerful sense of connectedness with people that Paul has referred to as our "new old friends." So I felt joy and hope as well.

Pedro, a Guerilla Fighter for Peace

◇◇◇◇◇◇◇

AS AN INSTITUTE WE WORK with many people the world over who have suffered terrible injuries, physical, psychological, and spiritual. Some are filled with bitterness, hatred, and despair; others are not. But I think all people, and I don't except myself, need to be reminded that it is possible for the human spirit to triumph over fearful odds. My own story offers one such example, but it is neither the best nor the only one. So I like to lift up other people whose stories have inspired me with the hope that they will inspire others as well. Pedro's life story is one such example.

I met Pedro at an international conference in Bogotá, Colombia, organized by La Fundación para la Reconciliación, whose director, Fr. Leonel Narvaez, a Roman Catholic priest, had invited me. For many years Colombia has been wracked by insurgencies and hit squads that have connections with a flourishing drug trade. Fr. Leonel's organization assists in reintegrating Colombian ex-combatants into their communities. I was particularly interested because ex-combatants in South Africa have had many problems finding their place in our society. The Institute for Healing of Memories a few years ago organized a program for them with goals similar to Fr. Leonel's organization. Unfortunately our effort had to close prematurely due to insufficient funding, but it remains a project dear to my heart. Many of the Colombian young men and women in Fr. Leonel's organization were recruited as children into paramilitary groups on both the right and the left. La Fundación provides counseling and social services including skills training to young soldiers, and through its Schools of Forgiveness it trains some of them to become peace workers as well. In 2006 La Fundación para la Reconciliación was recognized for its important work with an Honorable Mention for the UNESCO Prize for Peace Education.

On the first night of the conference in Bogotá, Pedro, a former guerilla fighter, was introduced and spoke briefly. Then he danced for us with his life-size doll, Matilde, with extraordinary tenderness. As I watched Pedro dance I thought, "Here is someone who is seeking to redeem his past in a way that would powerfully encourage and inspire others." I was determined to find the means to bring Pedro to South Africa. Not long thereafter that became a reality, and in 2007 we were fortunate to be able to invite him to become a featured participant at a conference of Healing of Memories facilitators from around the world that was held in Cape Town. This is Pedro's story.

When Pedro was a tiny infant his mother deposited him at the home of his grandfather and she left. It was not a happy home, and Pedro says that he never remembers anyone saying, "I love you," to him or hugging him. Instead he was beaten and abused. He became an angry, bitter little boy, and when he was only ten years old he ran away and thereafter he lived in the streets. Being a clever boy he began dancing with a doll and passersby gave him coins, and in this way he managed to survive. When he came of age, Pedro joined the army where he spent several years fighting against the FARC guerillas. When he got out, he found it impossible to find a job, partly because he had limited skills and partly because as a black Colombian of dark complexion he encountered racism.

After being unemployed for some time, he met a man who recruited him to work for the cocaine industry in a rural area that ironically was controlled by his former enemy, the FARC. The FARC gave him livestock and some land and gradually absorbed him into the guerilla force. Pedro says that the FARC became his family and that its revolutionary ideology appealed to his desire for revenge against those who had so mistreated him. Gradually, however, he became disillusioned as he saw that the guerillas were displacing peasant farmers who hesitated to join them. A turning point for him came when his best friend who had once saved his life was charged with a minor offense and the paramilitary group voted to execute him. Pedro could not bear to watch the proceedings, but he recalls vividly hearing the shots fired as he turned away. In that moment he swore that he would find a way to leave the FARC.

One day not long after his friend was killed, he was sent to a nearby town where he was tasked with killing one of the local civilians who had run afoul of the FARC commander. When he got to the town, he spied the man he was assigned to kill walking down the street and saw that he was carrying a small baby. In that moment he knew he couldn't kill this man. Instead he called out to him, confessed why he was there, and the two of them escaped together.

Of course, in some ways nothing had changed. As Pedro said, "I was still black, still poor, and still alone." On top of everything else, now he was an ex-combatant from the notorious FARC guerilla forces. One day a friend of his, also a FARC ex-combatant, invited him to a workshop at Fr. Leonel's foundation. On the first day he left the workshop early because "they asked us to hold hands and I didn't like that." Nevertheless, something in the workshop struck a spark with Pedro and he kept going back. Eventually he began working there. Although he was on a new path, he says he was still struggling mightily with forgiveness—forgiving all those who had mistreated him and forgiving himself for the dreadful things he had done.

Only a few months before I met Pedro a terrible thing happened that tested his new resolve. He got a call that his brother had been killed in Cali, a city controlled by drug lords where there is much violence. When he arrived for the funeral, his nephew handed him a gun and, as Pedro reported, "I started to feel like a guerilla again with thoughts of revenge racing through my mind." At a certain point he stepped out for some air and his nephew came up behind him and, pointing to a man across the street, said to Pedro, "I know that man. He provided the gun that killed your brother." For a long moment Pedro said it was as if two people inside him were struggling mightily.

One was the guerilla who thought nothing of killing; the other was the person who worked at Fr. Leonel's foundation and who was on a journey of forgiveness. Finally he put his hand down because he realized he couldn't kill the man, though for several more days he felt guilty as he coped with the feeling of being a coward and blamed himself for not avenging his brother's death.

Nevertheless, this was a decisive moment for Pedro, and his life began to change in fundamental ways. Not long afterward he tracked down his mother who had abandoned him and whom he had not seen for many years. Over time they have reconciled, and Pedro eventually grew to love her. Now, he says, "My family is my life project." Pedro still dances with Matilde sometimes. He did so at our conference and told the participants that he has traded his gun for a dance. Many, including Pedro, wept.

◇ 21 ◇

Looking Forward, Daring to Hope

◇◇◇◇◇◇

AS I WOUND UP MY VISIT to Australia some years ago, I preached a final sermon at the Anglican Church of the Ascension in Alice Springs. I began on that occasion by quoting from the Old Testament Book of Habakkuk in which there is a dialogue between the prophet and God about God's failure to act in the face of the triumph of injustice and violence. Why, one might ask, did God not stop the genocide in Rwanda? Why did God not step in to stop the genocide in the former Yugoslavia? Why did God allow Aboriginal children to be stolen from their parents or the violence and trampling of human rights to continue in Zimbabwe? And, of course, I might ask, why did God not prevent my bombing? These questions about personal suffering and collective injustice have troubled people through the ages. Our God does not step in to prevent terrible things from happening, but God accompanies us on the journey, whatever that may be. It then remains for us to decide how we respond. In my own case, when people sought to kill me and failed, I already had a victory. But the questions then became, How do I appropriate that victory? How do I make my bombing redemptive? How do I make it life giving for myself and for others? And so it is for all of us.

In South Africa there is a song that black people sang during the apartheid years, Senzeni Na, which means "What have we done?" What have we done that we should suffer? Is it because of the color of our skin? The book of Genesis asserts that God made all human beings—no exceptions—in God's own image and likeness, and therefore all share equal value. In the Gospel of Luke, Zacchaeus is considered to be a corrupt tax collector and is despised, but Jesus sees his fundamental value as a human being. Again and again Jesus affirms the common humanity of sex workers, the good Samaritan, the Roman soldier, the thief on the cross, and the woman caught in adultery. More often it was the respectable, religious people who struggled with Jesus' message.

Those of us who are church people are often slow learners. It took us nearly eighteen hundred years of Christian history to realize that slavery was wrong, and even then in England the bishops did not support its abolition, not so much because they believed in it, though perhaps some did, but because of an inherent conservatism, an inertia, an unwillingness to change. Yet who among us would want to defend slavery today? We also have the struggle of women for equality. New Zealand was the first country in modern times to give the vote to women. Then many years later women began to insist that God was calling them to be priests. Most people were not persuaded to support women's ordination by intellectual arguments but rather through meeting women who spoke of their experience of being called by God. And now it is same-gender loving people who are asserting their right to an equal place in the churches and in the sun. Once again what changes hearts and minds is not argument but rather human contact with gay or lesbian loved ones or friends. In my experience we are against all forms of oppression except the ones we are in favor of.

Archbishop Tutu often tells people that we live in a moral universe and that unjust regimes are destined to be relegated to the dustbin of history. During the worst of the "bad old days" it seemed unbelievable that this could be so, but just a few months after I gave that sermon in Alice Springs in 2004, the political party that created apartheid was dissolved and disappeared from the scene. Indeed, who could have imagined in 1976, at the time of the uprising of Soweto schoolchildren, that eighteen years later when most of them were still young adults they would be voting for Nelson Mandela to become president of their country? In a sense South Africa is a giant morality play. It is true that we are facing serious challenges now, but once upon a time everybody said we were going to kill one another and we didn't. Instead, 1994 came bringing democracy. So, our God is a God of history.

The lesson from Habakkuk says that God is sovereign, and there is always reason to hope; in the end good will triumph over evil and people are called to remain faithful. Hope is not utopian or naive. It requires commitment, hard work, struggle, and sacrifice. Jesus said, "The kingdom of God is among you." We are not called upon to recreate a Garden of Eden to which we can all seek to retire. In the book of Revelations there is a passage that says, "War arose in heaven. Michael and his angels fought against the devil and the devil was cast down." That is expressed in martial language, but the message is that good overcomes evil, and we are called upon to be warriors together in the struggle for a just world.

Our generation is bedeviled by the unfinished business of previous ages that has come back to haunt us. While the Institute's contribution is a modest one, I believe the time for Healing of Memories has come in the human family. In the wake of wars and strife there have to be just settlements of the political and economic issues that divide us, but complementary to these we must address the psychological, emotional, and spiritual aftermath of conflicts. As I make my way to many countries, leading Healing of Memories workshops, giving talks, and often meeting a cross section of society either personally or through the media, I attempt to raise some of the critical questions of our time. What is healing? What is the role of memory? Of faith? Should we forgive? Can forgiveness be reconciled with the struggle for justice? These are ancient questions that our generation must struggle with afresh.

In my early years I was a freedom fighter. When, as a priest, I joined the ANC it was because I believed in a God that took the side of the poor and oppressed against a narrow sectarian and brutal regime. We were fortunate in South Africa that our struggle became the world's struggle. That was so because people across the globe rightly recognized that universal values of human rights were at stake, and today South Africa's constitution is a model for the world. Now I am a healer and I work to free people from being prisoners of the past, to free them from being prisoners of a moment in time, and to allow them to become agents of history once again—to allow them to be free to create and shape their world. This endeavor, no less than being a freedom fighter, is a struggle for human liberation. The ground has shifted, but the prize is the same.

Unless we bind up the wounds of the brokenhearted, we cannot hope to create a just and durable society where everyone has a place in the sun, for the victims of the past too easily become the victimizers of the future. As the world prayed for me on my own healing journey and supported the struggle of South Africa's people, the Institute now attempts to return the compliment by offering healing in other countries recovering from wars and conflicts. We work with people experiencing discrimination and injustice in its many forms—with victims of violence whether domestic, criminal, or political, with war veterans and prison inmates, many of whom are deeply traumatized themselves and who may also need to face a burden of culpability and guilt in order to heal. We work too with members of the faith community, especially those working on social justice issues, who carry their own burdens. I believe that spiritually grounded, culturally sensitive, community-based methods of healing like ours are the wave of the future.

As the Institute's leader I have the responsibility for articulating its vision and sustaining its programs. It can be a lonely role. I cannot be controlled by my own needs to be loved and appreciated because at times it is necessary to say and do things that are not popular. Then there are also the inevitable mistakes for which I like all leaders have to take responsibility. Too much of my time is taken up as a professional beggar. My fondest dream would be that we would find an endowment that would give us the freedom to carry the work forward as need arises without having to worry about resources.

People sometimes see me as an icon and ask how it is that I do not become discouraged. The answer is that if I am an icon, I am a very human one with all my imperfections and contradictions. There are certainly moments when I despair about everything. It is easy to become discouraged about post-apartheid South Africa, even about the continent of Africa; it is easy to lose heart because of the economic system that is dominant in the world today and about the threats of war and poverty. But there are always signs of hope. I like to tell a

*With Archbishop Desmond Tutu at a mass in Capetown
to celebrate the twentieth anniversary of my survival.*

little story that is also a song, "Mud and Stars" by Dawn Landes. Once there were two men in a prison cell and they both looked out the window. One looked down and saw mud; the other looked up and saw stars. So I suppose on a bad day I too see mud, and on a good day I see stars, and maybe on a realistic day I see both.

Projecting well into the future, the issue for the Institute as an organization and for us as individuals is not to save the world but simply to do our best. I remind myself that in the Christian tradition there is only one Savior and I am not he. Other people in our organization make a huge contribution—our staff, our board, and especially our facilitators in whose hands the healing work rests on any given day. I will eventually pass from the scene, and the Institute may or may not survive me. If it does, other people will come forward, and they may turn out to be better leaders. Were I to return in fifty years, I might be delighted with what I found, or I might be appalled. Either way, it's God's world and our human journey continues.

One of the lessons I have learned from traveling the globe is the uniqueness of every context, but equally important, I have experienced again and again the commonality that we all share, whether in its ugliness or its beauty. Disability has taught me that we need one another to be fully human, and we can be healers of one another. I draw strength from extraordinary human beings who dare to live heroic and beautiful lives through their gentleness, kindness, and compassion. Many of them are unsung and hardly known, but they give me inspiration and courage. I think back, once again to South Africa. There were generations of women and men, but I think particularly of brave women, who never saw their lives get better. In fact, they only saw them getting worse, but they dared to hope. They dared to struggle. They dared to believe that even if they didn't see it in their own lifetimes, others would live to see things get better. And indeed many of us have lived to see constitutional racism dismantled in South Africa. Although we are at but the beginning of a journey that will take many decades, even many generations, we have borne witness to a turning point in history.

As I have said many times, my story is also the story of South Africa. April 28, 2010, was the twentieth anniversary of my bombing. Three days later Archbishop Emeritus Desmond Tutu presided at a mass of thanksgiving at Cape Town's Anglican Cathedral that celebrated my survival and recovery. The congregation included people from every walk of life and several continents. The world's major religions were represented in the service. Prayers of thanksgiving were said for my survival and for the Institute's work, and intercessory prayers were offered for victims of violence and torture everywhere. An interracial youth choir sang South African music so soulfully that it left the congregation and the choir director himself weeping. They were weeping not only with joy at my victory but also at the victory that is today's democratic South Africa and the example that its achievement, with all its blemishes, represents to a fractured world deeply in need of hope. I think as human beings we need a long-term perspective on the movement of history that we can neither fully control nor predict. Some things are known only to God. We are, however, called to be coworkers in God's project for our world. This is the meaning of hope, and it is for that reason that we continue to walk with others across the globe as they struggle to heal and make a better world.

Index